CLASSICS IN EDUCATION
Lawrence A. Cremin, General Editor

☆ ☆ ☆

THE REPUBLIC AND THE SCHOOL
Horace Mann on the Education of Free Men
Edited by Lawrence A. Cremin

AMERICAN IDEAS ABOUT ADULT EDUCATION
1710–1951
Edited by C. Hartley Grattan

DEWEY ON EDUCATION
Introduction and Notes by Martin S. Dworkin

THE SUPREME COURT AND EDUCATION
(Revised and enlarged)
Edited by David Fellman

INTERNATIONAL EDUCATION
A Documentary History
Edited by David G. Scanlon

CRUSADE AGAINST IGNORANCE
Thomas Jefferson on Education
Edited by Gordon C. Lee

CHINESE EDUCATION UNDER COMMUNISM
Edited by Chang-tu Hu

CHARLES W. ELIOT AND POPULAR EDUCATION
Edited by Edward A. Krug

WILLIAM T. HARRIS ON EDUCATION
(in preparation)
Edited by Martin S. Dworkin

THE *EMILE* OF JEAN JACQUES ROUSSEAU
Selections
Translated and Edited by William Boyd

THE MINOR EDUCATIONAL WRITINGS OF JEAN JACQUES ROUSSEAU
Selected and Translated by William Boyd

PSYCHOLOGY AND THE SCIENCE OF EDUCATION
Selected Writings of Edward L. Thorndike
Edited by Geraldine M. Joncich

THE NEW-ENGLAND PRIMER
Introduction by Paul Leicester Ford

BENJAMIN FRANKLIN ON EDUCATION
Edited by John Hardin Best

THE COLLEGES AND THE PUBLIC
1787–1862
Edited by Theodore Rawson Crane

TRADITIONS OF AFRICAN EDUCATION
Edited by David G. Scanlon

NOAH WEBSTER'S AMERICAN SPELLING BOOK
Introductory Essay by Henry Steele Commager

VITTORINO DA FELTRE
AND OTHER HUMANIST EDUCATORS
By William Harrison Woodward
Foreword by Eugene F. Rice, Jr.

DESIDERIUS ERASMUS
CONCERNING THE AIM AND METHOD
OF EDUCATION
By William Harrison Woodward
Foreword by Craig R. Thompson

JOHN LOCKE ON EDUCATION
Edited by Peter Gay

CATHOLIC EDUCATION IN AMERICA
A Documentary History
Edited by Neil G. McCluskey, S.J.

THE AGE OF THE ACADEMIES
Edited by Theodore R. Sizer

HEALTH, GROWTH, AND HEREDITY
G. Stanley Hall on Natural Education
Edited by Charles E. Strickland and Charles Burgess

TEACHER EDUCATION IN AMERICA
A Documentary History
Edited by Merle L. Borrowman

THE EDUCATED WOMAN IN AMERICA
Selected Writings of Catharine Beecher,
Margaret Fuller, and M. Carey Thomas
Edited by Barbara M. Cross

EMERSON ON EDUCATION
Selections
Edited by Howard Mumford Jones

ECONOMIC INFLUENCES UPON EDUCATIONAL
PROGRESS IN THE UNITED STATES, 1820–1850
By Frank Tracy Carlton
Foreword by Lawrence A. Cremin

QUINTILIAN ON EDUCATION
Selected and Translated by William M. Smail

ROMAN EDUCATION FROM CICERO
TO QUINTILIAN
By Aubrey Gwynn, S.J.

HERBERT SPENCER ON EDUCATION
Edited by Andreas M. Kazamias

JOHN LOCKE'S *OF THE CONDUCT
OF THE UNDERSTANDING*
Edited by Francis W. Garforth

STUDIES IN EDUCATION DURING THE
AGE OF THE RENAISSANCE, 1400–1600
By William Harrison Woodward
Foreword by Lawrence Stone

JOHN AMOS COMENIUS ON EDUCATION
Introduction by Jean Piaget

HUMANISM AND THE SOCIAL ORDER
IN TUDOR ENGLAND
By Fritz Caspari

VIVES' *INTRODUCTION TO WISDOM*
Edited by Marian Leona Tobriner, S.N.J.M.

THE THEORY OF EDUCATION IN
THE *REPUBLIC* OF PLATO
By Richard Lewis Nettleship
Foreword by Robert McClintock

UTOPIANISM AND EDUCATION
Robert Owen and the Owenites
Edited by John F. C. Harrison

SCHOOLS OF HELLAS
By Kenneth J. Freeman
Foreword by William M. Calder III

THE EDUCATIONAL THEORIES
OF THE SOPHISTS
Edited by James L. Jarrett

SIR THOMAS ELYOT'S
THE BOOK NAMED THE GOVERNOR
Abridged and Edited by John M. Major

JEWISH EDUCATION IN THE UNITED STATES
A Documentary History
Edited by Lloyd P. Gartner

HENRY BARNARD'S *SCHOOL ARCHITECTURE*
Edited by Jean and Robert McClintock

JOHN STUART MILL ON EDUCATION
Edited by Francis W. Garforth

RICHARD MULCASTER'S *POSITIONS*
Abridged and Edited by Richard L. DeMolen

THE GREAT AWAKENING
AND AMERICAN EDUCATION
A Documentary History
Edited, with an Introduction, by Douglas Sloan

The Great Awakening and American Education

A DOCUMENTARY HISTORY

Edited, with an Introduction, by
DOUGLAS SLOAN

CLASSICS IN

No. 46

EDUCATION

TEACHERS COLLEGE PRESS
TEACHERS COLLEGE, COLUMBIA UNIVERSITY
NEW YORK AND LONDON

370.913
SL 5g
89747
Sept 1974

FOR MY MOTHER AND FATHER

Foreword

The influence of the Great Awakening on education has been a continuing theme in American historiography, at least since the publication of Joseph Tracy's early account of the movement as it first appeared in New England. But just as Tracy devoted his educational commentary almost wholly to events at Harvard and Yale, so have most subsequent interpreters viewed the educational side of the Awakening largely in terms of its impact on the older colleges and its role in the founding of new ones. The emphasis is by no means misplaced, given the critical role of the colleges in the development of a vigorous provincial culture; but it is at best a restricting one, in view of the pervasiveness of the Awakening and its far-reaching effects on every aspect of American life.

It is the special merit of Professor Sloan's analysis that he approaches his subject broadly, considering the many institutions that educate and the many clienteles they serve. Following his earlier investigations in *The Scottish Enlightenment and the American College Ideal*, he points to the inextricable ties between the Awakening and the spate of academies that came into being during the 1740's, 1750's, and 1760's. Beyond that, he indicates the impact of the Awakening on the churches as teaching institutions, and on the networks of families and agencies associated with the churches. And most important, perhaps, he suggests the fascinating continuity of the issues and debates of the Awakening, through the nineteenth century and into the twentieth. "The Awakening was the initiation of a grand cultural dialogue that has yet to be completed," he observes. The fact that the terms of that dialogue have changed over ' the years should not obscure the stubborn persistence of the issues.

LAWRENCE A. CREMIN

Contents

The Great Awakening
and American Education

The religious revival that swept the American colonies in the 1740's was so widespread, so unsettling, that it has been known ever since as the Great Awakening. As observers at the time noted, it was "a great and general awakening," leaving no social class, no section of the country, no church body untouched. By the same token, although the issues of the Awakening were primarily religious and expressed in religious terms, they were intertwined with virtually all of the important social, political, and intellectual questions of mid-eighteenth century America. As a result, in the short space of two years, between 1740 when the revivals first erupted throughout the colonies and 1742 when they reached their peak of intensity, the Awakening had set in motion powerful forces that would affect the future course of American society.

Educational forces, of new direction and magnitude, were not the least of those released by the Great Awakening. So central, in fact, were educational ideas, attitudes, and institutions that the full dimensions of the revival itself can scarcely be grasped without reference to them. Conversely, no attempt at an adequate understanding of colonial education can avoid a careful appraisal of the broad cultural and social impact of the Great Awakening.

1

The modern reader who approaches the Great
Awakening with educational questions in mind, and
who makes the initially difficult effort to get inside the
conceptual world of eighteenth-century religion, may
find himself looking at intellectual and educational issues that bear a surprising resemblance to those of his
own time. For example, student dissent, struggles over
the control of educational institutions, charges of anti-
intellectualism and counter-cries of intellectual elitism,
debates concerning the social purposes and uses of education, disagreements of priority in the proper relationship between character and knowledge, discussions of the
nature of human psychology and the roles of intellect
and emotion, issues of academic freedom—all were present.

The temptation, in fact, might very well be to draw
parallels between the eighteenth and twentieth centuries that a careful regard for the uniqueness of historical
events would not entirely justify. Nevertheless, similar-
ities are certainly to be found. It is worth asking which
educational issues were peculiar to the time and circumstances, and which were indeed among those fundamental problems that recur again and again and must
be faced in new form by each succeeding generation.
Perhaps it would be best to begin with a broad sketch of
the main events of the Great Awakening, and then to
consider in detail the educational ramifications.

I

It has often been observed that at the time of the
Great Awakening, and even before, similar revivals had
been occurring in much of western Europe and Great
Britain. Viewed from one perspective, in fact, the Great

Awakening was the American version of evangelical pietism—a vigorous and widespread movement within all of
the churches of seventeenth and eighteenth-century
Protestantism. Though its specific expressions differed
somewhat from one denominational and national context to another, the central and unifying conviction of
pietism everywhere was that true Christian existence
derives above all else from an inner, personal experience
of divine mercy and concern. Without this personal, inner relationship with God, all theology, worship, even
good works, no matter how impressive they might otherwise appear, were for evangelical pietism useless, if not
actually hazardous, to authentic Christianity.

This experiential concern could find many opportunities and avenues for expression: as a demand for emotional warmth and vitality in worship and theology; as
an anchor of security in the midst of various forces,
natural and social, perceived as threats to the meaning
of personal existence; as a release from tensions gener-
ated by conflicts between ideals and practice; and as a
rejection of elitist tendencies in church and society, especially those that appeared to rest on outward distinctions among men rather than on inner personal realities.
Sometimes pietism could manifest itself in quietistic, almost mystic, retreat from the demands of the world. More
frequently, however, evangelical pietism made itself felt
in religious and social activism. This was true especially
of the Calvinist and English Puritan churches, in which
pietism was deeply rooted and where the experiential
impulse was firmly tied to concerns for scriptural fidelity, moral purity, and social reformation. Indeed, in
these churches pietism often seemed to flourish most as a
protest movement against the established order and the
status quo. It was also in the Calvinist and Puritan tra-

ditions of colonial America—in the Congregational, Presbyterian, and Reformed churches—that experiential religion erupted during the Awakening most violently and with the greatest social impact.

The European roots of the Great Awakening are important to note. The indigenous and local conditions of colonial society, however, must also be taken into account in order to understand better the full causes and the particular shape and consequences of the American revivals. The Great Awakening occurred at a time when colonial society had reached a stage of complexity that was upsetting many older assumptions and ways of life. It is against this background of fundamental social and cultural change that the revivals, with their intensity and almost simultaneous appearance throughout the colonies, must be viewed.

The churches were among the earlier major social institutions to experience the unsettling and reordering effects of this change. By the third decade of the eighteenth century colonial population growth itself was swelling the numbers of persons outside the churches and confronting the churches with an almost overwhelming missionary task. More and more families were pushing out into the isolation of the frontier, farther and farther from the older centers of village life—of which the church had often been the most important. Furthermore, the emergence of a genuine cosmopolitan, urban culture in such large seaport towns as Boston, Newport, New York, Philadelphia, and Charleston, was beginning to offer a serious challenge to traditional and more stable rural patterns of life and thought. The tendency of certain clergymen, especially among the Anglicans of Virginia and some of the older established Congregational churches of the northern cities, to align themselves with the more prominent members of society, accentuated growing class cleavages and further rendered the church's message irrelevant to large groups of people. A continuing flow of new and different religious and ethnic groups into the colonies was introducing all of the problems of religious pluralism, with its increased possibilities for sectarian strife and temptations toward religious indifference. As a result of such developments as these, all of them long underway by 1730, church discipline was being severely undercut and any sense of a vital, undergirding religious community was becoming extremely difficult to maintain.

The weakness of the churches in mid-eighteenth century should not, however, be exaggerated, the Jeremiads of their own preachers to the contrary notwithstanding. Despite many problems the churches enjoyed considerable prestige. The ministry was a highly respected profession, and the minister himself was frequently the most important intellectual leader in many colonial communities. More important, Christian morality and doctrine, even when honored only in the breach, continued to exert a powerful hold on large numbers of persons. The basic assumptions of Calvinist Christianity provided the only categories by which many people inside and outside of the churches could attempt to make sense out of their lives. In the hardships of frontier life and amidst the confusions of cultural change, great depths of religious feeling everywhere lay ready to be released. All that was needed under such conditions to make the doctrines existentially alive and powerful was for the right man to bring their meaning to bear in a vivid and compelling way upon the concerns of his listeners. More and more ministers began to make this discovery, sometimes more by accident than by design.

In 1720 Theodorus J. Frelinghuysen, a Dutch Reformed minister under the authority of the church in Holland, began to minister to churches in the Raritan Valley of New Jersey. Frelinghuysen's parish extended over nearly two hundred fifty square miles of wild, unculti- vated, sparsely settled country, in which, as he himself observed, "piety could not be expected to flourish."[1] As a student at the University of Lingen in Holland, Frelinghuysen had been an outstanding scholar, excel- ling in Greek, Hebrew, and theology, and becoming knowledgeable also in Aramaic and Syriac. At the university he had also become deeply influenced by the evangelical pietism of his favorite professors and church leaders, and he lost no time upon arriving in Raritan in trying to arouse piety and religious concern among his new congregations. For nearly twenty years Frelinghuysen preached warm evangelical sermons, stressing the need for personal religious experience and admitting to the communion table only the converted and the committed. Frelinghuysen's zeal brought con- tinual dissension and controversy into the church, but it also produced converts and growing congregations. When, in 1726, Gilbert Tennent, a passionate young Presbyterian minister, was assigned to gather a new church in nearby New Brunswick, he was so impressed by Frelinghuysen's method of preaching that he began to look to him for leadership.

Gilbert Tennent was the eldest of four sons of Wil- liam Tennent, an immigrant from North Ireland who be- came minister of a church in Neshaminy, Pennsylvania, the same year Gilbert undertook his New Brunswick

[1] Quoted in James Tanis, *Dutch Calvinistic Pietism in the Mid- dle Colonies, A Study in the Life and Theology of Theodorus Jacobus Frelinghuysen* (The Hague: 1967), p. 47.

pastorate. At Neshaminy, William Tennent erected a
schoolhouse where he taught his younger three sons and
other boys in the neighborhood, preparing most of them
for the ministry. The Tennents were firmly committed
to a warm evangelical faith and to preaching for conversion. Soon graduates of the Log College—as their
school came to be called in derision by its anti-revivalist
opponents among the Presbyterians—were joining the
work of the Tennents and Frelinghuysen, and leading
revivals throughout New Jersey and parts of Pennsylvania.

By the 1730's New England was also ripe for religious
renewal. The original concerns of the Congregationalists,
the dominant religious group of New England, had been
to carry the Reformation to completion in the New
World by building a church containing only true Christians and a society ordered according to Christian precepts. Combining the experiential tradition of English
Puritans with Calvinist theology these New Englanders
had demanded a personal religious experience as a mark
of divine election, and as a prerequisite to full church
membership. Over the years, however, this goal of a
purified church as the foundation of a Godly society
had proven ever more elusive.

Declining numbers of conversions eventually led many
ministers to blink, compromise, or abandon outright
their strict requirements for church membership. Con-
centration on leading a good life, always an integral
part of Puritanism, began in many a minister's sermon
to overshadow the necessity of entering a new life
through conversion. With the increased emphasis on
man's moral ability the door was also opened to rationalistic theological influences, emanating mainly from
England, that held a high estimation of the powers of

human reason and will in matters of religion. Both worked to throw the older Puritan and Calvinistic theology, with its emphasis on God's sovereignty and on human sinfulness and weakness, into disarray. Along with everything else a rising level of affluence among some New Englanders, and an accompanying desire for the social graces and amenities of a more urbane and genteel religion, prompted increasing numbers after 1690 to defect to the Church of England. The inevitable results of all of this were increasing indifference toward the church among the laity, and mounting uncertainty and confusion in the ranks of the clergy.

Although there had been flickers of revivalism in some churches from time to time, the first real suggestion that all New England might be about to awake from its "spiritual slumber" came in 1734 in Northampton, Massachusetts. In that year the young minister of the Northampton church, Jonathan Edwards, began a series of sermons for his congregation on such orthodox themes as "the sovereignty of God" and "justification by faith alone." Edwards was himself among those who had become convinced that religion in New England was rapidly losing its power and in serious peril. He was also certain that he detected the source of this decline in the growing influence of Arminianism. Originally a heresy of orthodox Calvinism, Arminianism by Edwards' time was a term applied rather loosely to all rationalistic theological thought which taught that man by the use of reason could discover God's will and by his own efforts cooperate with God in winning salvation. To Edwards this was pretentious and dangerous doctrine, for in his view it deceived man about his true plight as sinner and offered him the easy comfort of false hopes.

It was to combat such views that Edwards had begun

his series of sermons in 1734. The response startled Edwards himself as much as anyone. Religious concern gripped the congregation, within six months over three hundred persons had experienced conversion, and before the revival was over it had spread to other towns along the Connecticut River Valley in Connecticut and Massachusetts. On a journey to New York in the fall of 1735 Edwards had even met his Presbyterian counterparts from farther south, William and Gilbert Tennent, and had exchanged with them the inspiring reports of spreading revival activity. Already there were intimations that the revivals could become intercolonial and interdenominational in scope. Although the Northampton revival had played itself out by 1737, the stage had been set for still greater things to come.

The beginning of the Great Awakening on a scale of colony-wide proportions was triggered by the arrival late in 1739 of George Whitefield, the sensational young evangelist from England. Whitefield had begun his career as a preacher working with John and Charles Wesley among the poor of England and Wales. As his popularity and reputation as an evangelist grew, he was commissioned by the Wesleys in 1738 to sail for Savannah, Georgia, to assist the churches in their missionary work there and to found an orphanage for the colony. After several months in Georgia, Whitefield returned to England to raise money for the new orphanage, then embarked once more for the colonies. News of Whitefield's impending visit stirred great excitement among the colonists who had already heard many reports of his extraordinary preaching to audiences of tens of thousands assembled in open fields to hear him. Upon his arrival Whitefield spent some months traveling and preaching in the middle colonies, where he met the

Tennents, who helped to persuade him to undertake an evangelical preaching tour of all the colonies.

After a journey south, preaching all the way, White-field headed north in the autumn of 1740 to begin a three months' tour of New England that took him through the main cities and towns of Rhode Island, Massachusetts, and Connecticut, and as far north as Maine. Everywhere he went the effect was the same. At each stop crowds of increasing size turned out to hear him depict the terrors of damnation and the necessity and joys of the new birth. Everywhere the fires of revival spread, fanned by like-minded ministers who received his advent as a gift from God and an answer to America's religious decline.

Everywhere, too, there were doubters, people not so sure about the divine origins of the conversion experiences they were witnessing. To these persons the revivals seemed neither to have their source in an outpouring of the holy spirit, nor to be occasioned by a divine emissary in the person of George Whitefield. Rather, they seemed to resemble much more an overflowing of mass emotion under the promptings of a talented rabble rouser. As the revival spread, opposition also grew until the division between those who supported and those who opposed the Awakening was deep and cut across all denominational and sectional lines. In the congregational churches of New England the pro-revivalists and anti-revivalists came respectively to be dubbed "New Lights" and "Old Lights"; in the Presbyterian church the corresponding parties bore the names "New Side" and "Old Side."

From the beginning the controversies and divisions of the Great Awakening had major educational ramifications. There were two main reasons for this. In the first place, the theological and social ideas of Calvinism and Puritanism had traditionally found important expression in educational attitudes and policies. When religious disagreements erupted in the Great Awakening it was only natural that the debates frequently should be couched in explicit educational terms and lead to concrete educational policies and undertakings. Second, of less importance ultimately but often of overriding concern in the immediate press of events, there was an awareness on all sides that educational institutions were powerful instruments for propagating ideas and points of view. Consequently, as the Awakening gathered momentum, the struggle between the contending parties for control of the church increasingly spilled over into attempts to gain control of the existing institutions of education, or, when this failed, to create new ones.

It is not difficult to understand how religious issues could so quickly acquire educational significance. The Calvinist and Puritan churches of eighteenth-century America were rooted in a tradition that had long placed a high value on learning and education. From the time of the Reformation the Protestant notions of the authority of scripture and the priesthood of all believers had greatly encouraged the idea, strong in early New England, that every man should be able to read and write. Not only was literacy prized because it equipped men to read the Scriptures and encounter therein the truths of salvation, but the skills of reading and writing also enabled men to conduct their affairs in the world with the diligence and dispatch required of a good Christian. Calvinism, and English Puritanism in particular, had also been profoundly influenced by the Christian humanism of northern Europe and England with the humanists' dual faith in the rationality of God's created world and in the importance of the liberal arts for preparing devout and competent public leaders. Many Calvinists firmly believed that the world could be understood and church and society ordered according to the rational structures of God's creation. The ultimate truths of revelation themselves, they thought, would prove amenable to reason, even if they could not be commanded by reason. In this scheme of things the necessary complement to a literate congregation was a learned clergy thoroughly trained in the liberal arts. With such an education the minister would be able to expound the true meaning of the Bible, to spot and resolve theological inconsistencies, and to discern accurately the kind of church and civil government dictated by scripture. The idea that education and religion were inseparable was deeply ingrained in Calvinism. When Jonathan Edwards expressed his conviction that an advancement in learning had preceded and gone hand in hand with the recovery of "true religion" in the Reformation, he was simply repeating an attitude already commonplace among Protestants.[2]

This high regard for human learning, nevertheless, involved some knotty problems for both piety and intellectual rigor. One such problem lay in determining the proper relationship between the truth discovered by natural reason and that delivered by scriptural revelation. The various "covenant theologies" of the English Puritans, for example, represented, in part, attempts to make revelation reasonable, if not by divesting God of his ultimate mystery, at least by spelling out with as much precision as possible the terms on which God and man dealt with one another. An even greater source

[2] *The Works of Jonathan Edwards* (New York: 1829), III, 380.

of difficulty stemmed from the stress by many Puritans upon the necessity of conversion, that inner assurance of divine favor without which reason, rationality, and learning were in the end all of no avail. While a concern for logical order and rationality and an emphasis upon personal, emotional experience were not necessarily contradictory, they could be held together in the same individual consciousness or theological system only by dint of much intellectual and emotional effort. Finally, complicating the other two problems, was the additional question of how much authority laity and clergy should have in relation to each other. Clearly, if all sides of the Calvinist outlook were to be stressed equally, a precarious balance indeed had to be maintained in the church and in the individual. Of course the balance was rarely achieved, and once achieved, quickly upset.

An especially acute problem in the late seventeenth and early eighteenth centuries was that the rational and experiential elements in Calvinism were moving farther and farther apart. The very Arminianism against which Edwards launched his attack was in many ways the natural development of the traditional rationalist element in Calvinism under the stimulus of the new science and philosophy of the day. When the revivalists attempted to redress the balance by stressing inner awareness the gulf widened farther still. The anti-revivalists were quick to take advantage of the situation and very early began to depict the Awakening as a conflict between reason and emotion. The charges of anti-intellectualism which they hurled against the revivalists cast the dispute into an educational context from the beginning and made it inevitable that educational institutions and attitudes would be drawn quickly and directly into the swirls of controversy. The anti-revivalists

found it relatively easy to portray themselves as the
champions of reason and the defenders of order and decorum against the onslaught of blind passion and an-
archy. The main early issues and events of the Awakening lent themselves to such an interpretation, which,
though an oversimplification, carried enough truth to
make the task of defending the Awakening exceedingly
difficult. It was around three major issues in particular
that the lines of battle were first drawn: the debate over
the nature of the conversion experience itself, the attack on unconverted ministers, and the practice of itinerant preaching.

The nature of conversion quickly became a point of
great interest and contention, partly because of the unusual displays of weeping, fainting, and crying-out that
attended many revivals. The revivalists' novel method
of preaching, first introduced by Whitefield and rapidly
taken up by those who followed him, also focused attention on the experience of conversion. Whitefield had
startled his American listeners by using every rhetorical
device, intonation, and gesture at his disposal to make
the doctrine of God's sovereignty and his gift of grace
emotionally gripping. Soon, however, the doctrine was
being overshadowed as an item of major interest by the
manner of the preaching and the conversion experience
themselves.

The enemies of revivalism attempted to pin the label
of "enthusiasm" upon the Awakening. Originally a term
referring specifically to personal religious inspiration,
"enthusiasm" had come to carry all the pejorative over-
tones of religious fanaticism, wild-eyed emotionalism,
and doctrinal heresy. For proof that the Awakening was
nothing but enthusiasm run rampant, its critics charged
that the emotional outbursts of the revivals could only

be understood as the uncontrolled passion of confused men and hysterical women. To this the friends of the Awakening retorted that, far from being a fleeting moment of emotion, the conversion experience produced deep and beneficial changes in individual character and personality. As for unusual weeping and crying, they asked, was it unnatural for a man to be distraught at the moment when he confronted the meaning and ultimate destiny of his entire life? Neither side in the dispute was disposed to give much credence or to listen closely to the claims of the other.

A second major issue to divide the churches appeared when the revivalists started to attack unconverted ministers. As skeptical clergymen began to question the good taste and rationality of the revivalists, the latter retaliated by challenging the religious seriousness of their cultured despisers. Could anyone suppose, the revivalists asked, that a minister who had not experienced grace in his own soul could help others find salvation? Such miracles, they conceded, were possible, but highly unlikely. Indeed, they warned, an unconverted minister would almost certainly be not only a hindrance but a positive threat to the spiritual health of his congregation.

No other issue did more to mobilize widespread clerical opposition to the Awakening than this one. As early as 1740, Gilbert Tennent preached a sermon at Nottingham, Pennsylvania, entitled "On the Danger of an Unconverted Ministry," setting forth in unequivocal and even harsh terms the revivalists' position. He asked how "letter-learned pharisee-teachers," as he called his unconverted but educated clerical colleagues, "having no experience of a special work of the Holy Ghost upon their own souls," would be either able or desirous of talking about important religious subjects to their people. "Isn't an unconverted minister," he reasoned, "like a man who would learn others to swim, before he has learned it himself, and so is drowned in the act, and dies like a Fool?" Tennent's sermon raised a storm in his own Presbyterian synod. Within a few months, moreover, copies of the sermon had found their way to Boston and were being circulated by critics of the revival as prime evidence that the movement meant only censoriousness and divisiveness for the church.

Gilbert Tennent managed to make matters still easier for his opponents. In response to urgings from Whitefield himself, Tennent followed up the English evangelist's preaching tour of New England with one of his own. Tennent's preaching in Boston, undertaken in the excitement of what one historian has aptly called "the flood tide of the Great Awakening,"[3] was especially fervent and unrestrained. One unfriendly observer, without doubt underscoring for his own advantage the worst aspects of Tennent's performance, wrote that he stomped and brayed like a monster, shouting at his audiences that they were "damned, damned, damned."[4] It was now possible for persons hostile to the Awakening to attribute the responsibility for its excesses not only to second-rate imitators of Whitefield, but also to one of the most important American leaders of revivalism, Gilbert Tennent himself. Later Tennent acknowledged that his preaching had been somewhat injudicious; but the damage had already been done.

Tennent was not alone in following Whitefield's example of itinerating from place to place, and the grow-

[3] Edwin Scott Gaustad, *The Great Awakening in New England* (New York: 1957), p. 42.

[4] *Ibid.*, p. 33.

ing practice of itineration aroused still further hostility. The idea that ministers were to serve only those churches to which they had been duly appointed, either by call of the congregation or by assignment from other official church authorities, was deeply ingrained in the colonial mind. For ministers to range about the countryside conducting revivals was for the anti-revivalists an affront to any sense of order and decorum, and, worse, a threat to the very stability of society itself. The justification offered by the itinerants was simply that when men's souls are in peril, concern with propriety is of secondary importance. However, as inspired laymen with no theological training whatsoever began to itinerate and to invade the pulpits of regularly appointed ministers, even friends of the Awakening began to have misgivings.

The depth of discontent in the churches became fully apparent when many persons began to withdraw from older, established churches to form congregations made up only of the converted. The "Separates," as the radically independent congregations were called, posed problems both for the standing order in church and state as well as for the more moderate, or non-separating, revival leaders, who hoped for an inner purification of the church without actual schism.

As organized opposition to the Awakening began to form, it soon moved beyond argumentation and debate to actual coercion and suppression. In 1741 and 1742 clerical groups in Boston, Connecticut, and Philadelphia variously issued protests against the emotionalism and social disturbances of the revivals. Not content, however, with the mere passing of resolutions, the opponents of the Awakening began to mobilize the machinery of church and state to quash the revivals and their perpetrators.

In Connecticut, where the Separates were especially strong, official coercion was also most pronounced, with each extreme reinforcing the other. In 1741 an influential group of Connecticut ministers met and passed a resolution condemning itinerant ministers. These sentiments acquired the force of law the following year when the Connecticut General Assembly passed an act "for regulating abuses and correcting disorders in ecclesiastical affairs."[5] Subsequently, the Assembly clamped down still tighter by revoking the "toleration clause" of the Old Saybrook Platform, which had made it possible for dissenters to remain within Congregationalism. The result was to drive many Separatist churches to declare themselves Baptists in order to avoid paying taxes for the support of the Congregational minister whose leadership they had disavowed. Moreover, Yale and Harvard, after initially welcoming Whitefield, both turned against the entire Awakening, thus forcing the revivalists to look elsewhere for the higher education of their ministers.

The moderate, or non-separating, revivalists included many New Light Congregationalists in New England and all of the New Side Presbyterians farther south. Led by Jonathan Edwards and the Tennents, the moderates in both areas of the country moved very quickly to repudiate such radical groups as the extreme Separatists and Baptists, as well as a number of Moravians in Pennsylvania, for having distorted the true nature of the Awakening. The moderates viewed the radicals as too subjective—cultivating emotional experience for its own sake, rather than simply regarding it as a secondary accompaniment of conversion—and too schismatic—overly complacent about their own salvation and too ready to

[5] Joseph Tracy, *The Great Awakening* (Boston: 1842), pp. 70–72.

pronounce judgments on the state of other men's souls. Since it was the most cherished hope of the moderates that the Awakening would bind the American churches together in a new community of love, they could only look upon the radical Separatists as spoilers.

The complexity of the issues involved becomes especially clear in considering the situation of the moderate revivalists. They wanted to establish the validity of the Awakening, while at the same time dissociating themselves from its abuses. This required both the development of a compelling intellectual defense of revivalism and the repudiation of extremist groups with which the moderates did not agree. The necessity for this two-sided defensive strategy also underscored the seriousness of the factionalism that had beset the revivalist movement.

The fragmentation of the revivalist groups should not be allowed, however, to obscure the genuine dynamism inherent in the revivalist movement. This dynamic quality of the revivalist impulse manifested itself in different ways. For example, the Presbyterian church in the middle colonies was in the first years of the Great Awakening largely controlled by Old Side ministers. By 1758 the New Side revivalist party had gained almost complete control of the church, not primarily through political manipulation, but through the growth in numbers of revivalist clergy and congregations. The same dynamism found expression in higher education. Prior to 1740 the colonies had only three colleges—Yale, Harvard, and William and Mary. By 1776 there were nine colleges; and, of the six new ones, four had been founded by ministers and laymen with revivalist backgrounds and points of view. Moreover, scores of academies for the education of revivalist-oriented ministers and professional men were founded throughout the South and

West during the eighteenth century. Finally, the religious forces unleashed in the Great Awakening continued to inspire periodic waves of revivalism in the frontier regions of the West and South. During the 1740's and 50's New Side Presbyterians were especially active in winning converts in Hanover and adjacent counties of Virginia. A second wave of revivalism in the South began in the 1750's as Baptist preachers—the most important of their leaders being Separate Baptists from New England—itinerated through North and South Carolina, Georgia, and Virginia. A third wave of eighteenth-century revivalism, often designated as "the Methodist phase" of the Great Awakening, began in the 1770's in Dinwiddie County, Virginia, and spread quickly into the surrounding regions of Virginia and North Carolina.

The very dynamism characteristic of the revivalist movement should be kept in mind especially in attempting to assess the educational and intellectual significance of the Great Awakening. It supplied an energy to the educational undertakings of the revivalists—often lacking to their opponents—that vastly improved the chances of their educational ideals achieving concrete realization. Furthermore, the sheer force and sweep of the Great Awakening gave it an educative impact of a dimension that included, but also transcended, the ideas and efforts of specific individuals and groups.

II

The educational dimensions of the Great Awakening were soon manifest in the differing intellectual attitudes and commitments of the parties involved, and in the institutional strategies they developed in their efforts to promulgate their own views and to outflank one another. Many of the educational issues, intellectual and institutional, that were to figure so centrally in the divisions of the Awakening had already begun to appear in a theological dispute between two groups of ministers in the American Presbyterian church as early as the 1720's. This early disagreement not only foreshadowed the later crisis of the Great Awakening, but also contributed to it.

The major organizational body of the Presbyterian church in America at the time, the Synod of Philadelphia, included in its membership two groups of ministers with quite dissimilar backgrounds. The larger group in the synod was predominantly Scotch-Irish, as immigrants to America from the Scottish settlements in North Ireland came to be called. These men were graduates of Scottish universities and had grown up under the strict doctrinal and disciplinary standards of the Presbyterian church in Scotland and Ireland. The smaller group was composed mainly of ministers who had been born and reared in New England, had received their education at Yale, and had been Congregationalists before entering the Presbyterian ministry. Each group held views regarding theology and church government that were considerably different and that very early came into conflict.

These disagreements first began to emerge in the 1720's in the so-called "subscriptionist controversy" over whether ministers licensed by the synod should be required to subscribe without reservations to all of the doctrines of the Westminster Confession, the traditional standard of faith in the Scottish and Irish Presbyterian churches. The Scotch-Irish ministers favored subscription; the New England men opposed any requirement for unqualified subscription to the Confession. Fundamental issues were at stake with each side, as so often, emphasizing different aspects of their common Calvinist heritage.

The Scotch-Irish ministers tended to stress the objective and rationalist side of Calvinist theology, insisting that the truth of church doctrine be safeguarded from the vagaries of individualistic interpretation. The New England ministers, coming out of an English Puritan and Congregational background, placed more emphasis on the subjective elements of the faith. They valued highly a personal sense of the truth of doctrine, and feared the hypocrisy of an individual's subscribing to the Confession without genuine, inner conviction. Concerned to preserve doctrinal truth and order in the church, the subscriptionists accordingly also demanded a highly educated ministry and strong clerical rule in church government. The anti-subscriptionists, again revealing their Puritan and Congregational origins, regarded the participation of laymen in church affairs with greater favor, and were more concerned about the strength of a minister's personal faith than about his formal education. In the midst of heated controversy a serious split in the church was narrowly averted by a compromise agreement reached in the Adopting Act of 1729, which stipulated that candidates for ministerial licensing were to subscribe to the general outlook of the Westminster Confession, but could reserve the right to demur on specific articles of doctrine, if their consciences so required. Cases in question were to be adjudicated in church court.

This uneasy peace, which the Adopting Act had brought, was disturbed within a few years by the activities of William Tennent's new Log College graduates. Much closer in temperament and outlook to the New England than to the Scotch-Irish ministers of the synod, the Log College graduates became notorious in the 1730's for their fiery revival preaching and the emotionally charged responses they evoked. The Scotch-Irish ministers, to their dismay, saw control of the church slipping from their fingers as more and more congregations indicated their preference for ministers who were able and willing to preach like Log College men. Finally, in 1738, a proposal was passed in the synod requiring that all ministerial candidates possess a degree either from a European university (such as Edinburgh or Glasgow, which most of the Scotch-Irish had attended) or from a New England college. This action was patently an attempt to curtail the influence of the Log College graduates, none of whom had a traditional college degree, by denying them ministerial licenses. Thus the question of educational standards for ministers became one of the first issues in the Great Awakening.

As the converted clergy found their educational credentials challenged, they retaliated by questioning the religious commitment of the learned ministers. Gilbert Tennent's famous 1740 sermon "on the dangers of an unconverted ministry" was preached partially in response to the action of the Synod of Philadelphia in withholding ministerial licenses from Log College graduates. So pointed were the barbs directed by Tennent at the anti-revivalists that the latter in anger expelled the Log College ministers from the synod. Very early in the Awakening it was beginning to appear that the traditional ideal, affirmed, for example, by Cotton Mather as late as 1726, of the Puritan minister who was both learned and converted was in total jeopardy.[6]

[6] Cotton Mather, *Manuductio ad Ministerium, Directions for a Candidate of the Ministry* (Boston: 1726).

This pattern of reaction and counter-reaction repeated itself in New England as the revivals spread. The friendliness Yale and Harvard had initially shown toward revivalism quickly evaporated in the heat of the moment. Newly "awakened" students in both colleges expressed greater concern about the state of their professors' souls than the quality of their teaching. The authorities had little patience with their rebellious students—the disruptive consequence of their activities appeared too dangerous. President Clap of Yale even went so far as to expel the brothers John and Ebenezer Cleaveland for simply attending services at the Separatist church of their parents in Milford, outside of New Haven. At Harvard, too, at least one awakened student was expelled by the faculty for calling the local minister a "dumb dog that cannot bark."[7] George Whitefield, meanwhile, had aroused further resentment in the academic communities by permitting pages from his journal to be published in which he severely criticized the religious life of the New England colleges. When Whitefield returned to America in 1744 the Harvard faculty, with the later endorsement of the Yale faculty, roundly censured him in a fifteen-page pamphlet for his enthusiasm and censoriousness and for his extemporaneous and itinerant preaching.

Accused of being anti-intellectual enthusiasts, and with both Yale and Harvard closed to them, the revivalists found it necessary to make other arrangements for the education of their ministers. A two-stage revivalist educational counteroffensive was launched.

The first stage began with the founding of new acad-

[7] Samuel Eliot Morison, *Three Centuries of Harvard* (Cambridge, Mass.: 1936), p. 86.

emies as rival institutions of learning to the older, established colleges. In his 1741 sermon Tennent first issued the call for many little schools devoted to the preparation of revival-minded ministers. He was, in effect, asking for the founding of many new Log Colleges. A similar call was repeated the following year by Jonathan Edwards, who extended the plea for revivalist-oriented education even to the elementary level. Condemning the lack of piety at Yale and Harvard, in much the same terms Whitefield had used, Edwards also proposed "establishing and supporting schools in poor towns and villages," not only "to bring children up in common learning," but also to prepare them for conversion.[8]

In New England the attempts of the revivalists to set up rival institutions to Yale and Harvard were shortlived. Separatist groups established an academy at New London, Connecticut, in 1742, called the "Shepherds' Tent," to train their ministers. The Connecticut General Assembly, however, quickly acted to close down the Shepherds' Tent, and New England Separatists, thereafter, found themselves without any institutions of higher learning that would admit their ministerial candidates.

In the middle and southern colonies, however, the academy movement of the moderate revivalists began to take hold and to spread rapidly. Several academies founded by graduates of William Tennent's Log College achieved a special fame of their own, both for the quality of instruction they offered, and for the number of their alumni who later attained eminence as politicians, professors, even scientists, as well as ministers. These included the academy of Samuel Finley at Not-

[8] *The Works of President Edwards in Four Volumes* (New York: 1849), III, 414–416.

tingham on the Maryland–Pennsylvania border; the academy of Samuel Blair at Faggs Manor, Pennsylvania; and that of Robert Smith at Pequea, Pennsylvania. Finley and Blair, both early leaders of the Awakening and fervent evangelists, were graduates of the Log College, and Smith, also a New Side leader, had been a student under Blair at Faggs Manor. Although a few Old Side ministers also established academies—that of Francis Alison, the major spokesman for the Old Side, was especially outstanding—the New Side far outstripped the Old Side in the number of academies founded. The impetus given to academy founding by the New Side revivalists helped lead to the establishment of more than fifty Presbyterian academies in the middle and southern colonies by the end of the Revolutionary War. Several of these academies eventually evolved into regular, chartered colleges.

The second phase in the revivalists' strategy to secure their own centers of higher learning came with the decision to concentrate energy and resources in the creation of a full-fledged college. The result was the College of New Jersey (later Princeton University) founded under the leadership of important Log College graduates and outstanding ministers of New England background in the Presbytery of New Brunswick.

The New Side's decision to establish a college served more than one purpose. It was clear to the New Side leadership that unless they had access to a bona fide, chartered college capable of granting degrees that would command the respect of all, they could not hope to counter the accusations that they were the enemies of learning. Both the Log College graduates, whose education had been openly disparaged, and the New England men in the presbytery, who were proud of their Yale degrees, had good reason to want to make it plain that they were not opposed to learning and education, as was being charged. In addition, the need of the New Side for institutions of higher education found encouraging support in the desires of many local communities for institutions of higher education to serve their needs—institutions closer to home than Yale and Harvard. It was clear that a new college established in a thriving, young community could count on widespread local support if it offered an education that would be of benefit to the entire community. Thus it was that revival ministers, local lay leaders, and New Jersey officials all cooperated in securing for the College of New Jersey its second and permanent charter in 1748.

Other colleges were eventually founded under revivalist auspices. Dartmouth College grew out of an Indian mission school first conducted at Lebanon, Connecticut, by Eleazar Wheelock, a zealous Congregational New Light preacher and Dartmouth's first president. The College of Rhode Island (today Brown University) was established largely under revivalist Baptist sponsorship. Finally, Queen's College (today Rutgers University) was started by the revivalist wing of the Dutch Reformed Church. In each instance the pattern followed in the founding and chartering of these colleges was the same as that observed in connection with the College of New Jersey. The first inspiration for a new college came from an influential group of revivalists, who also supplied teachers and administrators; they were joined by sympathetic community leaders who helped to broaden support for the new institutions; and, finally, a general liberal arts curriculum was introduced that aimed not simply at the preparation of ministers but of other professional men as well.

A feature common to all of these colleges did not escape comment even at the time. Each of their charters stated explicitly that the colleges were intended to serve Protestants of all denominations and forbade religious tests for admission. Various reasons have been advanced to explain this clear movement in the direction of religious tolerance. Each probably contains a share of the truth. One suggestion has been that the colleges knew they needed students, if they were to survive, and, therefore, out of expediency attempted to appeal to the widest possible clientele. A second explanation, however, has stressed that the charters gave expression to a real and growing sense of the need for religious freedom and denominational cooperation. Even though it split the churches, the Great Awakening was, paradoxically, a genuinely interdenominational movement. It frequently became more important during the Awakening to know whether a man was revivalist or anti-revivalist, than to know whether he was Congregational, Presbyterian, or Baptist. Many of the revivalists also had a vision of an America unified in one great communal movement toward the realization of God's Kingdom on Earth. Sectarian requirements for college attendance could only subvert such a vision. Furthermore, many of the revivalist congregations and leaders had experienced persecution at the hands of the established churches and were determined to work toward greater separation of church and state. A final explanation for the expression of greater religious freedom in the college charters is that many of the most important revivalists did, indeed, contrary to accusations then and since, have a high regard for learning and were not willing to subordinate it entirely to religious and sectarian ends.

The attacks upon their intellectual respectability hurt

and rankled the moderate revivalists and forced them to the task, not only of founding their own institutions, but also of countering charges that they were anti-intellectual and emotional enthusiasts. Many supporters of the Awakening were graduates of Harvard and Yale, and these included some of the colonies' most respected and cultured ministers. These men did not at all relish being classed with fanatics and rabble rousers. Likewise, the graduates of the Log College resented the insinuations that their education was inferior to that of their Edinburgh and Glasgow-trained adversaries. The moderate revivalists also felt that the complaint about enthusiasm frequently served as an excuse for avoiding the deeper and more uncomfortable question posed by revivalism; namely, the fate of one's soul. For many reasons, therefore, it became extremely important for the moderate revivalists to be able to demonstrate the intellectual respectability and validity of the Awakening.

As already noted, this was no simple task since few of the moderate Awakeners themselves had been very careful in the beginning to guard against abuses. Their situation was made even more difficult by the bizarre antics of James Davenport, a young minister from Long Island, a graduate of Yale, and an admirer of Whitefield and Gilbert Tennent. In 1741 Davenport began his own New England preaching tour which was more flamboyant and, to increasing numbers of persons initially undecided in their attitude toward the Awakening, more offensive than anything previously witnessed. Davenport claimed direct inspiration from the holy spirit without the aid of human learning, a belief which inspired him, among other things, to lead a book-burning demonstration on the wharf at New London, and to assert that he could identify the unconverted by sight. It was, however,

when he began to accuse other ministers by name as
"carnal-minded" and "unredeemed" that the entire
Awakening fell under suspicion. Although Davenport
was jailed and declared *non compis mentis*, and although
he eventually recanted, the damage had been done.
Gilbert Tennent's belated condemnation of Davenport
merely led his critics to suggest that something was lacking either in Tennent's sincerity or in his wisdom—after
all, had not he himself encouraged such as Davenport by
first storming into Boston on the heels of Whitefield?
No matter how respectable many revivalist ministers
might be, the critics charged, their activities in the end
would only produce more and more spectacles of the sort
witnessed in Davenport and his followers. Now, as never
before, the moderate Awakeners desperately needed a
convincing and discriminating intellectual justification
of revivalism that would protect it both from its enemies
and its too ardent friends.

The burden of providing such a defense fell to Jonathan Edwards, to whom the major revivalists in all the
colonies looked for intellectual and spiritual leadership.
In this task Edwards had to contend with many sharp
and articulate critics, but the most formidable was the
Reverend Charles Chauncy of First Church, Boston. Like
many of his fellow Congregational ministers, Chauncy at
first welcomed the Awakening. Within a few months,
however, alarmed at what he saw taking place, much of
it contrary to his own conception of an urbane and rational Christianity, Chauncy began to lead the assault
against the revivals.

Edwards' defense of revivalism was two-pronged. Neg-
atively, he conceded that some of the criticisms of the
Awakening were well-taken. Fanaticism and factionalism, he admitted, were present, but he refused to admit

that they were intrinsic to revivalism as such. Instead, he attempted to establish criteria by which the permanent and beneficial results of conversion could be distinguished from both the merely incidental side-effects and the aberrantly harmful. Edwards first moved in this direction in 1741, in a sermon, delivered at the Yale commencement, on "The Distinguishing Marks of a Work of the Spirit of God." In this discourse Edwards contended that many of the physical and emotional manifestations of the Awakening were in themselves of no spiritual significance one way or another, and should not be cultivated for their own sake. The true "distinguishing marks," which he emphatically insisted were also present in the Awakening and demanded its support, were a deeper sense of divine truth and a greater "spirit of love to God and man." It was in making use of these distinctions that Edwards began to dissociate himself from the radical Separatists of New England and that the Tennents began to criticize the subjectivism of the Moravians of Pennsylvania.

Positively, Edwards argued that revivalism was based upon a more adequate understanding both of the scriptures and of human nature than was the religion of the anti-revivalists. In 1743 Edwards published his second major defense of the Awakening, entitled *Some Thoughts Concerning the Present Revival of Religion in New England*. One of Edwards' major concerns in this work was to show that the emotions, or affections, are at the very center of the religious life and, indeed, of all human activity. Following such an argument Edwards charged that his opponents, insofar as they deprecated the role of the emotions in religion, were basing their opposition to the Awakening upon a totally inadequate conception of human nature.

Charles Chauncy promptly responded to Edwards with a long work of his own. As the title of his book indicated —*Seasonable Thoughts on the State of Religion in New England* (1743)—Chauncy was writing in direct answer to Edwards. Drawing upon observations he himself had made on a tour of New England, Chauncy offered examples to document his earlier warning that the Awakening was nothing more than enthusiasm, "a bad temperament of the blood and spirits," "a disease, a sort of madness."[9] He also attacked Edwards' notion that vital religion is rooted in the affections. "Our people," Edwards had written, "do not so much need to have their heads stored, as to have their hearts touched. . . ."[10] It was this kind of thinking that in Chauncy's view lent encouragement to the most extreme emotional excesses of the revivals. Chauncy responded that there were two kinds of religion, one of the head and one of the heart, and that only the first was good. "There is the religion of the understanding and judgment and will," he wrote, "as well as of the affections; and if little account is made of the former, while great stress is laid upon the latter, it can't be but people should run into disorders."[11]

The essential difference between the two was that Edwards, unlike Chauncy, refused to view the head and heart as fundamentally distinct and separate. Chauncy held that the understanding is rational, the emotions irrational, and that it is the task of the former to check and control the latter. Against this psychological dualism Edwards was groping toward an understanding of hu-

[9] Charles Chauncy, *Enthusiasm described and caution'd against* (Boston: 1742), p. 3.

[10] Edwards, *Works,* III, 336.

[11] Charles Chauncy, *Seasonable Thoughts on the State of Religion in New England* (Boston: 1743), p. 422.

man nature as an interrelated whole, a unity in which the direction, quality, and very possibility of all human activity, including that of thinking itself, are grounded in the affections.

In his later *Treatise Concerning Religious Affections* (1746), Edwards developed still more carefully his view that the affections are the driving and unifying power of the self. The affections, he wrote, "are very much the springs of men's actions," and "are the things that put men forward, and carry 'em along in all their worldly actions." That man is simply deluded or rationalizing who believes that his total personality and underlying motives do not shape his every act and utterance. Thus, from Edwards' standpoint, the contrast drawn by his opponents between a higher religion of reason and a lower religion of emotion was a patent impossibility because it was founded upon a false view of the human mind and personality. "True religion," Edwards maintained, "consists in the affections"; therefore, the proper contrast to be drawn was between a higher religion grounded in "holy affections," the chief of which was love, and a lower religion of base and selfish affections. It was in conversion, he argued, that the religious affections are awakened, so that they, rather than other emotions, directed the thinking, willing, and acting self.

Although the full dimensions of Edwards' thought cannot be explored here, two aspects of his theology of conversion do deserve note. They indicate the direction his thinking, and that of his followers, would take when they turned explicitly to matters of education. And, they reveal those areas where Edwards and his followers were in fact vulnerable to charges of anti-intellectualism, as well as those where such charges could not justifiably be maintained without important qualifications.

In the first place, in refusing to pit the understanding against the emotions, Edwards was struggling with the difficult idea that reason and the emotions are integrally related and affect each other in a reciprocal and circular way. "Holy affections," he repeatedly stressed, "are not heat without light; but evermore arise from some information of the understanding, some spiritual instruction that the mind receives, some light or actual knowledge." The result of this "spiritual instruction" was "a new sense of the heart," a new vision of reality that paved the way for a re-direction of the emotions and a total restructuring of the personality—all of which, he was convinced, took place only in a genuine conversion experience.

To try to make clear what he meant, he drew upon analogies from the realms of physical and aesthetic experience. In the experience of learning, for example, Edwards distinguished between speculative and experiential knowledge—or what he called "notional" and "sensible" knowing. A man can have many correct notions, he argued, about "the justice of a speech, the goodness of style, the beauty of a poem, the gracefulness of deportment, etc.," but, if in such matters he has no "taste," his knowledge remains purely formal and external. Without a total rational, emotional, aesthetic response, correct reasoning is of little avail in the full appreciation of either an idea or a work of art. Similarly, in religion true rational knowledge is important—and neither Edwards nor his close followers slighted rational, doctrinal preaching—but without a "taste" for religious beauty, doctrine by itself is empty and formal. What Edwards seems to have been urging was that for all meaningful knowledge there must be a union of the cognitive and the affective powers of the personality in a new vision of reality—

whether reality be a picture, an idea, or the being of God.

Edwards was convinced that he was not deprecating rational understanding in defending the Awakening. This is particularly evident in the criteria he finally arrived at for judging the validity of the conversion experiences. In *Religious Affections* Edwards identified twelve positive signs which he thought pointed to the presence of genuine religious experience, all of which were guided by two central considerations. First, religious affections were never to be isolated from rationality; they were not "heat without light," and, if they did not conduce to a better and clearer understanding, they were rightly suspect. It was true, Edwards granted, that in the momentous restructuring of the personality in conversion, violent emotions might well be unleashed, but these, he insisted, were by-products of the main event and ought never to be pursued or encouraged for their own sake. Second, true religious affections would manifest themselves in love for others expressed in actual conduct. By maintaining the unity of understanding and emotional experience, Edwards was able simultaneously to mount an attack upon the empty and formalistic rationalism he discerned in much New England preaching, and to reject the uncritical and indulgent emotionalism of many revivalist groups.

In a real sense, Edwards and the revivalists who followed his leadership were attempting to deal with a much more complicated and intellectually and socially messy world than their opponents were willing to admit existed. The liberal-minded anti-revivalists displayed not a little of what Arthur O. Lovejoy has aptly called "the anti-intellectualism of Enlightenment rationalism"—the frequent readiness to ignore or belittle those aspects of experience not immediately illuminated by the clear light of reason.[12] This Edwards was not willing to do, and it is no surprise to find him chiding his adversaries for their cavalier dismissal of the genuinely obstinate puzzles of human experience. At the same time, Edwards was quite certain that he himself had been granted a clear vision of ultimate reality. His own consequent inclination to brand as opposers of God's work those who raised eyebrows at the Awakening contributed not a little to the hardening of his opposition and the breakdown of real dialogue between the two sides. Moreover, the complexities of his own exposition of the mystical "new sense of the heart" made it difficult to discourage the tendency of many radical revivalists and ordinary church folk to make their own strict separation between reason and emotion.

There was a second major aspect of the moderate revivalist theology that had educational importance. Even though Edwards' opponents faulted him for being too abstract, too metaphysical, his thought contained a strong pragmatic and utilitarian emphasis. After all, the revivalists did not talk about religious truth as something beyond experience, but as a reality that bore upon men's lives in the here and now. And they did get results—they produced conversions that could be actually observed, described, and tested. The very term, "experimental religion," which Edwards and the revivalists enjoyed applying to their outlook, made clear their conviction that, whereas their opponents were operating in a world of mere hypothesis and speculation, they were dealing with empirical fact.

[12] Arthur O. Lovejoy, "The Parallel of Deism and Classicism," *Modern Philology*, XXIX (1932), 287.

The same utilitarian strain was evident in the revivalists' belief that the coming millennium—God's reign on earth which the Great Awakening was helping to inaugurate—would be marked by new political and social arrangements and by a burgeoning of technological and scientific wonders. Although the revivalists seldom made a conscious connection between experimental religion and educational practice, they did place a high value, as will become clear in looking at the revivalist college curriculum, on scientific and utilitarian subject matter. Likewise, Edwards embraced without reservation the educational empiricism of John Locke in urging upon the Indian school at Stockbridge that "the child should be taught to understand things, as well as words."[13] The revivalists' rejection of mere speculative or "notional" knowledge in religion pushed them toward an appreciation of the experiential and pragmatic in other matters as well.

In becoming one of the major arenas within which the battles of the Awakening were fought, education increasingly reflected the underlying differences in social attitudes separating the friends and foes of revivalism. The logic of revivalism itself contained a built-in tendency toward social levelling, a fact quickly pointed out by persons who viewed the Awakening as a fundamental threat to the existent social order. If all persons, regardless of social status, were potentially candidates for conversion, then, the revivalists held, all should have access to the chief means of salvation—the preached and written word. Moreover, the Awakening was at bottom a mass movement which drew its main energy and strength

[13] Jonathan Edwards, "Letter to Sir W. Pepperell, November 28, 1751," in Sereno E. Dwight, *The Life of President Edwards* (New York: 1830), pp. 474–481.

from popular support inside and outside of established institutions. Thus, inner logic and popular pressure combined to help produce profoundly new views of the place and purposes of education in American society.

The popular base of the Great Awakening is nowhere better illustrated than in the "reading revivals" that occurred in newly settled Hanover County, Virginia, in the early 1740's. There, the initiative for revivalism came from unchurched laymen having no access at first to regular, ordained clergy. Having heard reports of the Awakening, groups of laymen in the frontier area began to assemble in private homes to read and discuss the meager religious literature they could put their hands on. As conversions began to take place spontaneously the reading group practice spread from one area to the next. Finally, only after the movement was under way were the people able to make contact with young Log College graduates venturing into Hanover County, and invite them to provide guidance and organize regular congregations from the reading groups.

The work of Samuel Davies, who followed the first wave of Log College men into Hanover County, exemplifies the popular and educational dimensions of the Awakening. Having received his own education at the Fagg's Manor Academy of Samuel Blair, another outstanding Log College revivalist, Davies arrived in Virginia in 1748, where he organized churches and eventually helped to found the Hanover Presbytery in 1755. Davies enjoyed the reputation of being one of the greatest pulpit orators of his day, but he is perhaps best known to students of American history for his success in arguing that dissenters in the colonies as well as in England were protected under the 1689 Act of Toleration. In gaining the support of English authorities against the colonial government, Davies' victory was an important landmark in the history of religious freedom in America. For ten years in Virginia Davies worked unceasingly— preaching revival sermons, organizing and instructing his many congregations, spending nearly eighteen months in Great Britain with Gilbert Tennent to raise funds for the College of New Jersey, and recruiting volunteers for the defense of the frontier against attack during the French and Indian War. In 1759 he became President of the College of New Jersey, but succumbed to illness and died in 1761, a few months after commencement.

After graduating from Fagg's Manor Davies not only continued his own self-study, in a program so rigorous that, along with his many other duties, it was said to have contributed to his early death, he was also incessant in his efforts to provide reading materials and instruction for his parishioners. He was particularly concerned that the poor whites and black slaves in his churches be able to continue their religious growth and that they be taught to read and write. Davies tirelessly solicited books and reading materials from friends in England and Scotland, and circulated them among his congregations. "Davies churches," reported one observer, "were little schools. . . . Households generally were furnished with a few standard works of good old times and were expected to study them carefully."[14] At the same time Davies did not stint his own sermon preparation. "Every sermon I think worthy of the name," he wrote, "cost me four days hard study."[15]

The moderate revivalists were also concerned that laymen have a thorough grasp of religious knowledge, even

[14] William Henry Foote, *Sketches of Virginia* (Philadelphia: 1850), I, 378–379.
[15] *Ibid.*, I, 303.

of difficult theological concepts. Ministers, in their view, had no monopoly on religious truth, and they were not to present theology as an esoteric subject which only they could understand. To be sure, ministers were called by virtue of their own religious experience and special training to provide spiritual and intellectual leadership for their people, but this was a responsibility, not a privilege. In one of his sermons Jonathan Edwards explicitly voiced the need for ministers and laymen alike to share the duties and benefits of study.

The differences in attitudes toward learning among the various factions of the Awakening were most vivid in their conceptions of ministerial education. The "learned ministry" controversies of the Awakening also exposed most clearly the extremist positions which could, and quickly did, develop toward clerical elitism in one direction and toward militant anti-intellectualism in the other.

The anti-revivalists' attitudes were generally the simplest and least ambiguous. Their view of the church as a guardian of social order, their conception of the minister as a cultural and intellectual standard-bearer, and their commitment to rational order in matters of belief —whether of the new liberal or older orthodox varieties —all led them to a straightforward and consistent demand that to qualify for a ministerial license a candidate must have a bachelor's degree from an established college or university and be able to pass an examination which frequently required further graduate training in theology.

The revivalists operated according to a different set of priorities, but they held both social order and scholarly ability in much higher esteem than their opponents were usually willing to grant. Conversion was their first concern; consequently, they took much less seriously than did the anti-revivalists many of the conventions and ideals whereby social stability had traditionally been maintained. In their attitudes toward ministerial education the moderate revivalists evinced an ambivalence they never quite surmounted. They valued conversion for ministers above all; yet they cherished the rhetorical skills conferred by a liberal arts education. They flayed "letter-learned Pharisee preachers" for their hypocrisy; yet were extremely sensitive to attacks on their own scholarly abilities. Their founding of academies and colleges in part reflected these anxieties about their own status in the eyes of the respectable.

The attitudes of Separates and Baptists, and later of the Methodists, toward the learned ministry were again much more radical and even more complex than those of the moderate revivalists. In their order of priorities the new birth consistently took first place over all other considerations. Compared with other revivalists their animosity toward college-educated ministers was more unbridled, and their willingness to accept conversion as the sole qualification required of the revival preacher was more complete.

Overt anti-intellectualism was most in evidence among these groups. However, much of their hostility to college-educated ministers can be seen in part as a reaction to the high-handed tactics of the established authorities who frequently left them little choice between holding to their convictions or abandoning them and educating their ministers. Denied admission to Yale and Harvard the Separates no sooner attempted to establish their own center for education, the Shepherds' Tent, than the Connecticut authorities moved decisively to close it down. It may be no accident that with the folding of the

Shepherds' Tent the tendency of the Separates to regard immediate inspiration as directly antithetical to learning became more pronounced. Recall, too, that Gilbert Tennent preached his own sermon "on the dangers of an unconverted ministry" partly in retaliation against the attempts of the Old Side to discredit the education of Log College graduates and to deny them ministerial licenses.

It should also be recognized that the radical Baptists themselves gave more thought to ministerial education than is sometimes supposed. It was, for example, none other than the Baptist leaders and outspoken critics of unconverted ministers, Morgan Edwards and Isaac Backus, who successfully marshalled support among Philadelphia and New England Baptists for the founding of the College of Rhode Island in 1764. Even in the frontiers of the South and West, where Baptists were especially active and where the demand for ministers— with or without a diploma—far outstripped the supply, Baptists were not oblivious to the need for good sense and sound intellect. Thus, John Leland, the Baptist leader in Virginia, urged his people to remember that, although grace was essential, the call to preach was, nevertheless, bound up with the personality of the whole man. If it were not, Leland wrote, "we should have as good reason to believe that God would call infants, idiots, or dumb men, as any other; but this we know is not the case."[16] As Leland tried to make clear, not all of the radicals by any means equated the lack of degree certification with the exaltation of ignorance.

It was in the colleges and universities founded by the

[16] Quoted in Winthrop Hudson, ed., *Baptist Concepts of the Church* (Chicago: 1957), p. 115.

revivalists that their attitudes toward learning took on specific content and institutional embodiment. A word of caution is perhaps in order at this point, however, for to suppose that the revivalists' educational programs were a direct, practical application of their particular religious outlook would be a mistake. The revivalists were also men of their time, and their own educational thinking drew upon the common currency of eighteenth-century educational ideals and practices. Rather than viewing their curricular programs, for example, as a kind of logical outgrowth or extension of underlying revivalist premises, it is much more fruitful to ask what currents in the world of eighteenth-century education did the revivalists find appealing and throw their support behind.

Initially the strongest motive in the founding of revivalist academies and colleges was to secure opportunities for the training of ministers. This was never the exclusive purpose of the revivalist-oriented institutions, however—even the first of the academies, the Log College, welcomed students seeking preparation for non-clerical professions—and, after the peak intensity of the Awakening had passed, they devoted still more attention to education for all the learned professions. This was true, certainly, of the College of New Jersey, which drew its board of trustees from the general community and received its purpose from its official charters as one of "encouraging and promoting a learned Education of Our Youth in New Jersey . . . for the Benefit of the *inhabitants of the* Said Province *and other.*"[17] In many of the smaller academies also, with student bodies some-

[17] Quoted in John Maclean, *History of the College of New Jersey* (Philadelphia: 1877), I, 176.

times numbering thirty to sixty boys, more than half the young men were preparing for other professions besides the ministry, even though these schools were under the direction of a single minister-teacher. Thus, the exhortations of revivalist orators, repeated in sermons and civic addresses, on the Christian duties of patriotism and public service, found one concrete avenue of expression in the offering of a broader range of educational opportunities to the settlements of the middle and southern colonies than would have otherwise been available.

The core of the curriculum in the revivalist academies and the College of New Jersey was, of course, that common to all eighteenth-century institutions of higher education: the classical languages and the liberal arts and sciences. These were the subjects considered essential for the development of a truly educated man and basic preparation for all the learned professions—the ministry, law, and medicine. Fundamental changes within the curriculum, however, were also beginning to take place in the mid-eighteenth century with the introduction of new teaching methods, such as the demonstration lecture, new scientific subjects, and new literary and modern language studies. Many of these changes were being pioneered by the universities of Scotland whose achievements were helping to make Scotland one of the leading centers of the European Enlightenment. By the time of the Revolution the influence of the Scottish universities was becoming increasingly important in American higher education, particularly in the middle colonies where the College of Philadelphia and the College of New Jersey were located.

Revivalist-oriented educators displayed a remarkable interest in these new educational developments, and some played a leading part in promoting the new science and progressive teaching methods. The earliest minister presidents of the College of New Jersey, for example, strove with some success to broaden the curricular offerings of the college and to improve its science and language instruction. "Religion and Useful Learning," "Religion and Science," "Religion and Public Spirit"—these themes were repeated in sermons, commencement addresses, and publicity pamphlets as the guiding ideals of the infant college. There was a good deal of promotional rhetoric in this, of course, but it was not so inflated as to be completely out of touch with reality. A first priority among the specific needs listed in a pamphlet used by Gilbert Tennent and Samuel Davies in 1752-54 to raise funds in Great Britain for the college was money for scientific equipment. Even more revealing of the revivalist educators' interests were the courses of study pursued in some of the outstanding New Side academies.

A good example was the Nottingham Academy, directed for nearly two decades by Samuel Finley, before his own election to the presidency of the College of New Jersey. Finley, of course, taught the classics, but he also included advanced instruction in English literature and composition, an innovation he later introduced at the college. Finley also attempted to instruct his students in science and mathematics, as competently as he was able, and he made up for deficiencies he may have had in these fields by guiding able students into later careers in science and medicine.

The revivalist schools were not alone in their interest in the new education. The outstanding spokesman for the Old Side Presbyterians and the most astute critic of the Log College, the Rev. Francis Alison, himself a graduate of Edinburgh University, was one of the first to introduce the latest Scottish philosophy and literary thought into American higher education, at his own academy and later as Vice-Provost of the College of Philadelphia. Under the joint leadership of Alison and its Provost, William Smith, also a Scottish university graduate, the College of Philadelphia developed one of the most comprehensive and modern college curricula in America at the time. What is interesting, then, about the revivalist educational outlook is not its uniqueness, but rather its being in the forefront of curricular change and innovation, despite what initially appears to have been the revivalists' overwhelming concern with matters religious.

Necessity was undoubtedly one important force behind the revivalists' efforts to provide a modern course of study and first-rate level of teaching: for one thing, they were extra-sensitive to attacks upon their scholarly attainments; for another, they needed students and were eager to offer instruction that would attract as large a number as possible. But these more ulterior motives do not obscure their genuine interest in the new education and the intellectual excitement that many of their schools exuded. The empirical, pragmatic strain in revivalism and its vision of a revitalized human community on earth (which many revivalists suspected was beginning in America) led them easily to support the new empirical and utilitarian science of the day.

In this respect the Great Awakening and the Enlightenment were not as diametrically opposed as the surface ructions of revivalist controversy seemed to suggest. Whatever their differences, the leading educators on both sides were drawn to support much the same kind of modern and progressive college curriculum. Both considered themselves scientific in their attitudes—the anti-revivalists appealing to the claims of order and rationality, the revivalists stressing the importance of experience and observation. Both sides favored the new literary studies with their cultivation of English literature and the modern foreign languages—the anti-revivalists promoting literary studies for the cultural elite and polished man of affairs, the revivalists adapting them to the realization of their ideals of the evangelical orator and public servant. Though they differed in their visions of society, both valued highly the promotion of useful knowledge for social purposes. Furthermore, the revivalist educators supplied their own pursuit of the new studies with the same formidable energies exhibited in their missionary zeal. Consequently, and perhaps somewhat paradoxically, the revivalist educators frequently rivalled and, occasionally, even outdistanced their opponents in the actual implementation of an "enlightened" curriculum.

It was in this last element—the missionary drive of the revivalists to remake society—that revivalism may have exerted its most significant and lasting influence upon American higher education. Important roots of the long-standing American propensity to look to institutions of education as a chief means of reconstructing society can be traced to the Great Awakening. In transferring to education their sense of mission and urgency the revivalists began to look to the college and academy as powerful instruments for the realization of their social ideal. Educational institutions had always provided one of the central bulwarks of civilized life—Harvard College, for example, was from its beginning intended to furnish leaders for church and state—but their function was traditionally one of maintaining and

strengthening an already accepted ideal of social organization. In the Great Awakening a subtle but extremely
important shift began to take place, from an essentially
conserving to a more dynamic view of the role of education in society. The social uses of education were increasingly conceived, not primarily in terms of maintaining the given society, but of creating a new social
order that did not yet exist. Thus, the eighteenth century
witnessed the beginning of a surge in college and academy founding on the newly settled frontiers that was
only momentarily interrupted by the Revolution and
that did not subside until the Civil War. Many old
assumptions about the social uses of education lingered,
to be sure, and in the nineteenth century were to reassert
themselves. But, the fifth decade of the eighteenth century was a crucial period in the emergence of the American faith in formal education as a socially dynamic and
reconstructing force.

III

Arising as it did out of the stresses and strains within
colonial society, the revivalist movement gave impetus
and direction to the fundamental changes occurring
within that society. While scholars have only begun to
assess the enduring influence of the Awakening, and still
disagree at important points in their interpretations, increasingly they have begun to inquire into its broader
formative influence on American culture. The Awakening has won renewed attention especially from those interested in probing the origins of the revolutionary spirit
of the colonies and the egalitarian temperament and
sense of manifest destiny in the new nation. And it is
here, perhaps, in its role in shaping the American char-

acter and society, that the full educational significance of the Great Awakening should be sought.

Certainly with the emergence of new religious priorities and attitudes in the Awakening, there also appeared a profound challenge to older assumptions regarding social order and authority. Time-honored social distinctions based on tradition and privilege, rank and place, prestige and parts, all paled in the minds of many persons before the one great distinction between the saved and the damned. Many were to affirm Samuel Davies' words that it was salvation from heaven on which men should "fix all their hopes, notwithstanding the great Diversity of their Circumstances as to Situation, Education, outward Instruction, etc." Long before the Awakening, of course, the mobility and cultural diversity of the colonial population had made the perpetuation of traditional, hierarchical social ideals extremely difficult. What strength these older ideals and assumptions did possess was further eroded by the demands of a populace aroused by the Awakening.

The challenge to custom quickly spread in new and unpredictable directions. Men who had learned to defy their regular, authorized ministers would find it but an easy next step to flout other laws of civil authorities they considered unjust. This they did. Ministers who braved the wilderness to carry the message to frontier settlers would quickly take on a hostile officialdom to protect their fledgling congregations from being suppressed. And this they did. Once older social assumptions had been thoroughly shaken, the readiness to challenge traditional authority in the name of equality and natural rights became unquenchable, even among those who would have otherwise been aghast to find themselves in league with enthusiasts. It was only natural, too, that the revivalists' insistence that God was beginning a special work in America would mingle with the conviction of many, revivalist and non-revivalist alike, that the emergence of the new nation was providential and bore a divine blessing.

New attitudes toward ideas and learning also emerged from the Great Awakening. A public dialogue began to take place with all the existing means of communication hauled into its service. Newspaper articles, printed sermons, pamphlets, and broadsides carried the dialogue forward, as from every quarter came demands to participate, to listen, and to be heard. Ministers and lawyers, merchants and farmers, all types entered the fray and thrust before the public their own opinions, positions, analyses, and denunciations. It had very quickly become evident that the discussion of abstract ideas and public issues of moment was no longer the prerogative of the learned and privileged few.

To be sure, the shadow side of the popular impulse was apparent from the beginning. The bitterness of diatribe and an anti-intellectualism that considered one man's opinion as good as another's, or even better if certified by conversion rather than a university degree, often throttled respect for rational argument. Nevertheless, there did appear, as seldom before, a general demand that contested questions of public concern be made directly available for public discussion.

Attaining the scale of an intercolonial movement, revivalism, during and after the Awakening, helped both to legitimate and to hasten the abandonment of older social relations and cultural attitudes. Revivalism also provided, as Timothy L. Smith has argued, a powerful means for creating new forms of communal solidarity amidst the flux and openness of colonial life. It helped to forge "a sense of spiritual and moral kinship, rooted in voluntary adherence to a congregation," that was, Smith writes, "to remain throughout the eighteenth century and long beyond the key to neighborhood stability, ordered family life, and the education of children."[18]

Moreover, revivalism gave expression and nourishment to a growing intercolonial spirit of oneness. A manifestation of this larger unity was the development in the eighteenth century of the peculiarly American pattern of religious denominationalism, in which various religious groups, despite continuing sectarian differences and rivalries, saw themselves bound together in a common experience and a common purpose. This denominational spirit and mode of cooperation sustained the pervasive Protestant ethos of early nineteenth-century America, with its merging of religion, patriotism, and education, and made possible the aggressive evangelistic and educational campaigns of the churches to mold a Christian nation in their own image.

In order to grasp fully the educational meaning of the Awakening, however, it may be necessary to look beyond actual historical events and developments by raising again the question posed earlier: Were there among the historically unique issues of the Awakening some that are of enduring and perennial human concern? From this perspective the Awakening began with what has been the rallying cry of many an educational reform movement. What good is knowledge that does not produce vital changes in the knower? "What have we had lately but a dry formality?" asked Samuel Finley, and

[18] Timothy L. Smith, "Congregation, State, and Denomination: The Forming of the American Religious Structure," *William and Mary Quarterly,* 3rd ser., 25 (1968), p. 167.

the question was taken up and repeated again and again.[19]

The debates of the Awakening were, of course, couched in terminology and concepts that today are mainly of interest to intellectual historians or to theologians and specialists in social and ethical theory. Yet, it is clear that these controversies at bottom rested on basic assumptions about human nature, the sources and ends of knowledge, and the future of society. The modern student concerned with education will recognize in them some of the most fundamental and perplexing educational problems of western culture: How to preserve and honor the tradition of accumulated knowledge—built up patiently and painstakingly over the course of generations—while at the same time remaining open to creative innovation and spontaneous inspiration? How to safeguard culture's frail hold on ordered and rational knowledge while empowering it with vital emotional and aesthetic experience? How to connect objective knowledge *about* with personal, subjective knowledge *of*? How to relate and adjust the frequently conflicting claims of immediate, pragmatic social problems and the long-range strategies and goals of a larger social vision? How to uphold standards of excellence and simultaneously remain responsive to popular needs, tastes, and demands? Such questions are with us still—in new form and with wider dimensions—and the demand for some workable solutions presses with greater urgency than ever.

Within the historical limitations of colonial America there existed for a brief moment the possibility for Americans to begin at the deepest level a protracted dialogue

[19] Samuel Finley, *Christ Triumphing and Satan Raging: A Sermon.* . . . (Philadelphia, 1741; Boston, 1742), p. 17.

over the nature and purposes of their society. The discussion, however, too soon went awry, positions polarized, too frequently argument regressed to polemic and inquiry to indoctrination. It remains unclear whether the full dialogue failed to develop because there was in fact, as Charles Chauncy alleged, too much "bad temperament in blood and spirit," or because the historical circumstances offered no real options but to choose one side or the other, or because the particular religious and social framework within which the dialogue began was too restrictive for it to move beyond a certain point. In any event Americans divided and the divisions persisted. From this perspective the Awakening was the initiation of a grand cultural dialogue that has yet to be completed. And, perhaps, the Awakening has a final meaning for our own time as a warning against allowing positions to polarize and harden to the extent that men cease to talk, regardless of how irreconcilable the lines of disagreement may appear.

Bibliographical Note

The best and most recent treatment of the Great Awakening and American education is to be found in Lawrence A. Cremin: *American Education: The Colonial Experience, 1607-1783* (1970), especially Chapter 10, "Modes of Enthusiasm." Placing the Great Awakening in the larger context of European and colonial pietism, Professor Cremin discusses the educational undertakings of American Quakers, the educational impact of the Great Awakening itself, and the influence of eighteenth-century American academies and colleges in the emergence of American denominationalism. Professor Cremin also provides a voluminous and up-to-date bibliographical essay.

Much older and concerned mainly with the new colleges of mid-eighteenth-century America is Wayland J. Chase: "'The Great Awakening' and Its Educational Consequences," *School and Society*, XXXV (1932), 443-449.

Many of the standard works on the Awakening provide not only general background, but also much useful information on the role of educational institutions and different attitudes toward learning in the Awakening. Charles Hartshorne Maxson: *The Great Awakening in the Middle Colonies* (1920) discusses the course of the revivals in that section of the country, including its effect on educational institutions. Joseph Tracy: *The Great Awakening: History of the Revival of Religion in the Time of Edwards and Whitefield* (1842, 1970) is still a useful treatment of the Awakening in New England, and contains material on the reactions of the Harvard and Yale faculties. A more modern examination of the same area is Edwin Scott Gaustad: *The Great Awakening in New England* (1957); Gaustad's clarification of the major parties involved is helpful in understanding revivalist and anti-revivalist attitudes toward learning. Wesley M. Gewehr: *The Great Awakening in Virginia, 1740-1790* (1930) discusses the Awakening in Virginia as having developed in three phases, Presbyterian, Baptist, and Methodist, each with its own distinct characteristics. C. C. Goen: *Revivalism and Separatism in New England, 1740-1800* (1962) suggests that the attitudes toward learning of the radical Separatists were complex and not to be written off merely as anti-intellectual. Richard Hofstadter concludes that, whatever appreciation for learning the revivalists may have had, their lasting influence was to lend decisive impetus to the currents of *Anti-Intellectualism in American Life* (1963). L. J. Trinterud: *The Forming of an American Tradition; A Reexamination of Colonial Presbyterians* (1949) examines many of the theological, social, and educational attitudes of Old and New Side Presbyterians. Two recent and provocative studies of the Awakening as a decisive influence in shaping the mind of the new nation are Alan Heimert: *Religion and the American Mind: From the Great Awakening to the Revolution* (1966), and Cedric B. Cowing: *The Great Awakening and the American Revolution: Colonial Thought in the 18th Century* (1971). Linking the Awakening with Revolutionary politics and an emerging democratic spirit, both Heimert and Cowing also contain many suggestive leads for an educational assessment of the Awakening. In a very important and detailed study of one colony, *From Puritan to Yankee: Character and Social Order in Connecticut, 1690-1765* (1967), Richard L. Bushman describes the Great Awakening as "a psychological earthquake" that reshaped the traditional social order and helped usher in the colonists' readiness for rebellion in 1775. Timothy L. Smith: "Congregation, State, and Denomination: The Forming of the American Religious Structure," *William and Mary Quarterly,* 3rd ser., 25 (1968), 155-176, discusses revivalism as a search for community, and as an agent in the creation of new institutional forms, within the cultural diversity and social mobility of colonial America. Alan Heimert and Perry Miller, eds.: *The Great Awakening* (1967) is a comprehensive collection of documents covering many facets of the Awakening, together with an excellent introduction by Heimert.

Among the multitude of works valuable for understanding the many specific movements, individuals, and institutions connected with the Awakening, several are especially useful from an educational perspective. Chapters in Perry Miller: *Errand into the Wilderness* (1956) offer succinct discussions of Puritan thought and belief. F. Ernest Stoeffler: *The Rise of Evangelical Pietism* (1965) is particularly helpful in placing the Awakening in the larger context of European religious movements. James R. Tanis: *Dutch Calvinistic Pietism in the Middle Colonies: A Study in the Life and Theology of Theodore Jacobus Frelinghuysen* (1967) complements Stoeffler's European focus and demonstrates Frelinghuysen's ties to the Reformed tradition of pietism. Modes of ministerial education in the colonies are dealt with in Mary L. Gambrell: *Ministerial Training in Eighteenth*

Century New England (1937) and in William O. Shew-
maker: "The Training of the Protestant Ministry in
the United States of America, before the Establishment
of Theological Seminaries," *Papers of the American Society of Church History, 2nd ser.,* VI (1921), 71-197.

The Presbyterian academies and the relationships
between European Enlightenment thought and that of
leading Presbyterian educators are discussed in Douglas
Sloan: *The Scottish Enlightenment and the American
College Ideal* (1971). A picture of the academy movement is also presented in Henry D. Funk, "The Influence of the Presbyterian Church in Early American History," *Journal of the Presbyterian Historical Society,*
XII (1924-27), 152-189. An early study of William Tennent's Log College is George H. Ingram: "The Story
of the Log College," *Journal of the Presbyterian Historical Society,* XII (1924-27), 487-511. Archibald Alexander: *Biographical Sketches of the Founder and Principal Alumni of the Log College* (1840) has provided the
basis for many later accounts, and is valuable for its
presentation of much contemporary material. Many primary materials from a variety of sources are collected in
Thomas C. Pears, Jr., and Guy Klett, compilers: *A Documentary History of William Tennent and the Log College* (1940). Articles dealing with other specific, individual academies include: Franklin B. Dwight: "The Early
History of the Educational Institutions of New Jersey,
The Newark Academy," *Proceedings of the New Jersey
Historical Society,* III (1898-1900), IV (1901-1905); Jacob
Newton Beam: "Dr. Robert Smith's Academy at Pequea,
Pennsylvania," *Journal of the Presbyterian Historical So-
ciety,* VIII (December 1915), 145-161; and George H.
Ryden, "The Relation of the Newark Academy of Del-
aware to the Presbyterian Church and to Higher Edu-

cation in the American Colonies," *Delaware Notes,* 9th ser. (1935), 7-42. Donald Robert Come: "The Influence of Princeton in Higher Education in the South before 1825," *William and Mary Quarterly,* 3rd ser., II (1945), 359-396, discusses many important academies and their relationship to the College of New Jersey.

Also extremely important for appraising the educational impact of the Awakening are several of the standard histories of major colleges founded after 1746, including: Thomas Jefferson Wertenbaker: *Princeton, 1746-1896* (1946); John Maclean: *History of the College of New Jersey from Its Origin in 1746 to the Commencement of 1854* (2 vols., 1877); Leon Burr Richardson: *History of Dartmouth College* (2 vols., 1932); Richard P. McCormick: *Rutgers: A Bicentennial History* (1966); and Walter C. Bronson: *The History of Brown University, 1764-1914* (1914). Colonial Harvard and Yale are treated in Samuel Eliot Morison: *Three Centuries of Harvard* (1946); Edwin Oviatt: *The Beginnings of Yale, 1701-1726* (1916); Franklin Bowditch Dexter, ed., *A Documentary History of Yale University Under the Original Charter of the Collegiate School of Connecticut, 1701-1745* (1916). Of special value for the relationship between religion and learning at Yale is Roland H. Bainton: *Yale and the Ministry: A History of Education for the Christian Ministry at Yale from the Founding in 1701* (1957). Lawrence A. Cremin: *American Education: The Colonial Experience, 1607-1783* (1971) contains exemplary discussions of the colonial colleges, including the College of Philadelphia and Kings College in New York, as they developed within the totality of colonial education and intellectual life.

Some of the best insights into the educational dimensions of the Awakening are to be found in studies of individual revivalists and of their opponents. Jonathan Edwards was, of course, the central intellectual figure of the Awakening—in some respects, of the entire colonial period—and works on him are multiplying. Selections from Edwards' major writings and a bibliography of his works, together with an interpretive introduction, are in Clarence Faust and Thomas Johnson, eds.: *Jonathan Edwards, Selections* (1935). Perry Miller's intellectual biography, *Jonathan Edwards* (1949), is fascinating, provocative, and, as several scholars have commented, is probably as much Miller as Edwards. Three articles in Miller's *Errand into the Wilderness* (1956) are also extremely helpful for understanding Edwards. Claude M. Newlin: *Philosophy and Religion in Colonial America* (1962) discusses Edwards and the rationalists, including Charles Chauncy.

The "great itinerant" is the subject of Stuart C. Henry: *George Whitefield: Wayfaring Witness* (1957). Important sermons by the Tennents, Robert Smith, Samuel Finley, and other Presbyterian revivalists are collected in Samuel Davies Alexander: *Sermons and Essays by the Tennents and their Contemporaries* (1855).

In his study of *Isaac Backus and the American Pietistic Tradition* (1967) William G. McLoughlin provides insight into Backus and the separate Baptists' struggle for religious liberty. Reactions to the Awakening in Connecticut, and its impact on Yale College particularly, are treated in Louis L. Tucker: *Puritan Protagonist: President Thomas Clap of Yale College* (1962). Edmund S. Morgan: *The Gentle Puritan: A Life of Ezra Stiles, 1727-1795,* is an excellent biography of a moderate Old Light president of Yale, and is especially illuminating of his attitudes toward religion and learning. George William Pilcher: *Samuel Davies: Apostle of Dissent in Colonial Virginia* (1971) is a biography of the Presbyterian revivalist, and Richard Gummere: *Seven Wise Men of Colonial America* (1967), chapter 4, discusses Davies' classical scholarship.

Other works useful for an educational interpretation of the Great Awakening include: Perry Miller: "From the Covenant to the Revival," in J. W. Smith and A. L. Jamison, eds., *Religion in American Life,* I, *The Shaping of American Religion* (1961), 322-368; Joseph Haroutunian: *Piety versus Moralism: The Passing of the New England Theology* (1932); William Warren Sweet: *Revivalism in America: Its Origin, Growth, and Decline* (1944); George William Pilcher: "Samuel Davies and the Instruction of Negroes in Virginia," *The Virginia Magazine of History and Biography,* LXXXIV (1960), 293-300; Leonard W. Labaree: "The Conservative Attitude Toward the Great Awakening," *William and Mary Quarterly,* 3rd ser., I (1944), 331-352; Robert Sklar: "The Great Awakening and Colonial Politics: Connecticut's Revolution in the Minds of Men," *Connecticut Historical Society Bulletin,* XXVIII (1963), 81-95; Frederick B. Tolles: "Quietism Versus Enthusiasm: The Philadelphia Quakers and the Great Awakening," *Pennsylvania Magazine of History and Biography,* LXIX (1945), 26-49; David S. Lovejoy: "Samuel Hopkins; Religion, Slavery and the Revolution," *New England Quarterly,* XL (1967), 227-243; William G. McLoughlin: "The American Revolution as a Religious Revival: 'The Millennium in One Country,'" *New England Quarterly,* XL (1967), 99-110; Edwin S. Gaustad: "The Backus-Leland Tradition," in Winthrop S. Hudson, ed., *Baptist Conceptions of the Church* (1959); and Cedric B. Cowing: "Sex and Preaching in the Great Awakening," *American Quarterly*, XX (1968), 624-644.

Editorial Note: In reprinting the following documents some abbreviations have been extended and capitalization has been modernized.

The Ructions of Revivalism

From its beginning the Awakening elicited different responses from different persons. Some were converted, some became revivalists themselves, others rejected the whole affair as madness, still others welcomed it, but with caution. The following selections reveal something of the kinds of responses evoked among different participants and observers, and introduce some of the main issues as they saw them.

The Itinerant Preacher

ELEAZAR WHEELOCK

Eleazar Wheelock was one of those fiery spirits who very early began to imitate George Whitefield's practice of preaching from place to place. During the years 1740-42, Wheelock itinerated constantly, preaching incessantly, frequently delivering as many as forty sermons in half that many days, while at the same time traveling, attending various conferences, and counseling individuals.

The exuberance and sheer drive of the revivalist is manifest in this excerpt from a journal that Wheelock kept of a preaching tour he made through Rhode Island to Boston in the fall of 1741. In 1743 Wheelock set up an Indian school in Lebanon, Connecticut, which he later helped transform into Dartmouth College at Hanover, New Hampshire. Wheelock served as president of Dartmouth until his death in 1779.

Oct. 19, 1741. O, that God would give me courage, zeal, and skill to deal faithfully with my friends.

Oct. 20. Preached at 10, with some enlargement [at a town near Plainfield]. Present, Rev. Messrs. Coit, Kirtland, Dorrance, Barker, Avery, Marsh, etc. The assembly large and considerably affected. Preached in the afternoon at Plainfield to a full assembly. A number cried out. Held a conference at night. Young Christians don't rise, as in some places. One converted. O, when shall I learn to live always upon God and be thankful for all the least enlargement and assistance.

Oct. 21. Had but little sleep. Arose before day. Rode with Mr. Coit and my friends to Voluntown. Courteously received and entertained by Mr. Dorrance. Went to meeting at 10. Heard Mr. Gideon Mills preach well. Preached after him. There is a great work in this town; but more of the footsteps of Satan than in any place I have yet been in: the zeal of some too furious: they tell of many visions, revelations, and many strong impressions upon the imagination. They have had much of God in many of their meetings, and his great power has been much seen and many hopefully converted. Satan is using many artful wiles to put a stop to the work of God in this place. Good Lord, let him be confounded. Let his mischiefs fall upon his own head. At their conference at night I mentioned some of these devices of Satan, which I apprehend they are in danger of, and heard the accounts of a number of new converts.

Oct. 22. Rose this morning refreshed. A pleasant day; found my soul stretching after God. The Lord has this day in some measure fulfilled my early desires. Preached twice with enlargement, by Mr. Smith's barn to great assemblies. Many cried out; many stood trembling; the whole assembly very solemn, and much affection; four or five converted. One woman, who came from Kingston against a great deal of opposition on purpose to hear me, came out clear, and went away rejoicing in God, longing to have her husband and others taste and see with her.

Oct. 23. Rose at 3; somewhat indisposed. Dear Lord, I commit my body, my soul, my life, health, and all to thee. Use me as thou wilt, only let me glorify thee and seek that as my last end. Left Voluntown about 7, accompanied by a great number of wounded and comforted. Came to Mr. Cooper's of Scituate in the county of Providence. Preached to a considerable assembly. I am always thronged with company, and want time to talk with the tenth part of those, who desire to converse with me. Dined, and rode with a great number of Voluntown people to Capt. Angel's. Preached there. The old man and woman violently opposed; called me antichrist, etc. Rode to elder Fish's; found him a bigoted, ignorant Baptist; his wife soon shot her bolt and told us all what she was. She seemed to look upon baptism in their way as the only evidence to be relied upon of a safe estate. Came about 8 to Mr. Henry's, seven miles from Providence.

Oct. 24. Rose early, prayed and sang. Discoursed with some wounded; afterwards exhorted a company, who came in. Sung a hymn, prayed, and rode with a great company of Voluntown people and others to Providence. About two miles from Providence met Mr. Knight and another man, who came out to meet us. His first salutation was, "God bless you, my dear brother." Went to his house. Rev. Mr. Cotton came, invited me to preach; felt freedom and sweetness in my soul.

Oct. 25. Rode with Mr. Knight into town in his calash. Preached three sermons, 2 Cor. 13:5; Mark 1: 2; Luke 10:ult. O, the dreadful ignorance and wickedness of these parts; O what a burthen dear Mr. Cotton has daily to bear.

Oct. 26. Rode with Mr. Cotton back seven miles to Mr. Bennet's: preached at 1 o'clock to a numerous and affected assembly. One converted. Returned with a great number to Providence. Preached to a full assembly: many scoffers present; one man hired for twenty shillings to come into the meeting-house and fall down, which he did and made great disturbance; ordered all, who had a real concern for the salvation of their souls, to follow me to Mr. Cotton's in order to have a conference with them. A considerable number came, who seemed considerably moved. Mark 16:16; Job 27:8.

Oct. 27. Went with Mr. Cotton and madam over the ferry to Rehoboth, upon Mr. Greenwood's invitation; preached at 1. Rode with Mr. C. etc. to Swansey.

Oct. 28. Brother Finney went to deacon Kingsley for liberty to preach in the Baptist meeting-house, but he refused it; but deacon ———— sent for the key, and I preached at 1, and again in the evening. O, poor, bigoted, ignorant, prejudiced people! Went after sermon to Capt. William Turner's, a separate Baptist; was exceedingly pleased with his wife, a true and shining Christian and a woman of great knowledge and prudence; her family exceedingly well governed by her: stayed with them and discoursed about their spiritual concerns, etc. I think, that the principles of the separate Baptists are the most uncharitable, unscriptural, and unreasonable, that I have yet met with. John 7:38; Ez. 22:14

Oct. 29. Came with Mr. Cotton and many others to Attleborough: very courteously received by Mr. Wells. Heard Mr. Turner of Rehoboth; preached after him; a great deal of affection and sobbing through the whole assembly; had great enlargement. Exhorted in the evening at Mr. Wells's. Matt. 6:33.

Oct. 30. Had a great sense of my own badness and unworthiness, of what a cursed heart I have. O, Lord, let me see and know more of it. Rode with Mr. Wells and many others to Norton; kindly received by Mr. Avery. Preached to a full assembly; much affection and sobbing through the whole assembly. Ezek. 12:14. Rode after lecture to Taunton. Lodged at madam Danforth's, who lives with her daughter Hodges. Preached at 10: a great outcry in the assembly; many greatly wounded. Dined at Mr. Danforth's, son to the former minister. Rode to Raynham with Mr. Wales and brother Byram.

Nov. 1. Preached in the forenoon to a full assembly; one cried out, many affected. Mark 1:2, 3. Advised those, who belonged to the assembly, not to follow me to Taunton, but stay and hear their own preacher. Went with brother Byram to Taunton; preached there, Job 27:8. One or two cried out. Appointed another meeting in the evening. Hos. 13:13. I believe thirty cried out. Almost all the negroes in town wounded; three or four converted. A great work in the town. Dear brother Crocker, a true servant of Jesus Christ, preaches here upon probation. I was forced to break off my sermon, before it was done, the outcry was so great: continued the meeting till 10 or 11 o'clock.

Nov. 2. Rode with Mr. Crocker to the tavern to see Capt. Leonard's negro (a slave), found him under a very clear and genuine conviction. Dear brother Rogers came to see me here. Rode with a great number to Bridgewater. Preached to a full assembly in Mr. Shaw's meeting-house. Present, the Rev. Messrs. John Wales, Jonathan Parker, John Cotton, Daniel Perkins, John Shaw, John Porter. Matt. 6:33.

Nov. 3. Rode with a great number to Mr. Perkins's meeting-house; a very full assembly. After sermon the lecture was appointed at Mr. Anger's; but so many wounded, that I could not leave them. Therefore preached again to a full assembly. Ez. 22:14. A great outcry: four or five converted.

Nov. 4. Rode to Mr. Porter's. A great multitude. Preached upon a stage. Hos. 13:13. One converted in sermon. After dinner rode with Mr. Belcher and a great multitude to Easton. Brother Rogers preached. John 5: 40. A very great outcry in the assembly. I preached after him. Acts 7:51; four or five converted. Lodged at Mr. Belcher's.

Nov. 5. Came to Mr. Niles's of Braintree. Preached with great freedom, 2 Cor. 13:5. Present, Messrs. Eells and Hancock; Mr. Worcester came in the evening.

Nov. 6. Set out for Boston. . . .

SOURCE: William Allen, "Memoir of Rev. Eleazar Wheelock, D.D.," *American Quarterly Register,* Vol. X, No. 1 (August 1837), pp. 12–17.

The Itinerant Listener

NATHAN COLE

As the Whitefields and the Wheelocks carried their message from place to place, crowds thronged from the surrounding countryside to hear them. This unlettered, but powerful, almost poetic account of Whitefield's arrival in Middletown, Connecticut, on October 23, 1740, is from the journal of Nathan Cole, a farmer in nearby Kensington Parish at the time. Few documents provide more eloquent testimony to the excitement of the day and to the almost desperate hunger that drove many like Cole to seek out the revivalists.

Now it pleased god to send mr. whitfeld into this

EDITORIAL NOTE: It was decided that the rhythm and force of this passage from the journal of Nathan Cole would suffer from any modernization of spelling and punctuation, and no editorial changes have been made in the original.

land & my hearing of his preaching at philadelphia like one of the old aposels, & many thousands floocking after him to hear ye gospel and great numbers were converted to Christ, i felt the spirit of god drawing me by conviction i longed to see & hear him & wished he would come this way and i soon heard he was come to new york & ye jases [Jerseys] & great multitudes flocking after him under great concern for their Soule & many converted wich brought on my concern more & more hoping soon to see him but next i herd he was on long iland & next at boston & next at northampton & then one morning all on a Suding about 8 or 9 o'clock there came a messenger & said mr. whitfeld preached at hartford & weathersfield yesterday & is to preach at middeltown this morning at 10 o'clock i was in my field at work i dropt my tool that i had in my hand & run home & run throu my house & bad my wife get ready quick to goo and hear mr. whitfeld preach at middeltown & run to my pasture for my hors with all my might fearing i should be too late to hear him i brought my hors home & soon mounted & took my wife up & went forward as fast as i thought ye hors could bear, & when my hors began to be out of breath i would get down & put my wife on ye Saddel & bid her ride as fast as she could & not Stop or Slak for me except i bad her & so i woud run untill i was almost out of breth & then mount my hors again & so i did several times to favour my hors we improved every moment to get along as if we was fleeing for our lives all this while fearing we should be too late to hear ye Sarmon for we had twelve miles to ride dubble in littel more than an hour & we went round by the upper housen parish & when we came within about half a mile of ye road that comes down from hartford weathersfield & stepney to middeltown on high land i saw before me a Cloud or fog rising i first thought off from ye great river but as i came nearer ye road i heard a noise something like a low rumbling thunder & i presently found it was ye rumbling of horses feet coming down ye road & this Cloud was a Cloud of dust made by ye running of horses feet it arose some rods into ye air over the tops of ye hills & trees & when i came within about twenty rods of ye road i could see men & horses Sliping along in ye Cloud like shadows & when i came nearer it was like a stedy streem of horses & their riders scarcely a horse more then his length behind another all of a lather and some with swet ther breath rooling out of their noistrels in ye cloud of dust every jump every hors semed to go with all his might to carry his rider to hear ye news from heaven for ye saving of their Souls it made me trembel to see ye Sight how ye world was in a strugle i found a vacance between two horses to Slip in my hors & my wife said law our cloaths will be all spoiled see how they look for they was so covered with dust that thay looked allmost all of a coler coats & hats & shirts & horses We went down in ye Streem i herd no man speak a word all ye way three mile but evry one presing forward in great hast & when we gat down to ye old meating house thare was a great multitude it was said to be 3 or 4000 of people asembled together we gat of from our horses & shook off ye dust and ye ministers was then coming to the meating house i turned and looked toward ye great river & saw the fery boats running swift forward & backward bringing over loads of people ye ores roed nimble & quick every thing men horses & boats all seamed to be struglin for life ye land & ye banks over ye river lookt black with people & horses all along ye 12 miles i see no man at work in his field but all seamed to be gone— when i see mr. whitfeld come up upon ye Scaffil he looked

almost angellical a young slim slender youth before
some thousands of people & with a bold undainted countenance & my hearing how god was with him every where
as he came along it solumnized my mind & put me in a
trembling fear before he began to preach for he looked
as if he was Cloathed with authority from ye great god,
& a sweet sollome Solemnity sat upon his brow & my
hearing him preach gave me a heart wound by gods
blessing my old foundation was broken up & i saw that
my righteousness would not save me then i was convinced of ye doctrine of Election & went right to quarel-
ing with god about it because all that i could do would
not save me & he had decreed from Eternity who should
be saved & who not i began to think i was not Elected
& that god made some for heaven & me for hell & i
thought god was not Just in so doing i thought i did not
stand on even Ground with others if as i thought i was
made to be damned my heart then rose against god ex-
ceedigly for his making me for hell now this distress
lasted almost two years.

SOURCE: George Leon Walker, *Some Aspects of the Religious
Life of New England with Special Reference to Congregationalists*
(Boston: Silver, Burdett and Company, 1897), pp. 89–92.

Enthusiasm

ANONYMOUS

*Perhaps no one person provided more ammunition
to the opponents of the Awakening than did James*

Davenport, whose fanaticism caused even many erst-while supporters of the revivals to draw back with mis-givings. The anonymous author of these letters to The Boston Evening Post *made the most of Davenport's an-tics to discredit everything about the Awakening as en-thusiastic, socially irresponsible, and wildly visionary ("colleges in the air"). Since Davenport was eventually judged mentally unsound and even came himself to re-pent of his earlier behavior, the foes of the Awakening may have used him to unfair advantage. Nevertheless, after Davenport no one could be entirely sure that in his extremes he had not revealed the inevitable end re-sult of the new way of preaching, if allowed to run its course unchecked.*

July 5, 1742

Dear Sir,

I am now sit down to fulfil the promise I made you some time ago, in case the Rev. Mr. *Davenport* should make his appearance in this town, to send you some ac-count of him. He came to this town last Monday in the afternoon, from Charlestown. He landed at New Boston (so called) near the causeway; as soon as he landed, he and his attendants, which were a rabble of men, women and children, began to sing, and walked through the street singing till he came to his lodgings. The ministers of the town happening at that time to be met together, and being acquainted with his arrival, they sent to de-sire to speak with him; he went to them, and was with them several hours that evening, and some considerable time the next morning. The conversation that passed between them I cannot pretend particularly to relate to you, nor is it necessary, that I should, since a number of the ministers have published a *Declaration* relating to that affair, which I send you herewith. However, one head of the discourse it may not be amiss to mention. Being asked with regard to some particular gentlemen in the neighbouring governments, who were well known here, whether he did not repent of his having declared them unconverted? he answered No, but thanked God that he had enabled him to declare them so. It seems it is a sufficient reason with him to pronounce any man unconverted, that they have not felt that they hated God, neither have had extraordinary joys and comforts.—

He has preached every day since upon the Common, to pretty large assemblies, but the greatest part very far from admiring him, or being willing to give him any countenance. When he first ascends the rostrum, he appears with a remarkably settled composed countenance, but soon gets into the most extravagant gesture and behaviour both in prayer and preaching. His expressions in prayer are often indecently familiar; he frequently appeals to God, that such and such impressions are immediately from his holy spirit, but especially his sermons are full of his impressions and impulses, from God. He does not seem to be a man of any parts, sprightliness, or wit. His sermons are dull and heavy, abounding with little low similitudes. He has no knack at raising the passions, but by a violent straining of his lungs, and the most extravagant wreathing of his body, which at the same time that it creates laughter and indignation in the most, occasions great *meltings, screamings, crying, swooning* and *fits* in *some* others. People in fits, though almost suffocated for want of air, in the crowd, are not suffered to be removed into more open air, lest the spirit should be disturbed in its operations. He boldly asserts, that a man cannot be convicted, and doubt about it, any more than have the air blow upon him and not feel it. He exhorts the people to meet together in private assemblies, and in despite of all family order and government, to spend whole nights till day-break in prayer: And I suppose some follow his advice; for I heard him yesterday upon the common publickly pray, that God would hear the prayers that had been going up the night before *till break of day.* Some think that he is crazy, others that he is not, but that he is a rank enthusiast, which last opinion I am the most inclined to. Though were you to see him in his most violent agitations, you would be apt to think, that he was a madman just broke from his chains: But especially had you seen him returning from the Common after his first preaching, with a large mob at his heels, singing all the way through the streets, he with his hands extended, his head thrown back, and his eyes staring up to heaven, attended with so much disorder, that they looked more like a company of bacchanalians after a mad frolick, than sober Christians who had been worshipping God. He has got a creature with him as a companion, whom some call an *Armour-bearer,* who assists him in praying and exhortations at private hours. He always stands with him upon the same eminence when he is preaching: For my part, when I see them together, I cannot for my Life help thinking of Don Quixote and Sancho-Pancha.

After this account, you will easily believe that he has but few admirers among the sober judicious part of the town. It is greatly to be wished, that those who deserve this character, after having satisfied their curiosity, would not attend his assemblies; and I persuade myself, that if they did but consider the mischief they do, in encouraging him by such a large appearance, and in encouraging others by their example, who are not so well able to defend themselves from the infection of *Enthusiasm,* they would be more careful of their conduct. And if he was left with none but his admirers, we should find them to be but few, and those such sort of company, as a man would almost be ashamed to be seen in. I need not ask your excuse for this long letter, since it is at your own request.

I am, Sir, *your sincere Friend,* etc.

Boston, July 30, 1742

Reverend Sir,

At your request, in a letter I lately received from you, I shall give you some short account of the famous Mr. D——t's late preachings in this populous place, and in the neighboring town of Dorchester. In the last mentioned place he held his first conventicle on Saturday the 17th Instant; and the next day being the time for administering the Lord's Supper, he declared the minister of the town to be an unconverted man, and warned the people not to attend the communion. Once or twice since I have heard him pronounce the said minister to be in a carnal unconverted state. He kept his meetings in an orchard, I think, twice on the Lord's Day, and once on the week days, beginning about 5 o'clock in the evening; and what was wanting in his preaching, was afterwards abundantly supplied, sometimes by his armour bearer, and sometimes by other zealous but ignorant and illiterate exhorters, to the great comfort and edification of the giddy audience.

As to his preaching in this town, it has, I think, been generally leveled against opposers and unconverted ministers; often signifying to the people, that a time of great persecution is speedily to be expected. His gestures in preaching are theatrical, his voice tumultuous, his whole speech and behaviour discovering the freaks of madness, and wilds of enthusiasm.

His audience at first was not great, and has, I think, been decreasing ever since, and is now chiefly made up of idle or ignorant persons, and those of the lowest rank, except some few who go out of mere curiosity, to hear something new. On Wednesday the 28th he had a collection in the common (as he had some days since at Dorchester, where 'tis said he picked up four pounds and half a crown) to carry on the building or seminary called by him the "Shepherds' Tent," wherein none are to be admitted but converted children. What the last collection amounted to, I cannot yet learn, but I believe to no great sum. However, 'tis past doubt some credulous folks were eased of their pence, which they could very ill spare, and 'tis certain one good woman put in two pairs of stockings. The wiser and better sort of people will, I think, scarce be wheedled a second time into collections for building castles or "colleges in the air."

When the exercise of the Common is over, the rabble follow their leader to his lodgings, (sometimes singing hymns as they pass) where praying, singing, exhorting, and consequent thereon, *falling down, screaming out, fits,* and *faintings* are the *nocturnal entertainment;* the night being best calculated to celebrate such dark and mysterious juggles.

Sometimes these meetings in the fields have been attended with very great disorders; several jangles and quarrels have happened among the multitude; the ferment has rose high, and not ended without blows: And I verily fear, that if these meetings continue, such quarrels will proceed to more dangerous lengths, unless the civil magistrates, whose duty it is to preserve the publick peace, interpose their authority to prevent them. For so far as a judgment can be formed from the behaviour and menacing speeches of some of Mr. D——t's adherents, their zeal is so *red hot,* that I verily believe they would make nothing to *kill opposers,* and in so doing, think they *did God service.*

While I am writing to you concerning these things, I cannot forbear expressing my thoughts, that this itinerant way of preaching, is by no means conducive to the interest of *true religion,* and *substantial godliness.* The engine which this sort of men artfully manage, is that of detraction; accordingly in every place where they come, in the course of their perigrination, their grand business is to persuade the people that their ministers are unconverted, to alienate their affections from them, and thereby utterly to destroy their usefulness among their hearers. From which practice it is very just to infer, that there is a design carrying on to subvert and eject the standing settled ministers; and that these itinerants and their accomplices are actuated by that well-known maxim of the Jesuits, "Divide et Impera."

The ministers of this land, I have often said, and continue still of the same opinion, are a set of gentlemen as sound in principle, and exemplary in their conversation, as any of the like number in the Christian world: And I confess it has sometimes raised in me the highest indignation to hear them reviled in so public and outrageous a manner, even in the presence of some of the most grave and eminent divines among us.

Thus I have several times heard Mr. T——t declare, that the greatest part by far of the ministers in this land, were carnal unconverted men, and that they held damnable Arminian principles; and have heard him pray, that the Lord would either convert them, or turn them out of his vineyard. Mr. D——t I heard declare on the hill near Charlestown Ferry, that the greatest part of the ministers in this country were unconverted, and that they were murdering of souls by thousands and by millions. In the Common I heard him say, The greatest part of the ministers in Boston were carnal unconverted men, and exhort the people to pray for the conversion of those miserable and wretched men. At another time, in the Common, I heard him say, the ministers of Boston were going to hell themselves, and drawing multitudes after them.

It has been no small surprise to me, when I have sometimes seen in these assemblies, a number of grave and serious men, members of our churches, who could hear these unjust and hard speeches belched out against their own proper pastors, not only with patience, but with pleasure. At the same time, if you were to ask those men, they would tell you, they highly esteem and value their own ministers: But can this possibly be true? Will any one believe them, while they not only caress and adore the itinerants, but continually pamper their bellies, clothe their backs, and fill their pockets?

I may further observe to you, what is indeed obvious to every one, that such great numbers of people running after every itinerant that comes, casts a great reflection on our faithful ministers, and has a tendency to weaken their hands, and discourage them in their work. I am sorry that I am obliged to say, this great slight and disrespect cast on our ministers, is in a considerable measure owing to themselves, and their own past misconduct, by too much caressing and giving into the measures of the first great itinerant, to whom they ought not to have given place by subjection, no not for an hour. And this, in my opinion, was the unhappy introduction to that

scene of enthusiasm, madness and disorder, which has
ever since been opening upon us.

I shall add no more at present, but if any thing
worthy of observation occurs, shall not fail to communicate it.

SOURCE: "A Letter from a Gentleman in Boston, to his friend in
the Country," and "A Letter from a Gentleman in Boston, to a
Minister in the Country, containing a brief Account of Mr.
D----t's late preaching in Boston *and* Dorchester, with some Remarks, etc." *The Boston Evening Post,* July 5, 1742, and July 30,
1742.

Rational Revivalism

SAMUEL BLAIR

*Samuel Blair, Presbyterian minister and later head of
a famous academy at Fagg's Manor, Pennsylvania, was,
along with such other leaders of the Awakening as
Edwards, the Tennents, Samuel Finley, and Jonathan
Dickinson, a different breed of revivalist from James
Davenport. While these men did not feel ill-at-ease with
the weeping and outcries of their listeners, they did not
encourage emotionalism for its own sake and they were
concerned to help their people understand the conversion
experience in rational and doctrinal terms. This description by Blair of the revivals at New Londonderry is
notable for several things: his efforts to provide sustained
pastoral counseling to the conscience-stricken and the
newly converted, his concern to maintain the standards*

*of rational theology, his observation of an apparent
connection between the revivals and an increased interest among the members of his congregation in reading
and study, and his constant attempt to distinguish the
rational and permanent from the purely emotional and
ephemeral results of the revivals.*

New-Londonderry in *Pennsylvania*, Aug. 6, 1744.

Rev. Sir,

I do most gladly comply with your desire in sending
you some account of the glorious appearance of GOD in
a way of special grace for us in this congregation, and
other parts of this country: And am of the same judgment with you and other pious and judicious people,
that the collecting and publishing of such accounts may
greatly tend to the glory of our REDEEMER, and the
increase of his triumphs. . . . I cannot indeed give near
so full and particular a relation of the revival of religion
here as I might have done had I had such a thing in view
at the time when God was most eminently carrying on
his work among us: I entirely neglected then to note
down any particulars in writing, for which I have been
often sorry since; so that this account must be very imperfect to what it might otherwise have been.

That it may the more clearly appear that the LORD
has indeed carried on a work of true *real religion* among
us of late years, I conceive it will be useful to give a brief
general view of the *state of religion* in these parts *before*
this remarkable season. I doubt not then, but there were
some sincerely religious people up and down; and there
were, I believe, a considerable number in the several
congregations pretty exact, according to their education,
in the observance of the external forms of religion, not

only as to attendance upon public ordinances on the Sabbaths, but also, as to the practise of family worship, and perhaps secret prayer too: But with these things the most part seemed to all appearance to rest contented; and to satisfy their consciences just with a *dead formality* in religion. If they performed these duties pretty punctually in the seasons, and as they thought with a good meaning, out of conscience, and not just to obtain a name for religion among men; then they were ready to conclude that they were truly and sincerely religious. A very lamentable ignorance of the main essentials of true practical religion, and the doctrines nextly relating thereunto very generally prevailed. The *nature* and *necessity* of the *New Birth* was but little known or thought of. The *necessity* of a *conviction* of sin and misery, by the HOLY SPIRIT opening and applying the law to the conscience, in order to a *saving closure* with CHRIST, was hardly known at all to the most. It was thought that if there was any need of a heart-distressing sight of the soul's danger, and fear of divine wrath; it was only needful for the grosser sort of sinners; and for any others to be deeply exercised this way (as there might sometimes be before some rare instances observable) this was generally looked upon to be a great evil and temptation that had befallen those persons. The common names for such soul-concern were, "melancholy," "trouble of mind," or "despair." These terms were in common so far as I have been acquainted, indifferently used as synonymous; and trouble of mind was looked upon as a great evil, which all persons that made any sober profession and practice of religion ought carefully to avoid. There was scarcely any suspicion at all, in general, of any danger of depending upon self-righteousness, and not upon the righteousness of CHRIST alone for salvation. Papists and Quakers

would be readily acknowledged guilty of this crime; but
hardly any professed Presbyterian. The necessity of being
first in CHRIST by a vital union, and in a justified state
before our religious services can be well pleasing and acceptable to GOD, was very little understood or thought
of: But the common notion seemed to be, that if people
were aiming to be in the way of duty as well as they
could, as they imagined, there was no reason to be much
afraid.

According to these principles, and this ignorance of
some of the most soul-concerning truths of the Gospel,
people were very generally through the land careless at
heart, and stupidly indifferent about the great concerns
of eternity. There was very little appearance of any
hearty engagedness in religion; and indeed the wise, for
the most part, were in a great degree asleep with the
foolish. 'Twas sad to see with what a careless behaviour
the public ordinances were attended, and how people
were given to unsuitable worldly discourse on the
LORD's holy day. In public companies, especially at
weddings, a vain and frothy lightness was apparent in
the deportment of many professors: and in some places
very extravagant follies, as horse-running, fiddling and
dancing, pretty much obtained on those occasions.

Thus religion lay as it were a dying, and ready to ex-
pire its last breath of life in this part of the visible
church: and it was in the spring, Anno 1740, when the
GOD of salvation was pleased to visit us with the blessed
effusions of his HOLY SPIRIT in an eminent manner.
The first very open and public appearance of this gracious visitation in these parts, was in the congregation
which God has committed to my charge. This congregation has not been erected above 14 or 15 years from this
time: The place is a new settlement, generally settled

with people from Ireland (as all our congregations in
Pennsylvania, except two or three, chiefly are made up of
people from that kingdom.)* I am the first minister they
have ever had settled in the place; having been regularly
liberated from my former charge in East-Jersey, above an
hundred miles north-eastward from hence (the Rev.
Presbytery of New-Brunswick—of which I had the comfort of being a member—judging it to be my duty, for
sundry reasons, to remove from thence). At the earnest
invitation of the people here, I came to them in the beginning of November 1739; accepted of a call from them
that winter, and was formally installed and settled
among them as their minister in April following. There
were some hopefully pious people here at my first coming, which was a great encouragement and comfort to
me.

I had some view and sense of the deplorable condition of the land in general; and accordingly the scope
of my preaching through that first winter after I came
here, was mainly calculated for persons in a natural unregenerate state. I endeavoured, as the LORD enabled me
to open up and prove from his word, the truths which I
judged most necessary for such as were in that state to
know and believe in order to their conviction and conversion. I endeavoured to deal searchingly and solemnly

* It may be convenient here, to observe; That in IRELAND
are three different sorts of people deriving from three several nations; (1) Those who descend from the ancient Irish; and these are
generally Roman Catholics. (2) Those who descend from ancestors
who came from England; and these are generally Church of Eng-
land-Men. (3) Those who descend from ancestors who came from
Scotland since the Reformation; and these are generally Presbyterians; who chiefly inhabit the northerly parts of Ireland: And
these are the people who have of late years in great numbers removed thence into these American regions.

with them: and through the concurring blessing of GOD, I had knowledge of four or five brought under deep convictions that winter.

In the beginning of March I took a journey into East-Jersey; and was abroad for two or three Sabbaths: A neighbouring minister, who seemed to be earnest for the awakening and conversion of secure sinners, and whom I had obtained to preach a Sabbath to my people in my absence, preached to them, I think, on the first Sabbath after I left home: His subject was the dangerous and awful case of such as continue unregenerate and unfruitful under the means of grace. The text was Luke 13:7. *Then said he to the dresser of his vineyard; Behold, these three years I come seeking fruit on this fig-tree, and find none; cut it down, why cumbreth it the ground?* Under that sermon there was a visible appearance of much soul-concern among the hearers; so that some burst out with an audible noise into bitter crying (a thing not known in these parts before). After I had come home, there came a young man to my house under deep trouble about the state of his soul, whom I had looked upon as a pretty light merry sort of a youth. He told me that he was not any thing concerned about himself in the time of hearing the above-mentioned sermon, nor afterwards, till the next day that he went to his labour, which was grubbing in order to clear some new ground. The first grub he set about was a pretty large one with a high top, and when he had cut the roots, as it fell down these words came instantly to his remembrance, and as a spear to his heart, *Cut it down, why cumbreth it the ground?* So, thought he, must I be cut down by the justice of GOD for the burning of hell, unless I get into another state than I am now in. He thus came into very great and abiding distress, which, to all appearance, has had a happy issue: his conversation being to this day as becomes the Gospel of CHRIST.

The news of this very public appearance of deep soul-concern among my people met me an *hundred miles* from home. I was very joyful to hear of it, in hopes that GOD was about to carry on an extensive work of converting grace amongst them. And the first sermon I preached after my return to them, was from Matt. 6:33. *Seek ye first the Kingdom of GOD, and his righteousness.* After opening up and explaining the parts of the text, when, in the improvement, I came to press the injunction in the text upon the unconverted and ungodly, and offered this as one reason among others, why they should now henceforth first of all seek the Kingdom and righteousness of GOD, viz. That they had neglected too long to do so already: this consideration seemed to come and cut like a sword upon several in the congregation; so that while I was speaking upon it, they could no longer contain, but burst out in the most bitter mourning. I desired them as much as possible, to restrain themselves from making any noise, that would hinder themselves or others from hearing what was spoken; and often afterwards I had occasion to repeat the same counsel. I still advised people to endeavour to moderate and bound their passions, *but not so as to resist or stifle their convictions.* The number of the awakened increased very fast: frequently under sermons there were some newly convicted, and brought into deep distress of soul about their perishing estate. Our sabbath assemblies soon became vastly large: Many people from almost all parts around inclining very much to come where there was such appearance of the divine power and presence. I think there was scarcely a sermon or lecture preached here through that whole summer, but there were manifest evidences of impressions on the hearers; and many times the impressions were very great and general. Several would be overcome and fainting; others deeply sobbing, hardly able to contain; others crying in a most dolorous manner; many others more silently weeping; and a solemn concern appearing in the countenances of many others. And sometimes the soul-exercises of some (though comparatively but very few) would so far affect their bodies as to occasion some strange unusual bodily motions. I had opportunities of speaking particularly with a great many of those, who afforded such outward tokens of inward soul-concern in the time of public worship and hearing of the word: Indeed many came to me of themselves in their distress, for private instruction and counsel; and I found, so far as I can remember, that with by far the greater part their apparent concern in public was not just a transient qualm of conscience, or merely a floating commotion of the affections; but a *rational fixt conviction* of their dangerous perishing estate. They could generally offer as a convictive evidence of their being in an unconverted miserable estate, that they were utter strangers to those dispositions, exercises, and experiences of soul in religion, which they heard laid down from GOD's word, as the inseparable characters of the truly regenerate people of GOD; even such as before had something of the *form of religion;* and, I think the greater number were of this sort; and several had been pretty exact and punctual in the performance of outward duties; they saw they had been contenting themselves with the form without the life and power of godliness; and that they had been taking peace to their consciences from, and depending upon *their own righteousness,* and not the righteousness of JESUS CHRIST.

In a word, they saw that true practical religion was

quite another thing than they had conceived it to be, or had any true experience of. There were likewise many up and down the land brought under deep distressing convictions that summer who had lived very loose lives, regardless of the very externals of religion. In this congregation I believe there were very few that were not stirred up to some solemn thoughtfulness and concern more than usual about their souls. The general carriage and behaviour of people was soon very visibly altered. Those awakened were much given to reading in the HOLY SCRIPTURES and other good books. Excellent books that had lain by much neglected, were then much perused, and lent from one to another: and it was a peculiar satisfaction to people to find how exactly the doctrines they heard daily preached, harmonized with the doctrines contained and taught by great and godly men in other parts and former times. The subjects of discourse almost always when any of them were together, were the matters of religion and great concerns of their souls. All unsuitable, worldly, vain discourse on the Lord's Day seemed to be laid aside among them: Indeed for any thing that appeared, there seemed to be almost a universal reformation in this respect in our public assemblies on the Lord's Day.

There was an earnest desire in people after opportunities for public worship and hearing the word. I appointed in the spring to preach every Friday through the summer when I was at home, and those meetings were well attended; and at several of them the power of the LORD was remarkably with us. The main scope of my preaching through that summer was, laying open the deplorable state of man by nature since the fall, our ruined exposed case by the breach of the first covenant, and the awful condition of such as were not in CHRIST,

giving the marks and characters of such as were in that
condition: And moreover, laying open the way of recovery in the new Covenant through a MEDIATOR,
with the nature and necessity of faith in CHRIST the
Mediator, etc. I laboured much on the last mentioned
heads; that the people might have right apprehensions
of the gospel-method of life and salvation. I treated much
on the way of sinners closing with CHRIST by Faith and
obtaining a right peace to an awakened, wounded conscience: showing that persons were not to take peace to
themselves on account of their repentings, sorrows, prayers, and reformations; not to make these things the
grounds of their adventuring themselves upon CHRIST
and his righteousness, and of their expectations of life by
him; and that neither were they to obtain or seek peace
in extraordinary ways, by visions, dreams, or immediate
inspirations; but, by an understanding view, and believing persuasion of the way of life, as revealed in the Gospel, through the suretyship, obedience, and sufferings of
JESUS CHRIST; with a view of the suitableness and
sufficiency of that mediatory righteousness of CHRIST
for the justification and life of law-condemned sinners;
and thereupon, freely accepting him for their Saviour,
heartily consenting to, and being well pleased with the
way of salvation, and venturing their all upon his medi-
ation, from the warrant and encouragement afforded of
God thereunto in his word, by his free offer, authoritative
command, and sure promise to those that so believe. I
endeavor to show the fruits and evidences of a true
faith, etc.

In some time many of the convinced and distressed afforded very hopeful satisfying evidence that the LORD
had brought them to a true closure with JESUS CHRIST;
and that their distresses and fears had been in a great

measure removed in a right gospel-way, by believing in the SON of GOD. Several of them had very remarkable and sweet deliverances this way. It was very agreeable to hear their accounts how that when they were in the deepest perplexity and darkness, distress and difficulty, seeking God as poor condemned hell-deserving sinners, the scene of recovering Grace through a redeemer has been opened to their understandings with a surprising beauty and glory, so that they were enabled to believe in CHRIST with joy unspeakable and full of glory. It appeared that most generally the Holy Spirit improved for this purpose, and made use of some one particular passage or other of the Holy Scriptures that came to their remembrance in their distress: some gospel-offer or promise, or some declaration of GOD directly referring to the recovery and salvation of undone sinners by the New-Covenant. But with some it was otherwise: they had not any one particular place of Scripture more than another in their view at the time. Those who met with such a remarkable relief, as their account of it was rational and scriptural, so, they appeared to have had at the time, the attendants and fruits of a true faith; particularly, humility, law, and an affectionate regard to the will and honour of GOD. Much of their exercise was in self-abasing and self-loathing; and admiring the astonishing condescension and grace of GOD towards such vile and despicable creatures, that had been so full of enmity and disaffection to him. They freely and sweetly with all their hearts chose the way of his commandments; their enflamed desire was to live to him for ever according to his will, and to the glory of his name.

There were others that had not had such remarkable relief and comfort, who yet I could not but think were savingly renewed, and brought truly to accept of and rest upon JESUS CHRIST, though not with such a degree of liveliness and liberty, strength and joy; and some of those continued for a considerable time after, for the most part, under a very distressing suspicion and jealousy of their case. I was all along very cautious of expressing to people my judgment of the goodness of their states, excepting where I had pretty clear evidences from them of their being savingly changed; and yet they continued in deep distress, casting off all their evidences. Sometimes in such cases, I have thought it needful to use greater freedom that way than ordinary; but otherwise, I judged that it could be of little use, and might easily be hurtful.

Beside those above spoke of, whose experience of a work of grace was in a good degree clear and satisfying, there were some others (though but very few in this congregation that I knew of) who, having very little knowledge or capacity, had a very obscure and improper way of representing their case in relating how they had been exercised: they would chiefly speak of such things as were only the effects of their soul exercise upon their bodies from time to time, and some things that were purely imaginary, which obliged me to be at much pains in my enquiries before I could get any just ideas of their case. I would ask them, What were the thoughts, the views and apprehensions of their minds, and exercise of their affections (at such times when they felt, perhaps, a quivering come over them, as they had been saying, or a faintness, or thought they saw their hearts full of some nauseous filthiness; or when they felt a heavy weight or load at their hearts, or felt the weight again taken off and a pleasant warmness rising from their hearts, as they would probably express themselves), which might be the occasions or causes of these things they spoke of. And then,

when with some difficulty I could get them to understand me, some of them would give *a pretty rational account* of *solemn* and *spiritual exercises;* and a thorough
careful examination this way, I could not but conceive
good hopes of some such persons.

But there were moreover several others, who seemed
to think concerning themselves that they were under
some good work, of whom, yet, I could have no reasonable ground to think that they were under any hopeful
work of the Spirit of God. As near as I could judge of
their case from all my acquaintance and conversation
with them, it was much to this purpose: They believed
there was a good work going on; that people were convinced, and brought into a converted state; and they desired to be converted too. They saw others weeping and
fainting, and heard people mourning and lamenting, and
they thought if they could be like these it would be very
hopeful with them; hence, they endeavoured just to get
themselves affected by sermons, and if they could come
to weeping, or get their passions so raised as to incline
them to vent themselves by cries, now they hoped they
were got under convictions, and were in a very hopeful
way. And afterwards, they would speak of their being in
trouble and aim at complaining of themselves, but
seemed as if they knew not well how to do it, nor what
to say against themselves; and then they would be looking and expecting to get some texts of Scripture applied
to them for their comfort; and when any Scripture text
which they thought was suitable for that purpose came
to their minds, they were in hopes it was brought to
them by the Spirit of God that they might take comfort
from it. And thus, much in such a way as this, some appeared to be pleasing themselves just with an *imaginary*

conversion of their own making. I endeavoured to correct and guard against all such mistakes so far as I discovered them, in the course of my ministry; and to open up the nature of a true conviction by the Spirit of God, and of a saving conversion. . . .

SOURCE: Thomas Prince, Jr., ed., *The Christian History, containing Accounts of the Revival and Propagation of Religion in Great-Britain and America.* For the Year 1744 (Boston: 1745), pp. 242-251.

The Learned Ministry Controversy

One of the first major, and most bitterly argued, controversies of the Awakening centered around an educational question: What constitutes the essence, the *sine qua non,* of ministerial qualification? Learning, a university degree, and certification by ecclesiastical authorities, or conversion and an inner call to preach? Both sides found the issue immensely difficult to handle. If the champions of learning went too far in rejecting the importance of genuine inner conviction, they could find themselves in the uncomfortable position of defending hypocrisy and an irrelevant and empty formalism. By the same token, if the proponents of conversion were too negligent of maintaining some objective standards of competence and training, they could quickly appear to be promoting ignorance and anti-intellectualism as positive goods. How to strike a meaningful balance without compromising everything away was the agonizing question faced by all those who refused to embrace the extreme on either side. One of the most difficult and yet most important of educational issues was brought to the surface in the learned ministry controversies: that of the relationship between inner conviction and objective competence, between personal conviction and public credentials.

The Danger of an Unconverted Ministry

GILBERT TENNENT

Few sermons during the entire Awakening stirred more controversy than that delivered by Gilbert Tennent at Neshaminy, Pennsylvania, on March 8, 1740. A blistering attack on unconverted ministers, the sermon was pointedly directed at the leadership of the Presbyterian Synod in Pennsylvania. The Synod had aroused Tennent's ire both because its leaders feared and opposed revivalism in general, and also because they had taken concrete steps to deny ministerial licenses to the revival-preaching graduates of his father's Log College, ostensibly on the grounds of their educational deficiencies. Depicting them as smugly reliant on academic training alone, Tennent denounced unconverted ministers as powerless to convert others. As means of countering the influence of a "dead ministry" he defended the practice of itineration, both by ministers and parishioners, and he called for the founding of many private, revival-centered schools. Delivered a short six months after Whitefield's arrival and at the height of the Awakening excitement, the sermon, excerpted here, set the terms and the tone, which Tennent himself was to regret, of later debates over ministerial qualification.

MARK 6:34. *And Jesus, when he came out, saw much people and was moved with compassion towards them, because they were as sheep not having a shepherd.*

As a faithful ministry is a great ornament, blessing and comfort, to the church of GOD; even the feet of such messengers are beautiful: So on the contrary, an ungodly ministry is a great curse and judgment: These caterpillars labour to devour every green thing.

There is nothing that may more justly call forth our saddest sorrows, and make all our powers and passions mourn, in the most doleful accents, the most incessant, insatiable, and deploring agonies; than the melancholy case of such, who have no faithful ministry! This truth is set before our minds in a strong light, in the words that I have chosen now to insist upon! in which we have an account of our LORD's grief with the causes of it.

We are informed that our dear Redeemer was moved with compassion towards them. The original word signifies the strongest and most vehement pity, issuing from the innermost bowels.

But what was the cause of this great and compassionate commotion in the heart of Christ? It was because he saw much people as sheep, having no Shepherd. Why, had the people then no teachers? O yes! they had heaps of Pharisee-Teachers, that came out, no doubt after they had been at the feet of Gamaliel the usual time, and according to the acts, canons, and traditions of the Jewish Church. But notwithstanding of the great crowds of these orthodox, letter-learned and regular pharisees, our Lord laments the unhappy case of that great number of people, who, in the days of his flesh, had no better guides: Because that those were as good as none (in many respects) in our Saviour's judgment. For all them, the people were sheep without a shepherd. . . .

First I am to enquire into the *Characters of the Old Pharisee-Teachers.* Now, I think the most notorious branches of their character, were these, viz. *pride, policy, malice, ignorance, covetousness,* and *bigotry to human inventions in religious matters.*

The old Pharisees were very proud and conceity; they loved the uppermost seats in the synagogues, and to be called Rabbi, Rabbi; they were masterly and positive in their assertions, as if forsooth knowledge must die with them; they looked upon others that differed from them, and the common people with an air of disdain; and especially any who had a respect for JESUS and his doctrine, and disliked them; they judged such accursed. . . .

Although some of the old Pharisee-Shepherds had a very fair and strict out-side; yet were they ignorant of the New-Birth: Witness Rabbi Nicodemus, who talked like a fool about it. Hear how our LORD cursed those plaistered hypocrites, Matt. 23:27, 28: *Wo unto you, scribes and pharisees, hypocrites; for ye are like whited sepulchres, which indeed appear beautiful outward, but are within full of dead bones, and of all uncleanness. Even so ye also appear righteous unto men, but within ye are full of hypocrisy and iniquity.* Ay, if they had but a little of the learning then in fashion, and a fair out-side, they were presently put into the priest's office, though they had no experience of the New-Birth. O Sad!

The old Pharisees, for all their long prayers and other pious pretences, had their eyes, with Judas, fixed upon the bag. Why, they came into the priest's office for a piece of bread; they took it up as a trade, and therefore endeavoured to make the best market of it they could. O Shame! . . .

Second general head of discourse, is to show, *Why such people, who have no better than the Old Pharisee-Teachers, are to be pitied?* And

1. Natural men have no call of GOD to the ministerial work under the Gospel-Dispensation. . . .

And Pharisee-Teachers, having no experience of a

special work of the Holy Ghost, upon their own souls, are therefore neither inclined to, nor fitted for, discoursing, frequently, clearly, and pathetically, upon such important subjects. The application of their discourses, is either short, or indistinct and general. They difference not the precious from the vile, and divide not to every man his portion, according to the apostolical direction to Timothy. No! they carelessly offer a common mess to their people, and leave it to them, to divide it among themselves, as they see fit. This is indeed their general practice, which is bad enough; but sometimes they do worse, by misapplying the word, through ignorance, or anger. They often strengthen the hands of the wicked, by promising him life. They comfort people, before they convince them; sow before they plow; and are busy in raising a fabric, before they lay a foundation. These fooling builders do but strengthen men's carnal security, by their soft, selfish, cowardly discourses. They have not the courage, or honesty, to thrust the nail of terror into sleeping souls; nay, sometimes they strive with all their might, to fasten terror into the hearts of the righteous, and so to make those sad, whom GOD would not have made sad! And this happens, when pious people begin to suspect their hypocrisy, for which they have good reason. I may add, that inasmuch as Pharisee-Teachers seek after righteousness as it were by works of the law themselves, they therefore do not distinguish, as they ought, between *Law* and *Gospel* in their discourses to others. They keep driving, driving, to duty, duty, under this notion, that it will recommend natural men to the favour of GOD, or entitle them to the promises of grace and salvation: And thus those blind guides fix a deluded world upon the false foundation of their own righteousness; and so exclude them from the dear Redeemer. All the doings of unconverted men, not proceeding from the principles of faith, love, and a new nature, nor being directed to the divine glory as their highest end, but flowing from, and tending to self, as their principle and end, are doubtless damnably wicked in their manner of performance, and do deserve the wrath and curse of a sin-avenging GOD; neither can any other encouragement be justly given them, but this, that in the way of duty, there is a peradventure of probability of obtaining mercy.

And natural men, wanting the experience of those spiritual difficulties, which pious souls are exposed to, in this vale of tears, they know not how to speak a word to the weary in season. Their prayers are also cold; little child-like love to God or pity to poor perishing souls, runs through their veins. Their conversation hath nothing of the savour of Christ, neither is it perfumed with the spices of Heaven. They seem to make as little distinction in their practice as preaching. They love those unbelievers that are kind to them, better than many Christians, and choose them for companions. . . .

Is a blind man fit to be a guide in a very dangerous way? Is a dead man fit to bring others to life? a mad man fit to give counsel in a matter of life and death? Is a possessed man fit to cast out devils? a rebel, an enemy to GOD, fit to be sent on an embassy of peace, to bring rebels into a state of friendship with GOD? a captive bound in the massy chains of darkness and guilt, a proper person to set others at liberty? a leper, or one that has plague-sores upon him, fit to be a good physician? Is an ignorant rustic, that has never been at sea in his life, fit to be a pilot, to keep vessels from being dashed to pieces upon rocks and sand-banks? *Isn't an unconverted minister like a man who would learn others to swim, before he*

has learned it himself, and so is drowned in the act, and
dies like a fool? . . .

4. The ministry of natural men is dangerous, both in
respect of the doctrines, and practice of piety. The doctrines of *original sin, justification by faith alone,* and
the other points of *Calvinism,* are very cross to the grain
of unrenewed nature. And though men, by the influence
of a good education, and hopes of preferment, may have
the edge of their natural enmity against them blunted;
yet it's far from being broken or removed. It's only the
saving Grace of GOD, that can give us a true relish for
those nature-humbling doctrines; and so effectually secure us from being infected by the contrary. Is not the
carnality of the *ministry,* one great cause of the general
spread of *Arminianism, Socinianism, Arianism,* and
Deism, at this day through the world? . . .

Third general head was to show, *How pity should be
expressed upon this mournful occasion?*

My Brethren, we should mourn over those, that are
destitute of faithful ministers, and sympathize with them.
Our bowels should be moved with the most compassionate tenderness over those dear fainting souls that are
as sheep having no shepherd; and that after the example
of our blessed LORD.

Dear Sirs! we should also most *earnestly pray* for them,
that the compassionate Saviour may preserve them, by
his mighty power, through faith unto salvation; support
their sinking spirits, under the *melancholy uneasinesses
of a dead ministry;* sanctify and sweeten to them the *dry*
morsels they get under such blind men, when they have
none better to repair to. . . .

And indeed, *my brethren,* we should join our endeavours to our prayers. The most likely method to stock
the church with a faithful ministry, in the present situ-

ation of things, the public academies being so much
corrupted and abused generally, is to encourage private
schools, or seminaries of learning, which are under the
care of skillful and experienced Christians, in which
those only should be admitted, who upon strict examination, have in the judgment of a reasonable charity, the
plain evidences of experimental religion. Pious and experienced youths, who have a good natural capacity, and
great desires after the ministerial work, from good motives, might be sought for, and found up and down in
the country, and put to private Schools of the Prophets;
especially in such places where the public ones are not.
This method, in my opinion, has a noble tendency, to
build up the church of God. And those who have any
love to Christ, or desire after the coming of his Kingdom,
should be ready, according to their ability, to give somewhat, from time to time, for the support of such poor
youths, who have nothing of their own. And truly, brethren, this charity to the souls of men is the most noble
kind of charity—O! if the love of God be in you, it will
constrain you to do something, to promote so noble and
necessary a work. It looks hypocrite-like to go no further,
when other things are required, than *cheap prayer*. Don't
think it much, if the Pharisees should be offended at
such a proposal; these subtle selfish hypocrites are wont
to be scared about their credit, and their kingdom; and
truly they are both little worth, for all the bustle they
make about them. If they could help it, they wouldn't
let one faithful man come into the ministry; and therefore their opposition is an encouraging sign. Let all the
followers of the Lamb stand up and act for GOD against
all opposers: Who is upon GOD's side? who? . . .

2. From what has been said, we may learn that such
who are contented under a *dead ministry* have not in

them the temper of that Saviour they profess. It's an awful sign, that they are as blind as moles, and as dead as stones, without any spiritual taste and relish. And alas! isn't this the case of multitudes? If they can get one that has the name of a minister, with a band, and a black coat or gown to carry on a sabbath-days among them, although never so coldly, and insuccessfully; if he is free from gross crimes in practice, and takes good care to keep at a due distance from their consciences, and is never troubled about his insuccessfulness; O! think the poor fools, that is a fine man indeed; our minister is a prudent charitable man, he is not always harping upon terror, and sounding damnation in our ears, like some rash-headed preachers, who by their uncharitable methods, are ready to put poor people out of their wits, or to run them into despair; O! how terrible a thing is that despair! Ay, our minister, honest man, gives us good caution against it. Poor silly souls! . . .

4. If the ministry of natural men be as it has been represented, then it is both lawful and expedient to go from them to hear godly persons; yea, it's so far from being sinful to do this, that one who lives under a pious minister of lesser gifts, after having honestly endeavoured to get benefit by his ministry, and yet gets little or none, but doth find real benefit and more benefit elsewhere; I say, he may lawfully go, and that frequently, where he gets most good to his precious soul, after regular application to the pastor where he lives, for his consent, and proposing the reasons thereof; when this is done in the spirit of love and meekness, without contempt of any, as also without rash anger or vain curiosity. . . .

That which ought to be the main motive of hearing any, viz. our souls' good, or greater good, will excite us, if we regard our own eternal interest, to hear there, where we attain it; and he that hears with less views, acts like a fool, and a hypocrite.

Now, if it be lawful to withdraw from the ministry of a pious man in the case aforesaid; how much more, from the ministry of a natural man? Surely, it is both lawful and expedient, for the reason offered in the doctrinal part of this discourse: To which let me add a few words more.

To trust the care of our souls to those who have little or no care for their own, to those who are both unskillful and unfaithful, is contrary to the common practice of considerate mankind, relating to the affairs of their bodies and estates; and would signify, that we set light by our souls, and did not care what became of them. For if the blind lead the blind, will they not both fall into the ditch? . . .

If it be opposed to the preceding reasonings, that such an opinion and practice would be apt to cause heats and contentions among people;

I answer, that the aforesaid practice, accompanied with love, meekness, and humility, is not the proper *cause* of those divisions, but the *occasion* only, or the cause by accident, and not by itself. If a person exercising modesty and love in his carriage to his minister and neighbours, through uprightness of heart, designing nothing but his own greater good, repairs there frequently where he attains it; is this any reasonable cause of anger? Will any be offended with him because he loves his soul, and seeks the greater good thereof, and is not like a senseless stone, without choice, sense, and taste? Pray must we leave off every duty, that is the occasion of contention or division? Then we must quit powerful religion altogether. . . .

Again it may be objected, that the aforesaid practice

tends to grieve our parish-minister, and to break congregations in pieces.

I answer, if our parish-minister be grieved at our greater good, or prefers his credit before it, then he has good cause to grieve over his own rottenness and hypocrisy. And as for breaking of congregations to pieces, upon the account of people's going from place to place, to hear the Word, with a view to get greater good, that spiritual blindness and death, that so generally prevails, will put this out of danger. It is but a very few, that have got any spiritual relish; the most will venture their souls with any formalist, and be well satisfied with the sapless discourses of such dead drones. . . .

And O! that vacant congregations would take due care in the choice of their ministers! Here indeed they should hasten slowly. The Church of *Ephesus* is commended, for trying them which said they were Apostles, and were not; and for finding them liars. Hypocrites are against all knowing of others, and judging, in order to hide their own filthiness; like thieves they flee a search, because of the stolen goods. But the more they endeavour to hide, the more they expose their shame. Does not the spiritual man judge all things? Though he cannot know the states of subtle hypocrites infallibly; yet may he not give a near guess, who are the Sons of *Sceva,* by their manner of praying, preaching, and living? Many Pharisee-Teachers have got a long fine string of prayer by heart, so that they are never at a loss about it; their prayers and preachings are generally of a length, and both as dead as a stone, and without all savour. I beseech you, my dear brethren, to consider that there is no probability of your getting good by the Ministry of Pharisees. For they are no shepherds (no faithful ones) in Christ's account. They are as good as none, nay, worse than none, upon some accounts. For take them first and last, and they generally do more hurt than good. They strive to keep better out of the places where they live; nay, when the life of piety comes near their quarters, they rise up in arms against it, consult, contrive and combine in their conclaves against it, as a common enemy, that discovers and condemns their craft and hypocrisy. And with what art, rhetoric, and appearances of piety will they varnish their opposition of Christ's Kingdom? As the magicians imitated the works of Moses, so do false apostles, and deceitful workers, the Apostles of Christ.

I shall conclude this discourse with the words of the Apostle Paul, 2 Cor. 11:14, 15: *And no marvel; for Satan himself is transformed into an angel of light: Therefore it is no great thing if his ministers also be transformed as the ministers of righteousness; whose end shall be according to their works.*

SOURCE: Gilbert Tennent, *The Danger of an Unconverted Ministry*. Philadelphia: Benjamin Franklin, 1740.

The Danger of an Unqualified Ministry

JOHN HANCOCK

John Hancock, pastor of the First Church in Braintree, Massachusetts, used an ordination sermon, which he was called upon to deliver in Connecticut, as an occasion to answer Tennent. Essential to the health of church and society, Hancock argues, is a learned and competent ministry, licensed and regularly appointed by duly constituted church authorities. A learned and educated ministry, he maintains, is no less committed than others, only less prone to superstition, confusion, and censoriousness.

This is the will of GOD our Saviour, in the institution of a standing ministry, in his church; that men be well qualified and spirited for this great and good work; that they give themselves to prayer, and to the ministry of the Word; that they make a business of it, that their profiting may appear to all, and that they may profit his people.

Such are pastors according to GOD's heart,† who shall feed his People with knowledge and understanding, which is food convenient for rational and immortal souls, angel's food. For *without knowledge the soul cannot be good:* It is pleasant to the soul, and understanding shall keep it; and if thou be wise, thou shalt be wise for thyself.

He is a good minister of Jesus Christ, who is nourished up in the words of faith and good doctrine, being able also to teach others. . . .

The Apostles of our Lord have been very careful to give the churches of Christ all the necessary qualifications of good ministers of Jesus Christ, that they may be furnished at all times with able and faithful pastors, and to be kept pure from a corrupt and bad ministry.

Indeed, whosoever has a just apprehension of the greatness, difficulty and importance of the evangelical ministry, needeth not arguments to convince him of the necessity of encouraging and supporting learned and

† Jer. 3:15.

godly pastors in the churches. It is therefore owing to ignorance, pride, and want of consideration and judgment, that any think and speak contrarywise, that men of mean abilities and attainments in knowledge are able to preach the unsearchable riches of Christ, open the great mysteries of godliness, and defend the Gospel.

Alas! It requires no small compass of reason and learning to be able to preach and defend the Gospel; for ministers are set to defend, as well as preach the everlasting Gospel. And if need be, they must contend earnestly for the faith, which was once delivered to the saints. The servant of the Lord must also be patient, in meekness instructing those that oppose themselves. . . .

For GOD's sake, brethren, what would have become of the Christian religion long ago, had it not been for the wise and learned defenders of it against its ablest adversaries? Such as the Apostle Paul, Origen, Justin Martyr, and others among the Fathers; and many since the time of the reformation of the church from popery.

God has raised up able advocates and apologists to espouse and defend his own cause from age to age, who have been valiant for the truth, and quitted themselves like men in the cause of God, so that truth has not fallen in the streets, but still prevails on the earth.

And indeed the revival of learning, since the glorious reformation, has been a great elucidation and establishment of the truths of our holy religion: So that the enemies of good literature are enemies to the true interest of Christianity, whether they know it or not.

It has been publicly observed, that the interest of religion and good literature have been wont to rise and fall together. . . .

Alas! How soon would the church of God be laid desolate, if the hedge of a learned, able and faithful ministry, which Christ hath set about it, were once taken down. Ignorance, error, heresy, superstition, confusion and every evil work, would soon cover the face of the vineyard of the Lord of Hosts. It would quickly be overgrown with thorns, and nettles cover the face thereof, when the wall thereof is broken down. With such awful severity and judgment, God threatens the church of Israel for their unfruitfulness under his most gracious cultivations in Isa. 5:5, 6. *And now——I will tell you what I will do to my vineyard, I will take away the hedge thereof, and it shall be eaten up, and break down the wall thereof, and it shall be trodden down, and I will lay it waste, it shall not be pruned, nor digged, and there shall come up briars and thorns, I will also command the clouds that they rain no rain upon it.*

Were the Gospel-Treasure put into broken vessels, it would soon run out and perish. If the teaching and government of the church were committed to unskilful and unfaithful guides, *ignorance would soon be the mother of devotion;* and heresy and confusion, the doctrine and discipline of the Christian Church. For to this purpose testifieth the Apostle Peter, by the spirit of prophecy, *There shall be false teachers among you, who privily shall bring in damnable heresies, and many shall follow their pernicious ways, by reason of whom the way of truth shall be Evil spoken of. And through covetousness shall they with feigned words, make merchandize of you.*†

How is it possible for a novice to magnify his office, and recommend religion to the esteem and practice of men? He that teacheth man knowledge should not he know? Because the preacher was wise, he still taught the

† 2 Pet. 2:1,2,3.

people knowledge, and sought to find out acceptable words. But how shameful is it for weak, raw, illiterate men to exalt themselves to the priesthood, and set up for teachers in the Church, who have need that one teach them which be the first principles of the oracles of God? And have need of milk, and should as new-born babes desire the sincere milk of the Word, that they may grow thereby?

Moreover, the setting up and sending forth such teachers in the Church of Christ, is the great reproach to Christianity, and the direct way to promote the contempt of the clergy, than which a greater injury can scarce be offered to the true interest of religion.

Thus I have finished the *doctrinal part of my subject,* and shall now close it with several useful reflections.

First, *We may learn, from what has been offered upon this argument, the great care that the glorious head of the church, has taken for its instruction and support.*

For to this end, Christ was pleased to raise up a succession of inspired prophets and teachers in the Jewish Church, and at sundry times, and in divers manners, spake unto the fathers by them. In the fulness of time, he manifested himself to Israel, full of grace and truth, as the Lord who teacheth us to profit, as the great teacher of the church, who spake as never man spake. When he had finished the work of GOD, and ascended up on high, he gave gifts unto men, *Some apostles, and some prophets, and some evangelists, and some pastors and teachers, for the perfecting of the saints, for the work of the ministry, for the edifying of the Body of Christ.*

Moreover, the Highest himself has established the security and safety of the church in opposition to the confederated powers of earth and hell, in that glorious promise, *That the gates of hell shall not prevail against it.*† Its defence is of GOD. GOD is in the midst of her, therefore the burning bush is not consumed. We have a strong City; salvation will GOD appoint for walls and bulwarks.

How beautiful and safe is the church in the favour and protection of the Almighty, under all the imperfection that cleaves to his ministers and members in this militant state? This is our hope, and this our confidence, that God will help her, and that right early.

Secondly, this doctrine gives a rule of conduct to the ministers of Christ in admitting persons into the sacred ministry; that they proceed with great care and caution in such a weighty affair, as they would approve themselves faithful to Christ and his interest. They are forbid to put a *novice* into the evangelical ministry. Lay hands suddenly on no man.

For any of the ministers of Christ then, to give their credentials to unworthy men, is to act directly in the face of Scripture canons, and betray the cause of Christ. It is really to expose their own souls and the souls of all they are concerned with to *Condemnation,* and doing infinite mischief to the true interest of religion.

I would use here great plainness of speech, for I apprehend the case requires it, and freely say, that I can't see how ministers can answer to GOD and their own consciences, their admitting raw, indiscreet, rash, illiterate and blind *novices* into their pulpits, and commending them to these churches, as useful instruments of carrying on the work of God, as hath been the manner of some more lately.

The overseers of the flocks of Christ, are indispensably obliged, by his holy Word, to commit this sacred

† Matt. 16:18.

treasure to faithful men who shall be able to teach others also, and not to cast these holy things to the dogs of the flock.

It is to be feared, that there has been too much indifference and coldness among the clergy of New-England, as well as elsewhere, in this important article, of examining and introducing candidates into the ministry; especially, in the years last past, has the sacred ministry been laid too common, as if it were not a sacred enclosure, and any bold intruder might take this honor to himself, without due qualifications, or a regular call; which in the nature of things bodes very ill to the church of Christ: Whereas the Scripture saith, *No man taketh this honor unto himself, but he that is called of God, as was Aaron.*

Were the ministry of the Gospel committed to ignorant, conceited *novices,* 'tis not unlikely that, within two seven years, the church would be reduced to a state of heathenism, thick darkness would cover the earth, and gross darkness the people.

And the present *unbounded license* of public teaching, I apprehend to be a leading step to the scandalous disorders and confusions of these times. And it's high time to correct and reform this shameful abuse of the ministerial authority.

But to the praise of the government of this colony, be it spoken, that they have expressed an examplary care in this matter of introducing candidates into the holy ministry, above all the provinces in New-England, and it is doubtless a great part of the beauty and strength of your good constitution. We rejoice, beholding your order, and the stedfastness of your faith in Christ. Upon this very thing depends the safety and prosperity of these churches.

Suffer me then, my reverend fathers and brethren,

(though most unworthy) to press it upon you to shew all good fidelity in this important affair. For this power of examining and putting men into the ministry is committed to you to exercise for the good of the church. Oh let it not be in vain, but approve yourselves faithful to Christ, and the souls of men, that you may both save your own souls, and be happily instrumental, in this way, of promoting the common salvation.

Thirdly, this doctrine also admonisheth the churches of Christ, to take heed of committing their souls to the care of unskilful novices. For hereby the souls of men are exposed to eternal ruin. Who then in his wits would be careless and unconcerned in the choice of a guide and pastor to his soul? There is surely no affair in the whole circle of life that requires more serious care and assiduous prayer, than this of choosing able, faithful, skilful guides for our souls. And as Christ has given these churches power of choosing their own pastors, so let them be exhorted to stand fast in the liberty wherewith he hath made them free, and not abuse it in a criminal manner.

Let the churches be advised to act with prudent care and caution in the exercise of this power. Be not fond of *novelties,* but covet earnestly the best gifts. Ask counsel of God, and take the best advice of the faithful ministers of Christ, who are commonly most able and ready to serve your best interest. Oh beware of heaping to yourselves teachers, and leaning to your own understanding. *For the time will come,* saith the Apostle, *when they will not endure sound doctrine, but after their own lusts shall they heap to themselves teachers, having itching ears; and they shall turn away their ears from the truth, and shall be turned unto fables.*†

† 2 Tim. 4:3, 4.

Verily, 'tis to be feared, we are fallen into this time, now so many of unstable minds are ready to forsake their own faithful and approved pastors, and the assembling themselves together, to follow the *sounding brass* of ignorant, conceited *novices. Verily, verily I say unto you,* saith our Saviour, the good shepherd, *he that entereth not in by the door into the sheepfold, but climbeth up some other way, the same is a thief, and a robber. But he that entereth in by the door, is the Shepherd of the Sheep. To him the porter openeth, and the sheep hear his voice.**

Fourthly, *This doctrine ministers reproof to every novice that is thrusting himself into the ministry.* For do but consider the infinite danger of so doing, lest being lifted up with pride, he fall into the condemnation of the devil. Such know not what they ask and seek, whilst they are striving for the mastery, to enter into the sacred ministry. My brethren, be not many masters, don't be too forward and hasty, in setting up for teachers, lest ye receive the greater condemnation.

Yet strange it is, that so many, in these days, apprehend themselves well qualified for the ministerial office without learning, or study, or any qualification for this good work; except ignorance, and confidence may be accounted such. It is to be suspected, that pride and self-conceit is at the bottom of such a stupid and wild conduct. What other cause but pride can be assigned for the very scandalous intrusions of illiterate *lay-men,* and *raw novices* into the labours of GOD's faithful ministers, in one place and another, to the great vexation and disturbance of the churches of Christ in this land? *Only by pride cometh contention. . . .*

* John 10:1, 2, 3.

Fifthly, *This doctrine may also serve to admonish all young unexperienced converts to take heed to themselves, watch and be sober; lest being lifted up with pride, they come into condemnation.* GOD resisteth the proud, but he giveth grace unto the humble. Be clothed with humility. Learn of Christ who was meek and lowly in heart, and has laid humility in the foundation of his heavenly doctrine. *Blessed are the poor in Spirit, for theirs is the Kingdom of Heaven.*† I say to every man that is among you, not to think of himself more highly than he ought to think, but to think soberly. This will be the best antidote against many irregularities and scandals that prevail in the present times, and even among many of those, who have been the subjects of the late religious commotion in the land. *Particularly,* a spirit of rash, censorious judging which is gone forth, and rages in the country? than which nothing can be more contrary to the spirit of Christ and his Gospel. . . .

And now from whence comes such a spirit of rash judging? Cometh it not hence, even of this lust of pride? And such as indulge it are in danger of falling into the condemnation of the devil.

There has been, of late, much talk about religion, and a remarkable work of GOD in the country; but it must be remembered, that "the Kingdom of GOD is not in word but in power." And, for my own part, I have been waiting to see the work prove itself in the power of godliness, and the genuine fruits of the spirit of GOD, in all goodness, righteousness and truth.

But indeed the unwearied pains taken by the friends of the late religious commotion among us, to persuade

† Matt. 5:3.

people, that GOD has remarkably revived his work in the land, is so far from being a confirmation of it, that, in my opinion, 'tis more apt to bring a suspicion upon it.

If there be such a happy revival of GOD's work, as some contend earnestly for, what need of calling of assemblies, and so much preaching and writing to possess the minds of people with the belief of it? For the work of GOD will prove itself, by producing a visible and glorious reformation among the happy subjects of it, which the Lord hastens in his time. . . .

I shall conclude with a serious address, To my Rev. and dear brother, whose consecration of God, in the Gospel of his Son, we are now attending.

First, dear sir, suffer the exhortation that speaketh to you, as to a son and candidate for holy orders. You have heard something of the great and necessary qualifications of a good minister to Jesus Christ, and the danger of admitting unqualified persons to take part of this ministry; and I doubt not, but that your heart is in some good measure affected with the sense of the difficulty and importance of the work upon which you are entering.

I have known your education, principles and manner of life from your youth up, and have had a good taste of your ministerial gifts and accomplishments, all which, in my judgment, are so many desirable qualifications to perfect you for the work of the ministry, for the edifying of the Body of Christ. These things, being in you and abounding, both free you from the imputation of a novice, and us from the guilt of putting such an one into the ministry.

But yet, there is room for growth; you must labour to increase in wisdom and the most useful learning; but above all things, grow in grace and in the knowledge of our Lord and Saviour Jesus Christ. My son, be strong in the grace that is in Christ Jesus. To this end give attendance to reading, to exhortation, to doctrine, meditate upon these things, give thy self wholly to them, that thy profiting may appear to all, and in all things. Study to show thyself approved unto God, a workman that needeth not to be ashamed, rightly dividing the Word of Truth.

I do this day, with sacred freedom and pleasure, act the part you have devolved upon me (however unequal to it) and in concurrence with other pastors and churches convened on this solemn occasion, join heart and hand in separating you to the Gospel of God. We bring you, dear sir, to this people, and bless you in the name of the Lord; may the Lord bless you out of Zion, and have respect unto your offering!

You enter sir, upon the work of the ministry, in a dark and difficult time, wherein you will find uncommon temptations to unfaithfulness; but be of good courage, and let none of these things move you. Do the work of a good minister of Christ, with all fidelity; and be valiant for the truth.

And as my subject leads me to give you this caution, so I would do it both for your own safety, and the safety of pure and undefiled religion: That is, guard your pulpit against every *novice;* exclude, if possible, all unqualified persons from the ministerial office. Lay hands suddenly on no man; be not partakers of other men's sins, keep thyself pure.

Finally, take heed unto thyself, and unto thy doctrine, continue in them, for in so doing this, thou shalt both save thyself, and them that hear thee. . . .

SOURCE: John Hancock, *The Danger of an Unqualified Ministry, Represented in a Sermon* . . . (Boston: Rogers and Fowle, 1743), pp. 16–17, 18, 19–24, 27, 28–30.

Learning and Grace

ANDREW CROSSWELL

Andrew Crosswell was one of the more radical New England Awakeners, a vigorous defender of James Davenport, and a fiery, evangelical orator himself. Crosswell always stressed the centrality of inner experience, and he supported the practice of church separations when absolutely necessary. But he also recognized that his singular emphasis on the New Light could lead to antinomian and anti-intellectual abuses, which he wanted to avoid. The selection below is taken from Crosswell's introduction to a sermon, entitled "What is Christ to Me, if He is not Mine," in which he argues that a general faith is not enough, if it is not accompanied by "a particular work" of grace in the soul. His attempts in the excerpted passage to explain his own convictions and practices indicate that even some of the most radical New Lights did not totally reject the importance of formal education for ministers, but that for them the problem of finding the right relationship between learning and grace was a difficult one indeed.

For my part, through grace, I have an universal love towards ministers (more especially those who appear to have been inflamed with the love of Christ, *whoever* they be, *wherever* they be, and *however*, in lesser matters, opposite to me); and have felt my heart wishing them well, and praying for them, even those who are most against me, a great part of the time that I have been writing this book. But though I *wish well to* all, I don't *think well of* all: On the contrary, I make no doubt but the colleges pour forth swarms of young men, who have spent their days in divers lusts and vanities, and have never had an *effectual law-work,* so that the light of the glorious Gospel of Jesus Christ hath shined into their souls. And these unhappy men (God pity them; my heart almost bleeds for them; such an one was I) come forth to *serve* the churches (but really to *serve them-selves*) and after a life spent in pleasure, pomp, and worldlimindedness, they go down to the dead, and the damned, and their people with them. And 'tis observing too many of this sort of ministers (for one must be *spiritually blind,* and very much *like* them, not to find a plenty of them in town and country) which Satan makes use of, to prejudice some persons against a learned ministry, causing them to separate from them, and to be ministers themselves, or at least to heap up teachers to themselves, some of whom had need be taught what are the first principles of the oracles of God: esteeming them highly for their ignorance sake, as if what came from the mouths of such men, must needs come immediately from the Spirit of God.

I would not be understood by this paragraph, to speak against the preaching of all those who are without academical learning; nor yet as if I was against all separations. As for those who appear to be no enemies to learning, but men of knowledge, and of a sound mind, and especially to be full of faith and of the Holy Ghost! I would as soon encourage their preaching, as if they had commenced doctors in divinity. Nor dare I be against all separations: For to be against all separations is to be against all reformations; and yet I make no question but a separating spirit is an antichristian spirit. 'Tis this, which hath made little brotherhoods and sisterhoods of about five or six in number; and the same principle will probably make their numbers still less. For my part I would bear with a great deal in a church, and in a minister before I would separate: a little of the language of Ashdod, which good ministers sometimes speak, joined with a great deal of the language of Canaan, would not drive me away. And inasmuch as the world calls me a promoter of separations (as well as thinks me to be a friend to many errors, which I have always been against). I shall take this opportunity to answer for my self, and to plead not guilty. I don't preach one word about separations, nor advise any to separate in private: But this one thing I do; I preach the glorious Gospel at home and abroad to as many as are disposed to hear me; though not before the consent of the ministers is asked. If they will allow me to preach to those people who desire to hear me; then, (to my rejoicing) the Gospel is preached without strife, or appearance of contention: But if they forbid my preaching because I preach that a poor sinner in order to his being justified, must believe that God for Christ's Sake doth forgive all his sins (which is sometimes the case) I preach notwithstanding. All men of reading know this to be the Protestant faith. And preaching the true Protestant faith will be likely to strengthen the hands of true Protestants.*

* This paragraph appears as a footnote in the original.

SOURCE: Andrew Crosswell, *What is Christ to Me, if He is not Mine? Or a Seasonable Defence of the Old Protestant Doctrine of Justifying Faith* (Boston: 1745), "Introduction," pp. 8–9.

An Internal Call

ISAAC BACKUS

*One of the leading Baptists of New England, histor-
ian of the church, and a foremost champion of the College of Rhode Island, Isaac Backus was self-taught and
without a formal education. He was converted in 1742,
joined the Separates a few years later, and feeling a call
to preach he began to itinerate and eventually became
a New Light Baptist. Backus, as did many of the Baptists, went one step farther than other revivalists in insisting not only on conversion for all true Christians, but
beyond that on a special call to preach for all true
ministers. This passage is taken from one of Backus'
pamphlets defending his notion of a special internal
call to preach as the essence of ministerial qualifications.
Backus does not despise learning, but he places it far
down in his order of essential priorities, and in so doing takes the opportunity to raise critical questions
about the quality of education being received by ministerial candidates of Harvard and Yale.*

Now 'tis likely that many when they see this discourse,
will be ready to deem it to be pride and arrogancy for
such a youth to come out in this form against so many
great, learned, yea and good men. But I can freely leave
that to my divine Master, to plead my cause, knowing

that a good conscience is better than all the applause of mortal men.

Some of the reasons of my coming forth in this manner, are as follow. Since the LORD was pleased to call me forth into this great work of preaching the Gospel, as I have had opportunity to improve in that work in various places, the question has often been asked me, especially by the common ministers of the land, What call I held to, whether ordinary or extraordinary, mediate or immediate? And when we have come to discourse upon it, it has appeared plain to me that what they hold to be an ordinary call is to be called only by men, and an extraordinary one is to be called of GOD, by the special influences of his SPIRIT. For I have heard them go through with a description of their call, and never mention GOD's SPIRIT in the case; but only that they were educated for that purpose, and then were introduced and ordained in an orderly way.

Indeed some of them will say that they have an internal call; but when they come to describe it, they say, " 'Tis a hearty disposition to serve GOD in that work." But is it not strange, that reasonable men should reckon this to be a call from GOD? Do they think there ever was a corrupt man in the world that went into that work without some disposition to it, which doubtless they called a disposition to serve GOD? Or should we allow it to be a sincere disposition, yet still that is not a call? The most that can be made of it is a willingness to be called. Every saint, when standing as they ought, are willing to do anything that GOD would have them; but something much further than that is needful in order to make them know that he would have them preach the Gospel publicly. I would not be understood to hold forth that there is none which hold fellowship with the scheme that I condemn that have truly experienced a call from the SPIRIT of GOD into the work of preaching the Gospel, for I believe there are some, though they may not be convinced of the evil of that method of going on. But a great part of the ministers in the land evidently run in the channel that I have described above.

Therefore to return, when I have heard them talk in such a form, it has put me upon a more close examination of the Scriptures, and to look more critically into the nature of these things (for much of what I have here written I knew experimentally before I did doctrinally, Prov. 16:23). And after much search and crying to the Lord for direction, though it never was my disposition from a child to appear singular from others, yet I have been constrained to appear against many in this point. I waited long and attended diligently to what others could say: I said, days should speak and multitude of years should teach wisdom. But great men are not always wise: therefore I said, I will answer my part, I also will show my opinion, Job 32:7, 9, 17. For I am persuaded that many guilty people, being traditionally trained up in that way, think it is a Gospel-Way; but being so clearly convinced that it is not, it has appeared clear duty to me not to hide my candle under a bushel, but to hold up the light which GOD hath given me, for the good of others. . . .

Let none think me to be an enemy to learning because of what I have said in this book, for true learning is what I highly prize. A clear understanding of the proper use of language, and the meaning of words, whereby men have such a privilege of conveying their ideas to each other, is very beneficial for all; and a clear knowledge of the things of nature, and of the affairs of mankind, etc. is good in its place, and I wish there was much more of it in the world than there is. But then there are a great many notions that some take much time to learn that do no good; and what is worse, it is evident that in our colleges many learn corrupt principles, not only about what makes a minister, but also about what makes a Christian; for it is too notorious to be denied that many scholars that have come out of college of late are rank Arminians. Yet were it not so, it is horrid presumption to pretend to limit the Most High to any schools or bodies of people whatsoever, and to say that he shall have none for his ambassadors but such as men have trained for that purpose in their way. . . .

One very great means that God has been pleased to make use of from the beginning for the recovery and salvation of lost men, has been the preaching of his Word. And therefore in every age he has called and set apart particular men for that purpose. *Jude* speaks of *Enoch's* prophesying, Jude 14. And *Noah* is called a *preacher of righteousness,* 2 Pet. 2:5. And we are told that *God at sundry times and in divers manners spake in time past unto the Fathers by the Prophets,* Heb. 1: 1. And in latter times, *though the preaching of the Cross is to them that perish foolishness: yet unto them that are saved, it is the Power of God,* 1 Cor. 1:18.

Hence it is a truth allowed in general by all persuasions, that the public preaching of the Word is an ordinance of divine appointment. But then there is a great diversity of sentiments about how men are to be qualified and introduced into this great work. Multitudes place their qualifications more in human learning than in divine enlightenings, and place their authority more in being externally called and set apart by men, than in being internally called by the Spirit of God. Yea, many seem to make no account of the latter, but set it aside as an extraordinary thing, not to be expected in these days. And the main argument that is commonly brought to prove this is, that the Bible is completed, and the days of inspiration are ceased; therefore to hold that any are by the Spirit and power of God in these days called and sent forth into this work, this they say is giving heed to new revelations: for it is nowhere expressed in Scripture that this or that man is, or ever will be, called to preach the Gospel. But though I believe with all my heart that the canon of the Scripture is full, and that there is a curse denounced against any that shall *add to or diminish from it,* Rev. 22:18, 19, yet I am far from thinking that it is just to conclude from hence that the Lord does not in these days as really call and direct his servants by his Spirit as he did in old time. . . .

Objection V. You speak much concerning a minister's call but say little about his qualifications which is the main thing, for a man must have learning and the understanding of the original tongues or else he does not know whether he preaches right or wrong.

Answer 1. If a man's having the treasure of God's Word opened and committed to his soul and having such a view of the worth of souls as to be constrained by divine power and love to go and spend his life and strength for God's glory and in laboring for their good, 2 Cor. 5:14; John 11:15, 16, 17; 2 Cor. 12:15; I say, if these things are not Gospel qualifications, I know not what are; yea such necessary qualifications as that without them, if a man had all the learning that men can give, he would be no ways fit for this great work.

Answer 2. As to the knowledge of the original tongues, though I do not despise it, for no doubt that may be improved to some benefit under the influence of the

Spirit of God, yet I am far from thinking it to be so essentially necessary as many would represent.

For though I have heard many (both ministers and others) assert that without the knowledge of the original tongues a man could not know whether he preached truth or falsehood, yet I shall not only assert, but prove, that every saint now has the same way to know the truth and certainty of God's Word that his people had of old, without which all the learning in this world will never bring any man to know certainly the truth of the Scriptures.

Christ told his disciples that the *Spirit of Truth would guide them into all truth,* John 16:13. And when the *Jews* said of Him, *How knoweth this man letters, having never learned?* Christ (after asserting that his doctrine was not his own but his that sent Him) says, *If any man will do his will, he shall* KNOW *of the doctrine, whether it be of God, or whether I speak of myself,* John 7:17. The way that the *Thessalonians knew and received the Gospel not as the word of man but (as it is in truth) the Word of God was by its coming to them in power, and in the* HOLY GHOST, *and in much assurance,* 1 Thess. 2:13, and 1:5. Once more, *Paul* tells the *Corinthians* (who reckoned as much upon learning and wisdom as many do in this day) *That he determined to know nothing among them save Jesus Christ and Him crucified, and* (says he) *my speech and my preaching was not with enticing words of man's wisdom but in demonstration of the spirit and of power.* And again, *What man knows the things of a man save the spirit of man that is in him? Even so the things of God knoweth no man but the Spirit of God. Now we have received not the spirit of the world but the Spirit which is of God that we might know the things that are freely given to us of God. Which things also we speak not in the words which*

man's wisdom teacheth but which the HOLY GHOST
*teacheth, comparing spiritual things with spiritual. But
the natural man receiveth not the things of the Spirit of
God, for they are foolishness unto him; neither can he
know them, because they are spiritually discerned,* 1 Cor.
2:2, 4, 11-14.

This is the only way by which God's people in every
age have known the truth and certainty of his Word
which hath been given in to by Protestants in general
both at home and abroad since the reformation. The
Westminster Confession of Faith, after mentioning sundry arguments that may induce us to believe the Scriptures, say, "Yet notwithstanding, our full persuasion and
assurance of the infallible truth and divine authority
thereof is from the inward work of the Holy Spirit bearing witness by and with the Word in our hearts," chap.
1, sect. 5.

If we cannot know certainly that the Bible is true
without understanding of *Hebrew, Greek,* and *Latin*
(which *Pilate* set over Christ's head when he was crucified, Luke 23:38; Matt. 27:37), then alas! we are in a
woeful case indeed, for (according to this) if we hear a
man preach that says he knows not only them tongues
but twenty more beside, and he tells us that this or that
is truth, we have only a man's testimony for it. And God
says we worship Him in vain when our fear is taught by
the precepts of men, Isa. 29:13 compared with Matt.
15:9. But it is the common privilege of God's people
(and then much more of his messengers) to have the
divine Spirit given them, to seal his truth to their hearts
without which, if a person has never so many of the
learned tongues, how does he know that them books
which we call the Word of God are not *cunningly de-
vised fables* and nothing but a piece of priestcraft as some
men of great human learning really call them? Or, if he

allows that they were first written by the direction of God's Spirit, yet how does he know that they have not been altered since, for he has not the first copies? If it should be said that great care has been taken to transmit them down to us without any alteration, I answer, so has there been great care and pains used in translating them into our language as exactly as possible.

As for the argument that many bring from the apostles having the miraculous gift of tongues given them to prepare them to preach among the gentiles for to prove that men must learn the tongues now before they may preach among us, I can see no reason in it at all. To them was given the knowledge of the people's language that they were to preach to, and so undoubtedly persons now must have some clear understanding of the meaning and use of the tongue he speaks in or else he will be a barbarian to his hearers and they to him, 1 Cor. 14:11. This argument is much stronger to prove that men in our land ought to learn the *Indian* tongue, or other languages in these parts of the world, before they preach that they might be able to hold forth salvation to such poor souls than it is to prove that men must learn *Hebrew, Greek* and *Latin* before they may preach to English hearers. But some will say that though the Bible is very well translated into our language, yet a clear understanding of the original tongues may be of benefit as a person thereby may be able to view the different readings that there are in some places, and so may illustrate some things more clearly than others can.

To which I reply that I allowed this before, that such knowledge may by the help of the divine Spirit, be improved for the good of others. But then it is no argument against every one's improving the gift which God has given him, for each soul will have a dreadful account to give up, if they do not faithfully improve every talent which their Master hath given into their hands, Matt. 25:15; Luke 19:13. Yet let no man pretend to what he has not nor put what he has in a wrong place, both of which are abomination to the Lord. Spare me a word to each of these, and I will have done with this head.

First, Let no man pretend to what he has not, which certainly is the case of some, if not many, in this land with regard to this matter. They pretend that none may preach without they understand the original tongues, and yet many take their degrees at college and are ordained, who have no clear understanding of the *Hebrew* tongue at all (in which above half the Bible was written) so that, according to their own plea, they must never preach out of the Old Testament. If they do, they know not whether they preach right or wrong. And further, sundry persons that have gone through the college and are well acquainted with these things I have heard own that there is not one to ten among their scholars that are such masters of the original tongues as to be able to make any corrections if in any places the scriptures are not translated exactly right. But they possibly will read the remarks of some learned expositor (which common Englishmen can read) and then impose upon the common people, with a pretence of knowing much about the original of the Bible.

Secondly, Again, what learning men have is often put in a wrong place, namely, to supply the want of the Spirit of God, who alone can teach us all things, as no man can teach us, 1 John 2:27. *But the world by wisdom knew not God,* 1 Cor. 1:21. . . .

SOURCE: Isaac Backus, *All true Ministers are called into that Work by the special Influences of the Holy Spirit. A Discourse Shewing the Nature and Necessity of an Internal Call to Preach the Everlasting Gospel . . .* (Boston: Fowle, 1754), pp. viii–x, xii, 15–16, 66–72.

The Crisis in the Colleges

All parties in the Awakening soon recognized that control of educational institutions was vital for the success of their cause. The ejection of revivalist students from Yale and Harvard led to attempts on the part of the revivalists to found institutions of their own. In the middle colonies the success of the revivalist schools and academies spurred anti-revivalists to renew their educational efforts in turn. In the process many of the newer institutions became channels for the latest intellectual and pedagogical currents of the time.

Student Dissent

DAVID BRAINERD

*The Awakening produced severe disturbances among
the students at both Harvard and Yale. One of the students at Yale was David Brainerd, who criticized the
character of one of his tutors and was expelled for his
pains. Brainerd subsequently devoted himself to missionary work among the Indians. The publication of Brainerd's Diary by Jonathan Edwards in 1749, two years after
the young man's death at the early age of twenty-nine,
helped turn Brainerd into a folk hero of evangelicals everywhere.*

*The excerpt below taken from Brainerd's Diary begins
with Brainerd's own entry, and is followed by Edwards'
editorial comment. In addition to its description of the
circumstances of Brainerd's expulsion, the passage is also
of interest in that Edwards does not attempt to disguise
Brainerd's almost stereotypic, sophomoric self-righteousness. Instead, he uses the events as one more opportunity
to further his program of defending the revivals while
trying to stem their excesses.*

Tuesday, December 9. . . . Sometime towards the latter end of January, 1740/1, I grew more cold and dull in
matters of religion, by means of my old temptation, viz.
ambition in my studies. But through divine goodness, a
great and general awakening spread itself over the college, about the latter end of February, in which I was

much quickened, and more abundantly engaged in religion.

[This awakening here spoken of, was at the beginning
of that extraordinary religious commotion through the
land, which is fresh in every one's memory. This awakening was for a time very great and general at New-Haven;
and the college had no small share in it: That society
was greatly reformed, the students in general became
serious, and many of them remarkably so, and much
engaged in the concerns of their eternal salvation. And
however undesirable the issue of the awakenings of that
day have appeared in many others, there have been man-
ifestly happy and abiding effects of the impressions then
made on the minds of many of the members of that college. And by all that I can learn concerning Mr. Brainerd, there can be no reason to doubt but that he had
much of God's gracious presence, and of the lively actings of true grace, at that time. But yet he was afterwards
abundantly sensible, that his religious experiences and
affections at that time were not free from a corrupt mix-
ture, nor his conduct to be acquitted from many things
that were imprudent and blamable; which he greatly
lamented himself, and was willing that others should
forget, that none might make an ill improvement of
such an example. . . .

It could not be otherwise than that one whose heart
had been so prepared and drawn to God, as Mr. Brainerd's had been, should be mightily enlarged, animated
and engaged, at the sight of such an alteration made in
the college, the town and land, and so great an appearance of men's reforming their lives, and turning from
their profaneness and immorality, to seriousness and concern for their salvation, and of religion's reviving and

flourishing almost everywhere. But as an intemperate imprudent zeal and a degree of enthusiasm soon crept in, and mingled itself with that revival of religion; and so great and general an awakening being quite a new thing in the land, at least as to all the living inhabitants of it; neither people nor ministers had learned thoroughly to distinguish between solid religion and its delusive counterfeits; even many ministers of the gospel, of long standing and the best reputation, were for a time overpowered with the glaring appearance of the latter. And therefore surely it was not to be wondered at, that young Brainerd, but a sophomore at college, should be so; who was not only young in years, but very young in religion and experience, and had had but little opportunity for the study of divinity, and still less for observation of the circumstances and events of such an extraordinary state of things: A man must divest himself of all reason, to make strange of it. In these disadvantageous circumstances, Brainerd had the unhappiness to have a tincture of that intemperate indiscreet zeal, which was at that time too prevalent; and was led, from his high opinion of others that he looked upon better than himself, into such errors as were really contrary to the habitual temper of his mind. One instance of his misconduct at that time, gave great offence to the rulers of the college, even to that degree that they expelled him from the society; which it is necessary should here be particularly related, with its circumstances.

In the time of the awakening at college, there were several religious students that associated themselves one with another for mutual conversation and assistance in spiritual things, who were wont freely to open themselves one to another, as special and intimate friends. Brainerd was one of this company. And it once hap-

pened, that he and two or three more of these his intimate friends were in the hall together, after Mr. Whittelsey, one of the tutors, had been to prayer there with
the scholars; no other person now remaining in the hall,
but Brainerd and these his companions. Mr. Whittelsey
having been unusually pathetical in his prayer, one of
Brainerd's friends on this occasion asked him what he
thought of Mr. Whittelsey; he made answer, "He has no
more grace than this chair." One of the freshmen happening at that time to be near the hall (though not in
the room) overheard those words of his; though he heard
no name mentioned, and knew not who the person was,
which was thus censured. He informed a certain woman
that belonged to the town, withal telling her his own
suspicion, viz. that he believed Brainerd said this of some
one or other of the rulers of the college. Whereupon she
went and informed the rector, who sent for this fresh-
man and examined him; and he told the rector the words
that he heard Brainerd utter, and informed him who
were in the room with him at that time. Upon which the
rector sent for them: They were very backward to inform
against their friend, of that which they looked upon as
private conversation, and especially as none that they
had heard or knew of whom he had uttered those words;
yet the rector compelled them to declare what he said,
and of whom he said it. Brainerd looked on himself
greatly abused in the management of this affair; and
thought, that what he said in private, was injuriously ex-
torted from his friends, and that then it was injuriously
required of him (as it was wont to be of such as had been
guilty of some open notorious crime) to make a public
confession, and to humble himself before the whole college in the hall, for what he had said only in private
conversation. He not complying with this demand, and

having gone once to the separate meeting at New-Haven, when forbidden by the rector, and also having been accused by one person of saying concerning the rector, that he wondered he did not expect to drop down dead for fining the scholars who followed Mr. Tennent to Milford, though there was no proof of it (and Mr. Brainerd ever professed that he did not remember his saying anything to that purpose) for these things he was expelled the college.

Now, how far the circumstances and exigences of that day might justify such great severity in the governors of the college, I will not undertake to determine; it being my aim, not to bring reproach on the authority of the college, but only to do justice to the memory of a person who I think to be eminently one of those whose *memory is blessed.* The reader will see, in the sequel of the story of Mr. Brainerd's life, what his own thoughts afterwards were of his behaviour in these things, and in how christian a manner he conducted himself, with respect to this affair; though he ever, as long as he lived, supposed himself much abused in the management of it, and in what he suffered in it.

His expulsion was in the winter anno 1741/2, while he was in his third year in college.]

SOURCE: Jonathan Edwards, ed., *An Account of the Life of the Reverend David Brainerd* (Worcester, Mass.: Leonard Worcester, 1793), pp. 31–35.

The Governor's Commission

CONNECTICUT GENERAL ASSEMBLY

Yale was thrown into turmoil by the Awakening. Emotionally excited students held prayer meetings, roamed the halls, as did Brainerd, questioning fellow students and tutors, and ignored college traditions in order to sing, discuss religion, and attend the preaching of itinerants in and around New Haven. President Clap had at first welcomed the revivals and had made college facilities available to itinerants. After Gilbert Tennent preached at Yale on his New England tour in the spring of 1741 and successfully stirred the students to new heights of excitement, Clap began to withdraw his support and to clamp down on New Light activity in the college. But he enjoyed little success. So tumultuous did life in the college become that in the spring of 1742 President Clap was forced to suspend classes and ordered the boys to their homes. The Connecticut General Assembly immediately became alarmed, and responding to a request from the Governor, appointed a Commission to inquire into events on the Yale campus. The Commission's report to the General Assembly of their inquiry is reprinted here.

The Committee appointed to take into consideration that paragraph in his Honor's Speech (made to this Assembly) relating to the unhappy circumstances of the

College, pursuant to the order of this assembly, have made inquiry of the Reverend Rector of said College, and of others likely to inform us respecting the state thereof, and after deliberation, take leave to report to your Honor, and to this Honorable Assembly, as follows.

That sundry of the students of said College, have as the Reverend Rector informs us by the instigation, persuasion, and example of others, fallen into several errors in principle and disorders in practice, which may be very hurtful to religion, and some of them inconsistent with the good order, and government of that Society.

Particularly: 1. Some of the students have fallen into the practice of rash judging and censuring others, even some of the governors, teachers and instructors of the College, as being unconverted, inexperienced and unskillful guides, in matters of religion, and have thereupon contemptuously refused to submit to their authority, and to attend upon and harken to their religious exercises and instructions, but rather to attend upon the instructions and directions of those to whom the care of instructing the students is not committed.

2. Some undergraduate students have made it their practice by day and night, and sometimes for several days together, to go about in the town of Newhaven, as well as in other towns, and before great numbers of people, to teach and exhort, much after the same manner, that ministers of the Gospel do, in their public preaching.

3. That much pains have been taken, to prejudice the minds of the students, against our ecclesiastical constitution and to persuade them to dissent and withdraw from the way of worship and ministry established by the laws of this government, and to attend to private and separate meetings and that sundry of the students have so done, in contempt of the laws and authority of the College.

4. That these things have occasioned great expense of precious time, by disputes among the scholars, and neglect of their studies and exercises at College, and have been a hindrance to the flourishing of religion and vital piety in that Society, and if tolerated, may defeat the good ends and designs of its institution.

Your Committee thereupon are humbly of opinion, that it is of great importance, both to our civil and ecclesiastical state that the true principles of religion and good order be maintained in that seminary of learning. And that it be recommended to the Reverend Rector, Trustees and others concerned in the government and instruction of the College, to be very careful to instruct the students in the true principles of religion, according to our confession of faith and ecclesiastical constitution; and to keep them from all such errors as they may be in danger of imbibing from strangers and foreigners, and to use all such proper measures, as are in their power, to prevent their being under the influence and instruction of such as would prejudice their minds against the way of worship and ministry established by the laws of this government, and that order and authority be duly maintained in that Society; and that those who would not enjoy the priviledges of it, who contumaciously refuse to submit to the laws, orders and rules thereof, which have been made, or shall be made, according to the powers and instructions given in their charter, but we think it highly reasonable, that all proper means be first used with such scholars, that they may be reclaimed and reduced to order, before they be dismissed from the College as incorrigible.

Your Committee are also informed, that at a late meeting of the Trustees, they concluded, that in order to the removing the difficulties of the College, it was proper that some experienced grave divines repair to Newhaven, and there to instruct the scholars by their sermons, they may be by them prepared for that end; and for as much as such divines must be taken from other pulpits, and the Trustees not having money in their treasury, sufficient to hire a person, to supply such pulpit or pulpits; we therefore recommend it to this assembly to grant to the Trustees a sufficient sum, to enable them to hire a meet person to supply such pulpit or pulpits.

All which is submitted by your humble servants.

> James Wadsworth
> Joseph Whiting
> Jeremiah Miller
> E. Williams
> Samuel Hill
> Jonathan Hait
> J. Griswold
> Ebenezer Gray

In the Upper House. The aforegoing Report read, accepted and approved.
Test George Wyllys Secrecy
Concurred with in the Lower House.
Test J. Fowler Clerk

SOURCE: Connecticut Archives, Colleges and Schools, I:269.

The Shepherds' Tent

CONNECTICUT GENERAL ASSEMBLY

Excluded from Yale and Harvard the New Lights at-
tempted to provide education for their ministerial candi-
dates by founding their own school, dubbed the Shep-
herds' Tent, at New London, Connecticut, under the di-
rection of Timothy Allen. Already, alarmed at the
spreading turmoil of the Awakening, which they per-
ceived as a threat to social stability and the standing
order, Old Light clergy and the General Assembly of
Connecticut, acting in collusion, had begun to take of-
ficial steps to put an end to the revivalist activity. In 1742
the General Assembly passed an act for "regulating
abuses and correcting disorders in ecclesiastical affairs"
which aimed to halt itinerants and church separations.
This was soon followed by another act, printed here,
tightening ministerial educational requirements and en-
abling the Assembly to close down the Shepherds' Tent.
Moved to Rhode Island, but unable to sustain itself, the
Shepherds' Tent folded within a few months.

AN ACT RELATING TO, AND FOR THE BETTER REGULATING SCHOOLS OF LEARNING

Whereas by sundry acts and laws of this Assembly, they
have founded, erected, endowed and provided for the

maintenance of a college at New Haven, and inferior schools of learning in every town or parish, for the education and instruction of the youth of this Colony, which have (by the blessing of God) been very serviceable to promote useful learning and christian knowledge, and, more especially, to train up a learned and orthodox ministry for the supply of our churches: And inasmuch as the well ordering of such publick schools is of great importance to the publick weal, this Assembly, by one act entitled An Act for the encouragement and better improvement of town schools, [passed, Oct. 1714] did order and provide, that the civil authority and selectmen in every town should be visitors, to inspect the state of schools, and to enquire into the qualifications of the masters of them and the proficiency of the children, to give such directions as they shall think needful to render such schools most serviceable to increase that knowledge, civility and religion, which is designed in the erecting of them; and in case those visitors shall apprehend that any such schools are so ordered as not to be likely to attain those good ends proposed, they shall lay the state thereof before this Assembly, who shall give such orders thereupon as they shall think proper; as by the said act may more fully appear: And whereas the erecting of any other schools, which are not under the establishment and inspection aforesaid, may tend to train up youth in ill principles and practices, and introduce such disorders as may be of fatal consequence to the publick peace and weal of this Colony: Which to prevent,

Be it enacted by the Governor, Council and Representatives, in General Court assembled, and by the authority of the same, That no particular persons whatsoever shall presume of themselves to erect, establish, set up, keep or maintain, any college, seminary of learning, or any publick school whatsoever, for the instruction of young persons, other than such as are erected and established or allowed by the laws of this Colony, without special licence or liberty first had and obtained of this Assembly.

And be it enacted by the authority aforesaid, That if any person shall presume to act as a master, tutor, teacher or instructor, in any unlawful school or seminary of learning erected as aforesaid, he shall suffer the penalty of five pounds lawful money per month for every month he shall continue to act as aforesaid. And every grand-jury, within any county where such school or seminary of learning is erected, shall make presentment of all breaches of this act to the next assistant, justice of the peace, or county court.

And be it further enacted by the authority aforesaid, That the civil authority and selectmen in each town, or the major part of them, shall inspect and visit all such unlawful schools or seminaries of learning, erected as aforesaid, and shall proceed with all such scholars, students or residents in such school, and all such as harbor, board or entertain them, according to the laws of this Colony respecting transient persons or inmates residing in any town without the approbation of the selectmen.

And be it further enacted by the authority aforesaid, That if any student or resident in such school shall pretend that he is bound as by indenture an apprentice to learn any manual art or trade, and the said civil authority or selectmen shall suspect that such indenture was given only as a color to reside in said town contrary to law, that then it shall be in the power of the said civil authority to examine all the parties to such indenture under oath, in all such questions which they shall think proper, relating to the true intention of such indenture and their practice thereon; and if it shall appear to the said authority or selectmen, or the major part of them, that such indenture was given upon a fraudulent design, as aforesaid, that then such authority shall proceed as if no such indenture had been made.

And be it further enacted by the authority aforesaid, That no person that has not been educated or graduated in Yale College, or Harvard College in Cambridge, or some other allowed foreign protestant college or university, shall take the benefit of the laws of this government respecting the settlement and support of ministers.

Always provided, Nothing in this act be construed to forbid or prevent any society allowed by law in this Colony to keep a school, by a major vote in such society to order more parish schools than one to be kept in more places than one in such society.

This Act to continue in force for the space of four years from the rising of this Assembly, and no longer.

SOURCE: Charles J. Hoadley, ed., *The Public Records of the Colony of Connecticut, From October, 1735, to October, 1743, Inclusive* (Hartford: Press of the Case, Kockwood and Brainerd Company, 1874), pp. 500–502.

The Colleges Censure George Whitefield

THE YALE FACULTY

In his Journal, *published and widely circulated in the colonies the year following his preaching tour of New*

*England, George Whitefield had written of Harvard and
Yale, "As for the Universities, I believe it may be said,
their Light is now become Darkness, Darkness that may
be felt, and is complained of by the most godly Ministers." Whitefield had not only disrupted the serenity of
life in the colleges, he had accused them of rank impiety.
News that Whitefield was returning to New England in
1744 for another revival tour gave the Harvard and Yale
faculties a chance to even the score. Harvard led off first
with a fifteen page pamphlet denouncing Whitefield, and
the Yale faculty followed with a* Declaration *of its own
shortly thereafter. The Yale* Declaration, *excerpted below, was probably written by Clap, and it catalogued
once more the chief complaints against the man who had
been a prime cause in ripping apart the frayed fabric of
New England Puritanism. The* Declaration *also marked
the end of the most tumultuous period of the Great
Awakening.*

THE
DECLARATION, ETC.

To the Rev. Mr. *George Whitefield.*

Rev. SIR,

The *Rector* sent you a letter some time ago, mentioning sundry things exceptionable in your principles and
conduct, and desired some satisfaction. In answer to
which you send him a short letter in writing, and three

of your printed letters, viz. two to the Right Reverend the Bishops, and one to the Rev. Dr. Chauncy; all which we have read and considered, and can't find any satisfaction in them.

We have therefore thought it proper to signify and declare our minds to you as follows, viz.

We have read the several declarations of the Reverend and Honored the President, Professors and Tutors of Harvard College, of the Reverend the ministers of four associations near Boston, and of the Rev. Mr. Walter of Roxbury, and others, and do in substance agree and concur with them in our sentiments, and think it proper more largely to insist upon two things,

First, It has always appeared to us, that you and other itinerants have laid a scheme to turn the generality of ministers out of their places, and to introduce a new set of such as should be in a peculiar manner attached to you; and this you would effect by prejudicing the minds of people against their ministers, and thereby induce them to discard them or separate from them.

And this appears to us,

I. Because the principles which you and the other itinerants laid down did naturally and necessarily produce this effect; ———— which are these.

1. That *the generality of ministers are unconverted.* The scope and design of a great part of your preaching, when you were in this country before, was to represent them as carnal Pharisees, and run a parallel between them and the Pharisees and false prophets of old. And, in your *Journal,* Pag. 70 and 95. you say, that *they don't experimentally know Christ, and preach an unfelt and unknown Christ.* And in the same *Journal* (Oct. 12) you say, that you *will hereafter come to be more particular in your application to particular persons.* In your letter to

Dr. Chauncy, Pag. 9. where you take notice, that the Dr. mentions it as an aggravation of your fault, in judging the ministers to be unconverted, "that you did it as you passed through the country in post-haste, having neither opportunity or advantage to know the real character of one tenth part of the ministers you thus freely condemn"; In answer you say, *I confess this was too unguarded. For whether in fact it was or is true or not, yet I ought to have taken more time before I delivered my judgment.*

Here is a plain acknowledgment that it was *then* your declared judgment, that most ministers in New-England were unconverted, and an implication, that your judgment is the same *now*. For you make no acknowledgment that the judgment was wrong, or that you are any ways faulty in forming of it, but only that you were too unguarded in delivering of it before you knew the men. But had you taken more time before you delivered your judgment, there would have been no fault at all. And inasmuch as you have never yet publickly declared any alteration in your judgment, (as we have seen) we presume it is the same *now* it was *before*.

Mr. Tennent, in his Nottingham Sermon (which you, in your *N.E. Journal,* Oct. 21, say is unanswerable) declares the ministers to be unconverted in very strong and even scurrilous terms, and says, Pag. 17. *That they are blind who don't see this to be the case of the body of the clergy of this generation.* Yea, so far has this matter been carried, perhaps in this beyond your first intention, that those itinerants who at first declared other ministers to be unconverted, were afterwards declared unconverted themselves, by those who ran greater lengths than they; in so much that we suppose that there is scarce one minister in a hundred, if any one at all, in all North America, but what has by some of your followers been judged to be unconverted. To be sure we are credibly informed, that one of the Separatists in Boston declared, that all the Ministers in Boston were unconverted, and gave that as the reason of their separation.

2. Another principle which you have advanced is, *That all unconverted ministers are half beasts and half devils, and can no more be the means of any man's conversion, than a dead man can beget a living child*: And though we should understand this comparison, as you explain yourself in your Letter to Dr. C—— Pag. 14. not as implying the thing to be absolutely *impossible,* but only very *unlikely; that they are seldom made use of to convert others,* (perhaps *as often as the Devil is,* according to your comparison in your Jour. Pag. 70.) we suppose it comes to the *same thing* in effect. And in the same letter to Dr. C—— Pag. 8. you say, *that unconverted ministers are the bane of the Christian-Church.* Mr. T——t in his Nottingham Sermon says, "that natural men have no call of God to the ministerial work, Pag. 7. That God sends not such hypocritical varlets, Pag. 8. That they are as unfit for it as a dead man to bring others to life, as a madman to give counsel, or a possessed man to cast out devils." Pag. 11.

Now from these two principles, which you have laid down, viz. that the generality of ministers are unconverted, and that all unconverted ministers are such baneful and pernicious men, it naturally and necessarily follows, that *people ought to discard them, or separate from them.* And we think that Mr. T——t's second inference from the foregoing premises is very just, viz. "from what has been said we may learn, that those who are contented under such a ministry, are as blind as moles, and dead as stones, without any spiritual taste or relish." And accordingly upon the publication of these principles, people are filled with the greatest prejudices against their ministers, and a multitude of separations immediately and necessarily followed.

II. This consequence, that people *should discard or separate from their Ministers,* not only necessarily and in fact follows from the foregoing principles, but it was also intended and designed. Indeed a man's intention can never be directly and absolutely proved, yet his words or actions may carry with them such a strong presumption as may prove his intention in the law, and that even to take away his life. Thus, if a man in a passion charges a gun with powder and ball, and discharges it directly at another, or at a company of men, seeing of them there, and kills a man, the law in that case presumes malice, and that he designed to murder him. And especially, if after he had seen some killed or struck, he should charge again and do the like over and over. If he should plead, that he designed only to scare them, or to bring them to better terms, it would signify nothing. Now these two principles, that *the generality of ministers are unconverted,* and that *they are such baneful and pernicious men,* as you have declared, when discharged among the multitude, and received into their minds, do as naturally and necessarily tend to make them *discard their ministers* as a brace of bullets discharged into their hearts has *to take away their natural lives.* It is utterly inconceivable to us that men should from time to time zealously propagate such principles, and yet never design or think that they should have any such effect. But Mr. *Ten--t,* not only lays down these principles, but expressly draws this consequence; and spends one half of his Nottingham Sermon in proving, that it is the indispensable duty of people to discard and separate from unconverted ministers; and among other things says, *that unconverted men*

have a fixed enmity against others, and that it is not pos-
sible that any harmony should subsist between them,
pag. 25. *and that unity in such a case would be like the*
unity of the devils, a legion of which dwelt peaceably
with one man, pag. 26.

This sermon, you say, is unanswerable (and condemn
the Rev. Mr. Stoddard for writing to the contrary) and
doubtless you concerted these principles with the T--t's
in the Jersies before you came into New England, and
there and here you saw the visible effects of them; and
by your practice you have ever since visibly approved of
them. For the Separatists every where set you up for
their oracle, pattern and patron; the great promoters of
them are among your chief favourites; and even to this
day, wherever there is any number of your disciples who
have a minister who does *not cry you up,* they are constantly endeavoring, by all ways and pretences whereby
they can seem to get any color of advantage, to get him
out. And you have never yet in any print, that we have
seen, condemned these separations, although they have
been so often complained of among the mischiefs of your
itinerations.

Indeed in your letter to Dr. C——y you say, "But
that I had a design either in preaching or writing, to
alienate people's minds from their standing ministers,
I utterly disavow." And in your letter to the Rector
you say, "I never had any scheme or design of turning
out any ministers in New England, and placing some of
my own choosing in their room——Such a thought,
as I know of, never entered into my heart."

Here we have your professed principles and practices
on one side, and your solemn declarations on the other.
We must ask your pardon, Sir, if we can find no possible
way to reconcile these two together, and therefore think

our selves at liberty, which of them to believe. For to persuade people that their ministers are half beasts and half devils, near as unlikely to be the means of their conversion as the devil himself, and that they are the bane of the Christian Church, and yet have no thought in your heart of alienating people's minds from them, appears to us to be an inexplicable contradiction!

It seems to us, that your avowing these principles, and practically encouraging the consequent effects, and yet denying the consequence in words, is acting too much like the papists: They say, 1. *That the Pope has power to excommunicate kings.* 2. *That every excommunicated king forfeits his crown and kingdom;* and yet absolutely deny that they hold that *the Pope has power to depose kings;* and that notwithstanding he has sundry times exercised that power. Mr. Locke in his Letter upon Toleration, says, the reason is because such a proposition nakedly proposed would awaken all mankind to a sense of their danger; and therefore they'll choose to express the same things in other words.

It seems to us, that you would be much more fair and consistent with your self, if you would freely own your design; For if those two principles are right and true, we are satisfied your design is good, and we would readily join with you in it.

And if all unconverted ministers must be discarded and separated from, a new set or supply must necessarily be introduced; these must be such as you judge to be converted, or otherwise there will be the same necessity, that you should be strengthened to lift up your voice against unconverted ministers, as there was before. Our colleges can do but a very little towards such an extraordinary supply; especially, since, as you say, *the light in them is but darkness, even thick darkness that may be felt.* This supply must therefore be either of exhorters or foreigners: You publicly told the people in New England, that they might expect, in a little time, some supply from your orphan house; and you told the Rev. Mr. Edwards of North-Hampton, that you intended to bring over a number of young men fom England to be ordained by the Tennents. Whether any more were to come from Scotland or Ireland, we think is not material. And it has been the constant practice of the Tennents, and their Presbytery, of late years, to send ministers to supply the separations in New England; particularly Messieurs Finley, Sacket, Blair, Treat, and sundry others, to preach to the separations at Milford, New Haven, etc. and some of them showed written orders for it, from that Presbytery. Yea, so violently were they engaged to supply us with their ministers, that they would do it in direct opposition to the civil and ecclesiastical government. Thus the scheme appears to us evident in every part of it, both from the principles you have laid down, and by the constant endeavours from time to time to put them in practice.——Especially considering,

Secondly, It has always appeared to us, that you and other itinerants have laid a scheme to vilify and subvert our colleges, and to introduce a set of ministers into our churches, by other ways and means of education. In your *Journal,* page 96. you say, *As to the universities, I believe it may be truly said, that the light in them is now become darkness, even thick darkness that may be felt.* Mr. T——t, in his aforesaid sermon, p. 16. says, "That the most likely method to stock the church with a faithful ministry, the public academies being so much corrupted, is to encourage private schools, or seminaries of learning, which are under the care of skillful and experienced Christians."——He adds, "Don't think it much, if the pharisees should be offended at this proposal; these subtle selfish hypocrites are wont to be scared about their credit and their kingdom, and truly they are both little worth."——Indeed we don't look on this to be a direct reflection upon the present rector, because one of these aspersions was made before he came here, and the other so soon after, that it could not be supposed that he should then have had much influence upon the College; but we look upon them to be a very abusive reflection upon his worthy predecessor, and we should choose (if it needful) that he should answer for himself.

Upon the best information, we suppose, that although at the first erection of this College, and while it was for some years destitute of a resident rector and complete government, there were sundry instances of vice and irreligion; yet by the good government of the late rector, under the inspection of the venerable trustees, it was by degrees brought into a very well regulated state as to learning, religion and manners. And that as many learned and godly ministers have been educated here as at any college or private seminary in the world, of no longer standing. But this is certain, that soon after the publication of these slanders upon the colleges, this was upon several accounts in a worse state than it was before. Sundry of the students ran into enthusiastic errors and disorders, censured and reviled their governors and others; for which some were expelled, denied their degrees, or otherwise punished; and some withdrew to that thing called the Shepherds' Tent. And we've been informed that the students were told, that there was no danger in disobeying their present governors, because there would in a short time be a great change in the civil government, and so in the governors of the College.

All which rendered the government and instruction of the College, for a while, far more difficult than it was before.

Now as these were the natural consequences of the dark representations made of the colleges, so we must here again suppose that they were intended and designed. This it may be you will flatly deny: Yet permit us, *Sir,* to put two or three questions to your conscience.

1st. Did not you design that this dark account which you gave of the colleges should be believed?

2ly. Did you not expect and design that this account when believed, should make all mankind entertain a low and mean opinion, if not abhorrence of an education for the ministry in such dark and corrupt colleges?

3ly. Did you not design to make mankind believe that those who are educated at your orphan house should be far better qualified to be our ministers, than those who are educated at these colleges? And didn't multitudes of your followers in this country speak very slightly of the colleges and humane learning, and favor that wild scheme of the Shepherds' Tent? And what could the design of all this be, but to *vilify and subvert our colleges, and to introduce a set of ministers by other ways and means of education?*

In your letter to Dr. C——cy, page 9. you say, "My whole design in preaching was to show the unspeakable danger of persons taking upon them to preach Christ to others, 'till they were acquainted with him themselves. And in my writings to give an impartial account, as far as I was informed, how the affairs which concerns the Kingdom of God stood in New England." We can't possibly reconcile this with your conduct; for you seldom gave any advice to persons just entering the ministry; but your main design was evidently levelled against the ministers already settled. And if you had been informed that the generality of them preached an unknown unfelt Christ; yet the 4th Chapter of the 1st. of Corinthians would have told you that you ought not to have received and published such an information from *any mortal men,* but to have waited 'till the *day when the secrets of men's hearts shall be revealed by Jesus Christ.* And if you had been informed of such things concerning the colleges, your informers were either ignorant or prejudiced; and you could not impartially publish such an information, without making some enquiry of the governors of the College, or giving of them some advice, which you did not, although you dined and went into the library with the Rector and Tutors. And therefore we can't help thinking, that your proceeding to publish such false and scandalous things concerning the colleges, must proceed from some ill design.

Perhaps you will say that you were indeed too unguarded, imprudent and rash, in publishing such reflections upon the ministers and colleges; but meant no harm in it. But is not this to represent yourself like Solomon's madman, *who casteth firebrands, arrows and death,——and faith, am I not in sport?* Prov. 26:18. Alas! the miseries, confusions, disorders and convulsions which you have, by these means, laid the foundation of in our churches, can scarce be paralleled in ecclesiastical history.

As by the permission of providence, we have committed to us the care of educating youth for the work of the ministry in these churches, whose peace and purity lies near to our hearts, we have thought it our duty thus to declare our apprehensions to you and to the world; that so all our ministers and churches may be fully upon their watch against all divisive plots and designs, carried on by specious pretences, and may *mark those who cause division and offences—and avoid them, who by good words and fair speeches deceive the hearts of the simple.*

We are, *Rev. Sir,*
Your humble Servants,
in all that we may,

Thomas Clap	Rector
Chauncy Whittelsey	
Jonathan Whiting	Tutors
Thomas Darling	

New-Haven,
Feb. 25. 1745.

SOURCE: *The Declaration of the Rector and Tutors of Yale College in New-Haven, Against the Reverend Mr. George Whitefield, His Principles and Designs. In a Letter to him* (Boston: T. Fleet, 1745).

The Log College

WILLIAM IRWIN

Greater opportunity existed in the more recently settled regions of the middle and southern colonies, than in New England, for the creation of revivalist-oriented institutions of education. The most famous and earliest of all the revivalist academies founded in the eighteenth century was the Log College of William Tennent, at Neshaminy, Pennsylvania, the model for dozens of subsequent academies and the progenitor of the College of New Jersey. One of the earliest descriptions of the Log College, the following account was written by the Reverend Nathaniel Irwin, himself a later minister of the Neshaminy Church.

The Presbyterian Church of Neshaminey is so called from its situation on the south branch of the Neshaminey Creek. It has also been called "the Forks of Neshaminey," as the building is situated, and the worshippers generally reside, in the forks of that Creek. The house of public worship is in Warwick Township in the County of Bucks about three miles distant from the line of Montgomery County and about twenty miles nearly due North of the City of Philadelphia. A religious society was first formed in this place about the year 1724 by the occasional preaching of the Revd. Wm. Tennent, (the oldest of that name).

This venerable patriarch had been a regular minister of the established Church of Ireland; which he left and came to America about the year 1715. His first permanent residence was at Bedford in the state of New York, where he continued about three years directing his attention chiefly to farming. In the year 1718 he appeared before the Synod of Philadelphia, then the highest court of judicature in the Presbyterian Church of America, and expressed his desire to join that body. The Synod after examining his credentials and receiving a profession of his faith and the reasons which induced him to renounce the Episcopal Church (which last are on rec-

ord) received him as a Member.[1] Soon after this he was
settled as stated pastor of the Church of Bensalem near
the mouth of the Neshaminey Creek. Being thus naturally led to explore the sources of the stream on which
he resided, he came at length to minister occasionally in
the *forks* and the vicinity. In the year 1725 (whether by
private contract or presbyterial settlement does not appear) Mr. Tennent undertook to preach statedly to the
people collected there, every other sabbath. For two
years and an half he continued thus to officiate at Mr.
James Cravens about three miles and an half south
east from the place where the church now stands: using
the barn in the summer, the dwelling house in the winter.

Mr. Craven was a low Dutch man late from Long Island and had been connected with the Dutch church subordinate to the Classis of Holland. Having now had "the
Church in his house" for so long a time, he became a
zealous member of the Presbyterian Church and his de-
scendants and connections have formed a small but respectable branch of this society ever since.

In 1727 the foundation of a house for public worship
was laid a few poles distant from the place where the
church now stands. So vigorous did this society appear,
even in the cradle, that this their first church was an elegant stone building 40 feet by 30 fitted for galleries and
the front of hewn stone.[2] It was finished so that divine
service began to be statedly performed in it in the sum-

[1] It is supposed that his wife who was a Presbyterian and de-
scended from a long line of Presbyterian Ministers had considerable
influence in bringing her husband to embrace the Presbyterian
faith. (Irwin's note)

[2] Considering the numerous wants of the people and the general state of building at this day, such a Church was noble for the
first effort of a society scarcely founded. (Irwin's note)

mer of the year 1728. Mr. Tennent at this time lived on a farm which had been given him by his friend Mr. (Growden) Logan, about equidistant from Neshaminey and Bensalem. But as he was now advanced in years and found the supplying two churches 14 miles distant from each other too much for his diminished strength, he resigned the charge of Bensalem and devoted his whole attention to the favorite child of his gray hairs—the infant Church of Neshaminey. Suited to this plan, his generous friend (Growden) Logan accommodated him with a new plantation (in lieu, of the former) situated on the old York Road in Warminster Township about one mile and a quarter south east of the church. This spot became famous as the seat of an academy called by some the Log College erected there by Mr. Tennent in or near the year 1730. Such an academy would scarce be *known* at this day; but it was justly celebrated at a time when there was hardly its superior south of New England.

Mr. Tennent was a master in the Latin and Greek languages and had some acquaintance with the liberal arts and sciences. These he taught in person for a time; as the school increased he employed one or more assistants. Many of the scholars after completing at this academy such a course of liberal learning as the place afforded and the day required, studied divinity with Mr. Tennent or others and became eminent in the church, especially as instruments in the revival of religion which succeeded. Among these were a Robertson, a McKnight, a Campbell, a McCrea, a Laurence, a Roan, a Rodgers, and, superior to all, Mr. Tennent's own sons,[3] four of whom were devoted to the service of the sanctuary. Foremost among

[3] Several persons who became eminent in their secular profession received their education in arts and languages at this academy. Distinguished among these stands Doctor John Redman, President of the College of Physicians, Philadelphia. (Irwin's note)

these stood Gilbert Tennent, late Minister of the second Presbyterian Church of Philadelphia whose fame is in all the churches. John Tennent, after preaching a few years and raising the fondest hopes of future eminence, was translated to the church triumphant above. Nor will the names William and Charles Tennent soon be forgotten by the friends of Zion.

About the year 1740 Mr. Tennent, being very far advanced in years, was desirous to resign the pastoral office, and signified to the church his opinion that they ought to [illegible] a minister to serve them in this place. This was not easy to do, considering the animosities that now existed in the Presbyterian Church, in consequence of what was called the revival of religion. Neshaminey was the nursery of the revival. Gilbert Tennent was among the first of Mr. Whitefield's admirers and successful imitators: He followed his steps; preached in his spirit and power; his crow-egg sermon[4] delivered at Nottingham will long be remembered as a monument of his zeal. As he, his brothers and other pupils of the aged Tennent (all favorers of the revival) often preached at Neshaminey, the people in general caught the holy fire and zealously espoused the cause of reformation. A respectable number, however, of very respectable people favored what was called the old side. . . .

                                                        Dated 1793

[4] Text—Scribes and Pharisees sit in Moses seat etc. Design: to expose certain ministers of that day by comparing them to the Scribes and Pharisees. Having painted the characters he said, they were as like as one crow-egg to another 'tis in print. (Irwin's note)

SOURCE: Thomas C. Pears, Jr., and Guy Klett, eds., *Documentary History of William Tennent and the Log College,* Mimeographed MSS (Philadelphia: Presbyterian Historical Society, 1940), pp. 164–166. Reprinted by Permission of the Presbyterian Historical Society.

The Old Side Academies

THE SYNOD OF PHILADELPHIA

To counter the influence of the Log College, the Synod of Philadelphia, under control of the Old Side, set up its own school in 1744. In taking this action the Synod did not actually establish a new academy, but rather took under its official care an academy which the Reverend Francis Alison had already been conducting in his home in New London, Pennsylvania. The leading Old Side educator, Francis Alison probably drafted the following letter to President Clap explaining the Synod's 1744 action.

May 30, 1746

Letter to President Clap, Philadelphia

"Some years ago our Synod found the interest of Christ's Kingdom likely to suffer in these parts for want of a college for the education of young men. And our supplies either from Europe or New England were few in proportion to the numerous vacancies in our growing settlements. Mr. William Tennent set up a school among us, where some were educated, and afterwards admitted to the ministry without sufficient qualifications as was judged by many of the Synod. And what made the matter look worse, those that were educated in this private way decried the usefulness of some parts of learning that we thought very necessary. It was therefore agreed to try to erect a college, and apply to our friends in Britain, and Ireland, and New England, to assist us. We wrote to the Association of Boston on this head, and had a very favorable answer. But when we were thus projecting the thing, the war with Spain was proclaimed, which put a stop to our proceedings then. The Synod then came to a public agreement to take all private schools where young men were educated for the ministry, so far under their care as to appoint a committee of our Synod to examine all such as had not obtained degrees in the European or New England colleges, and give them certificates if they were found qualified, which was to serve our Presbyteries instead of a college diploma, till better provision could be made. Mr. Gilbert Tennent cried out that this was to prevent his father's school from training gracious men for the ministry; and he, and some of his adherents, protested against it, and counteracted this our public agreement, admitting men to the ministry which we judged unfit for that office, which course they persisted in though admonished and reproved by us for such unwarranted proceedings. While these debates subsisted, Mr. Whitefield came into the country, who they drew into their party to encourage divisions. And they and he have been the sad instruments of dividing our churches. And by his interest Mr. Gilbert Tennent grew hardy enough to tell our Synod he would oppose their design of getting assistance to erect a college wherever we should make application, and would maintain young men at his father's school in opposition to us. This, with his and his adherents' divisive practices, obliged the Synod to exclude him and other of his stamp, from their communion. In this situation our affairs grew worse; for our vacancies were numerous, and we found it hard in such trouble to engage such gentle-

men either from New England or Europe to come among
us, as our best friends in those places would recommend
as steadfast in the faith, and men of parts and education.
Upon this the Synod erected a school in the year 1744. It
was agreed that the said school should be opened under
the inspection of the Synod, where the languages, philosophy, and divinity be taught gratis, to all that should
comply with the regulation of the school, being persons
of good character and behaviour . . ."

SOURCE: Thomas C. Pears, Jr., and Guy Klett, eds., *Documentary
History of William Tennent and the Log College*, Mimeographed
MSS (Philadelphia: Presbyterian Historical Society, 1940), p. 162.
Reprinted by permission of the Presbyterian Historical Society.

Samuel Finley: New Side Educator

BENJAMIN RUSH

*Samuel Finley was one of the most passionate of the
New Side Presbyterian preachers. In 1744 he established
an academy at Nottingham, on the Maryland–Pennsylvania border, which he conducted until he himself was
called to the presidency of the College of New Jersey
seventeen years later. Designed at first for older students,
the Nottingham Academy, after the founding of the College of New Jersey in 1746, concentrated mainly on providing college preparatory instruction for younger boys.*

*The alumni of Finley's academy included as distin-
guished a group of men as could be desired by any teacher,
among them outstanding ministers, businessmen, govern-*

ment officials, two signers of the Declaration of Independence, at least three state governors, and some of the most important early medical educators in America: John Morgan and William Shippen, founder of the first medical school in America; Benjamin Rush, physician, social and educational reformer, and the first professor of chemistry in America; Gerardus Clarkson, founder and president of the Philadelphia College of Physicians; Thomas Ruston, author of works on smallpox and yellow fever; and John Archer, founder of the Medical Faculty of Maryland.

This fond description of life at Nottingham was written by Finley's nephew, Benjamin Rush. Profoundly influenced by Enlightenment thought Rush eventually adopted a more universalistic religious outlook than that of Finley, but Rush's life-long work as one of the new Republic's most activist educational and humanitarian reformers bore always the unmistakable stamp of the revivalists' millennial faith in social progress.

My only surviving brother, Jacob Rush, and myself were sent to a country school in Nottingham, now in Cecil County in the State of Maryland, a few years after our father died. This School was taught by the Revd. Dr. Samuel Finley, afterwards President of the College of New Jersey, and who had married one of the sisters of my mother. It was then the most respectable and flourishing of any in the middle provinces of America. The character of Dr. Finley as a minister of the gospel and Scholar

SOURCE: George W. Corner, ed., *The Autobiography of Benjamin Rush: His "Travels Through Life" together with his Commonplace Book for 1789–1813* (Princeton University Press, copyright 1948 by the American Philosophical Society), pp. 28–35. Reprinted by permission of Princeton University Press.

is well known to thousands in this country, but he is less known as a teacher of an academy, and a master of a family. Few men have ever possessed or displayed greater talents in both those capacities. His government over his boys was strict but never severe nor arbitrary. It was always by known laws which were plain, and often promulgated. The object of a law, whether it related to great or little matters, was never taken into consideration in the trial of an offender. I remember he once issued an order forbidding his boys to throw stones at his fruit trees in order to obtain fruit from them. Soon afterwards he observed a boy flinging stones up an apple tree. He came up to him, and struck him with his hand on the side of his head. The boy remonstrated against his punishment, and said the tree had no fruit on it, and that he was only amusing himself by trying to hit a decayed apple of the last year's growth which hung upon one of the highest branches of the tree. "This is no excuse for your offence (said the Doctor). By throwing at that decayed apple you injure the tree. You have moreover broken the law, which though apparently trifling, will lead you to break laws of more importance." In the infliction of punishments in his school, he always premised them by a discourse upon the nature, heinousness, or tendency of the offence. Sometimes he made all the scholars in the school give their opinions upon the nature of an offence, before he gave his own, and now and then he obliged them to pronounce sentence of punishments, before he inflicted it. The instrument with which he corrected was a small switch which he broke from a tree. The part he struck was the palm of the hand, and that never more than three times. The solemn forms connected with this punishment were more terrible and distressing than the punishment itself. I once saw him spend half an hour in exposing the folly and wickedness of an offence with his rod in hand. The culprit stood all this while trembling and weeping before him. After he had ended his admonitions, he lifted his rod as high as he could and then permitted it to fall gently upon his hand. The boy was surprized at this conduct. "There, go about your business (said the Doctor). I mean shame, and not pain [to] be your punishment in the present instance."

He took uncommon pains to promote good manners among his Scholars. The slightest act of incivility was reproved. This he did at his table and in so elegant and delicate a manner as not to expose the person who was rebuked. He selected a number of artificial characters with which he connected all the usual follies and improprieties of boys. To these he gave the names of Thomas Broadbrim, Ned Short, Bill Slovenly, and the like. These characters he constrasted by the history of Johnny Courtley, who was an example of all that was proper and amiable in the conduct of a young man. His manner of describing these characters was so agreeable as to fix even the most volatile and desultory of his boys to their chairs. Sometimes his descriptions were interspersed with anecdotes that excited a burst of laughter. If in his walks and in his study he occasionally overheard an improper expression, or saw an improper act in any of his boys, he never failed to take notice of it at the ensuing meal, but in such a manner as not to excite a suspicion that a personal application of what was said, was intended. One evening I recollect he dwelled chiefly upon the character of Ned Short. Among other things, he informed us that he was of a quick temper, and very prone to give rude answers to the most innocent questions. "For instance (said he), if one of his companions asked him if he knew where his book was, he would answer 'Ask about.' " Here he paused. A blush appeared in the countenance of one of his boys, who had on that day given that answer to a question of a similar nature. The Doctor did not appear to be conscious that the rebuke had produced its intended effect. But his table was not made subservient only to this mode of instruction. He made it a constant practice to admit his boys to eat with all the strangers who visited him. The benefits derived from the news, anecdotes, and general conversations which young people are thus permitted to hear are much greater than is generally supposed. "Conversation (said a wise man) is education," and one of the first geniuses in Britain has declared that he learned more from the conversation of one man whom he named, than from all the books he ever read in his life. I could repeat an hundred things I heard at the table of my master to which I then was constrained to lend a reluctant and impatient ear, but which have since become the seeds of useful knowledge. I owe my present ideas of the misery connected with great wealth, to a dream which the Revd. Mr. Richard Treat related at his table when I was about 12 years old.

He inculcated at all times a regard to the common forms of good breeding. For this purpose, he frequently exercised his pupils in delivering and receiving letters, and in asking and receiving favors. He extended his attention to forms, to the composition, folding, and direction of letters. These had their rules, and were applied by him to different ranks and subjects according as they were upon business, or mere letters of friendship.

His method of teaching the Latin and Greek languages was simple. He taught several of the arts and sciences usually taught in colleges. In these he was unfortunately tied down to the principles and forms that were common in the schools of that day. He had studied the English language, and taught the reading, writing, and speaking of it with great care and success.

In the government and instruction of his family he exhibited an example of apostolical prudence, piety and zeal. He read and explained the whole or part of a chapter in the Old or New Testament every morning and evening before prayers in his family. Many of the remarks that he made upon passages in the Bible, which then passed hastily through my mind, have occurred to me many years afterwards, and I hope not without some effect. He obliged all the boys who lodged in his house to commit the Shorter Catechism of the Church of Scotland to memory, and to repeat it every Sunday evening. Upon each of the answers, he made pertinent and instructing or pious remarks. He likewise obliged all the members of his family to repeat what they remembered of the sermons they had heard at church. I cannot commend this practice too highly. It created habits of attention and recollection. I was much struck in observing how much we improved in the knowledge we brought home of the sermon by exercise. Two of his scholars I recollect frequently gave, between them, every idea mentioned in a sermon.

The Instructions of the Sunday evening were usually closed by delivering in a plain way some of the most striking and intelligible evidences of the truth of the Christian Religion. Many of his arguments upon these occasions, though clothed in simple language, were the same which are to be met with in the most logical writers upon that subject, and to the impressions they made upon my understanding, I ascribe my not having at any time of my life ever entertained a doubt of the divine origin of the Bible. I wish this mode of fortifying the reason of young people in the principles of Christianity were more general. The impressions which are made upon their fears, or their faith, by sermons and creeds soon wear away, but arguments fixed in the understanding are indelible. They operate upon the judgement, and this process of the mind we know to yield as necessarily to the impression of truth as vision in a sound eye succeeds the impression from the rays of light.

One more branch of education remains to be mentioned which was taught in the Doctor's family, and that is practical· agriculture. All his boarders shared in the labors of harvest and hay making. I bear on one of my fingers to this day the mark of a severe cut I received in learning to reap. These exercises were both pleasant and useful. They begat health, and helped to implant more deeply in our minds the native passion for rural life. Perhaps it may be ascribed in part to their influence, that not a single instance of death, and not more than two or three instances of sickness occurred in the Doctor's family during the time I lived in it, which was five years. The family seldom consisted of less than thirty persons.

The comfort and reputation of a boarding school depends so much upon the conduct of the wife of its master, that the account I have given would be very defective without mentioning that my aunt (with a small deduction on account of the irritability of her temper, occasioned by bad health) was eminently qualified for her station. She was industrious, intelligent, frugal, and in every other respect a good housewife. She possessed information upon many subjects, and some wit, which rendered her agreeable in conversation. She kept a plentiful table of country food dressed in a pleasant manner. The record of this fact will not appear trifling to those who know that the appetite is the ruling principle in

young people, and that no advantages in point of education will be duly appreciated where it is not pleased, nor
any acts of injustice committed by boarding schools remembered with less forgiveness, than scanty, or ill-dressed
meals. I quit the history of this delightful haunt of my
youth with reluctance. There is not a fruit tree, nor a
rivulet of water on it that was not dear to me. Some years
after I left it, I rode several miles out of my way to visit
it. I rambled with a melancholy pleasure slowly over the
fields and meadows and orchard in which I had shared
with my master and schoolmates in rural labors and fes-
tivity. I sat down in the dining room of the old mansion
house, and stood silent and motionless for a considerable
time in the schoolhouse, which was then used as a weav-
ers' shop. Most of the members of that once happy family
are now no more. Seven out of eight of Dr. Finley's children sleep with their father and mother in the grave.
Many of my schoolmates filled important stations, and
discharged the duties of useful professions with honor to
themselves and benefit to their country. I avoid naming
them lest by omitting any I should give offence. One
thing only damps the review of the time I spent at this
school, and that is that I profited so much less than I
might have done from all the opportunities I enjoyed
of literary and moral instruction. An education at a
country school has many advantages, but it has one dis-
advantage, which operates with peculiar force upon city
boys, and that is the facility with which the amusements
of hunting, gunning and the like are to be obtained is
so great as to overpower the relish for study. From much
reflection upon this subject I am satisfied that it would
be wise in country schoolmasters to forbid those amusements altogether. They are all attended with more or
less risk to health and morals. Rural employments might

easily be substituted in their room. These establish early ideas of a connection between industry and property, and they lay a foundation for those agricultural pursuits or pleasures, which are often the result of necessity, or of independence and leisure.

The mind of a boy could as soon cease to exist, as cease to be active. Shut out from play, it retreats of choice to study. One of the most accomplished scholars I ever knew, was an idle boy 'till he was 14 years of age. He always ascribed his fondness for books to his being confined for bad behaviour two or three days in his grand father's library. To obviate the ennui of idleness, he took down a book which he found entertaining. He read it through, by which means he suddenly acquired a taste for reading and knowledge that continued during the remainder of his life.

In taking leave of the school and family of my venerable preceptor, I have only to add that he died in the city of Philadelphia in the month of July in the year 1766 in the 51st year of his age. I sat up with him every other night for several weeks, and finally performed the distressing office of closing his eyes. The annals of Christian biography do not furnish an instance of more patience in sickness, nor of a greater triumph in death. His conversation for several days before he died was elevated, pious, and eloquent in the highest degree. It was carefully recorded by one of his attendants, and afterwards published by Mr. Aitken in the United States magazine. The character and manners of this excellent man commanded respect and affection from his numerous pupils. I never met with one of them who did not admire, esteem and love him. Some of them expressed their respect for his memory in terms bordering upon idolatry. I endeavoured to show my gratitude to him by adopting and educating his youngest son, who is now a respectable physician and citizen of South Carolina. His picture forms a part of the furniture of my house.

My classmates at this school were the Revd. Charles Cummins and Joseph Alexander of South Carolina, Dr. Wm. Williams of Virginia, Dr. John Archer of Maryland, and Dr. Thomas Ruston and Ebenezer Hazard of Philadelphia, all of whom are now living, July 1800. A similar instance of seven persons connected in any way, living 44 years after being separated, and in a country that had been exposed to war and pestilence has not probably often occurred in any part of the world.

Francis Alison: Old Side Educator

MATTHEW WILSON

Alison was a graduate of Edinburgh University and his learning as a classical and literary scholar was widely respected. He remained in charge of the New London Academy for nine years, when he was called, perhaps at the instigation of Benjamin Franklin who knew and admired Alison, to become head of the Academy of Philadelphia and Vice-Provost and professor of the College of Philadelphia. At both the New London Academy and the College of Philadelphia, the curriculum and teaching methods followed by Alison reflected the modern philosophical, scientific, and pedagogical influences of the Scottish universities where he had been trained.

In later years Alison could count among the alumni of

his academy such outstanding figures as Charles Thomp-
son, Secretary of the Continental Congress; John Ewing,
President of the University of Pennsylvania; Hugh Wil-
liamson, physician and educator; David Ramsay, physi-
cian and historian; George Read, Signer of the Declara-
tion of Independence; and Thomas McKean, Governor
of Pennsylvania. The following tribute to Alison, de-
scribing his course of study and methods of instruction
at the New London Academy, was written for the Pennsylvania Journal *by Matthew Wilson, also a pupil of*
Alison's and a leading Presbyterian minister.

The death of this great man is just announced to us in
a distant state, by Mr. *Bradford*'s impartial *Journal*, with
this just and comprehensive character, viz. "In him the
College has lost a learned and laborious teacher; the
Church of Christ a faithful minister; and society a very
useful and honest man." To this let me only add a few
indisputable truths, not in the point of oratorical and
poetic encomiums, but [in] that simplicity and truth,
which becomes philosophers and Christians, from my own
knowledge, for the imitation of others in public offices.

Dr. Alison's natural genius and powers of mind, appeared to every observer, great and excellent, beyond the
common race of learned men. His apprehensions prompt,
quick and clear. His judgment penetrating, solid, stable
and firm. His reasoning acute and expert. How oft have
we seen him, in synodical, or other debates, quick as
lightning, viewing the case on all sides, and forming in
an instant, a clearer judgment than most other men after
long disquisition? So clear and distinct his understanding, that it would penetrate at once into knotty difficulties, with the greatest facility. Nor were his notions
only borrowed from books and systems, or taken on

trust, but formed by "reason comparing balance," as if truth were more connatural to him, much sooner digested, made his own, and inwrought in his mind. His memory in younger years was admirable too, so as to prepare or commit his sermons in a few minutes, which were always rational; not inelegant; affecting; carrying full conviction to every attentive hearer's mind; and agreeable to the sacred oracles, which he could excellently explain and defend, against the errors of the superstitious, the enthusiast, and the libertine. He had a surprizing readiness and copiousness of speaking in private or public. His style though proper, expressive, clear and concise, yet was nobly negligent. Warmed with his subject, he could not stoop to the affected eloquence of words. Indeed every man's style in general is almost as peculiar to himself as his voice and features. He esteemed an affected style awkward, and thought it better to creep humbly according to nature, than attempt to fly on stolen pinions, which he used to call "prose run mad." *Purpureus pannus,* etc. Hor.

His wit was facetious among chosen friends, and his fancy vigorous and lively. He did not banish pleasantry from his conversation, for which he had superior advantage from his great reading, and variety of story, both ancient and modern. But his wit was more usually displayed in keen satire on some vice or folly, for the good of the company.

His great and accurate learning and acquired knowledge in the Latin and Greek languages (with some Hebrew) and all the liberal arts and sciences evinced that he had in his own country of Ireland, and in the colleges of Scotland, where he also went for improvement, been taught by very learned and correct teachers. Yet he continued a devourer of books, and adding to his rich treasure of knowledge, through all his lengthened life. He could well direct others to select a library, for himself was a living one. He read almost all books of any note, and being an excellent judge and critic, he could recommend the best.

Nor did he look with a careless glance on the public affairs of his country, but would speak of them as a man of prospect and large thought, before his strength of body and mind were worn out by long and severe afflictions. He never failed to implant the love of civil and religious liberty deep in every heart of his pupils, near forty years ago.

He had a great aversion to appearing in print, so that his friends could never extort any thing from him for the press that I recollect, except a Synodical Sermon to excite love and union among Christian Churches, which was recommended by the ingenious Dr. Smith, of another Society. Yet several of his anonymous publications met with public applause, in the Magazine, etc., etc.

Dr. Alison was a man of such stoic or rather Christian virtue, he could in nothing prevaricate with his own settled judgment, so that he came over a poor man to the wilds of America, rather than accept the rich emoluments of an establishment kindly offered him by his friends in power, with an infringement of his conscience. Yet he continued in strict friendship with worthy men of the Episcopal communion.

He was a man of warm and steady friendship; and so scrupulous his fidelity, his word was sacred as an oath. He hated all dissimulation and hypocrisy, and could seldom forbear affronting those he esteemed guilty of it, whether in high or low life.

He was exceeding punctual to his appointments, even when too arduous for his declining constitution, and his compliance with his word, if possible, was punctual as the returns of day and night. Hence he often censured young men for want of public spirit. And hence his friends knew it was in vain to urge his stay with them beyond his appointed hour.

His hospitality and charity were large and diffusive to proper objects, especially to youth, whom he hoped to improve for the service of God and their country. For in the school of poverty he well knew that great men could only be formed, as in ancient Greece and Rome. He greatly despised luxury and dissipation in young men, whom he represented as the most useless drones, and the most contemptible burdens of the earth, *"Frages con-sumere nati,"* etc. And after he accepted a Professorship in the College of Philadelphia he often lamented, that he could not in the city advance the interest of learning, as in the country. This was the true reason why he labored for, and obtained a charter and fund for an Academy at New-Ark, which he esteemed a suitable healthy village, not too rich and luxurious, where real learning might be obtained.

His greatest ambition was to do good, from a largeness of soul which comprehended at once the various interests of his God, of the world, his country and his friends, ready to serve them all to his utmost.

But that "he might not be exalted above measure," by these great abilities and virtues, he was ever afflicted and kept humble by his temper, which was very choler-ick, and gave him great trouble to restrain; yet he would often restrain it to admiration, when he was warned of something expected to ruffle it; however, though on some unexpected occurrences it would carry him too far, yet he would make ample amends, by doing greater favors to those who had taken in dudgeon the keenness of his satire, while his temper greatly stimulated youth to correctness and learning.

Reader, cast a veil on the afflictions and misfortunes of this great man, and thank Heaven, if you are more happy. I only add, his children are blest with fine geniuses, that may be greatly useful to their country, if they imitate their father's virtues.

The most important part of the Doctor's character is yet to be mentioned, his indefatigable labors and assiduous application in promoting a liberal education, and good learning in America. Many men of learning had before come over to America, and some had made some feeble, unsuccessful attempts to teach youth here; but it must be owned by all, they had not Dr. Alison's talents, resolution, perseverance or success. It is certain, he was the first who introduced real learning, not only Latin and Greek, with great exactness, but also diffused the knowledge of all the liberal arts and sciences, which enlarge and improve the mind; not only through Pennsylvania, but in all the neighboring states, so that almost all men of real learning, in these parts of the world, who are natives of the country, were either taught by him, or his pupils, or their scholars; as not only the Honorable The Secretary of Congress, and Chief Justice of Pennsylvania, Dr. Ewing, George Reed, Esq. etc., etc., but many who have filled with honor the first places in the churches, colleges, and Republic, army, law and medicine, of whom many of the finest talents have withdrawn from our world before their venerable master.

He first opened a seat of learning in New London, Chester County, of great and deserved renown in those days, (I think it cannot want much of 40 years since) on the most generous and broad bottom, for all denominations of Christians equally; which was visited, examined and encouraged by the Synod of Philadelphia, sometimes every year, until colleges were erected, where youth resorted from all the cities, provinces and colonies around.

His public spirit was coextended with his life. Not only anxious to promote his own seminary of learning, he sent such of his pupils as he could recommend, to teach public schools wherever he could influence; also to be assistants to other teachers then beginning the important task; and to be tutors in other schools and colleges, when erected, who thought themselves happy to get some of his pupils to put masters and scholars, on the Doctor's most correct and successful methods of teaching.

From Dr. Alison the love of learning, "catched a happy contagion of his virtue," spread through the new world, and founded all the colleges and academies around; which I hope the rage of war will never extinguish.

Permit me to offer a few hints, respecting his first synodical seminary, which may be improved by all other teachers of youth.

To his first seminary, though he had often great numbers under his care, and frequently two or more assistants, yet his own attention to every class, and every student, seemed nevertheless unremitted.

The great Mr. Locke, and many since have objected against losing "several years getting a critical knowledge of the dead languages, Latin, Greek, and Hebrew, while our own tongue is neglected, etc."—But had Mr. Locke known so happy a plan of teaching as Dr. Alison's, he would have found that no time was lost; for while the Latin and Greek were in teaching, we were not only taught the English grammar, by comparing it with the Latin; with the principles, difficulties, beauties, and defects of our mother tongue; but also we were taught to write and speak correct English; nay, while the English, Latin, and Greek grammars were accurately taught and exemplified in every lesson of our classics, every part of the belles lettres, as the Pantheon or heathen mythology, rhetoric and figures, geography and maps, chronology and Gray's *Memoria Technica,* Kennet's tóms; Veriot's Roman revolutions and other history (which we were not only obliged to read but answer any questions out of them he chose to interrogate) and besides all these, characters, actions, morals and events were taught and explained by him in every lesson.

As knowledge and composition, or writing and speaking, are the greatest ends of a liberal education, we received the greatest advantage from his critical examination every morning of our themes English and Latin, epistles English and Latin, descriptions in verse, and especially our abstracts or abridgements of a paper from the Spectators or Guardians (the best standards of our language) substantially contracted into one of our exercises.

When languages were accurately taught, we entered on a course of philosophy, instrumental, natural, and moral, in all which, the Doctor contented not himself with giving only lectures; he also examined us daily, and obliged us to write abridgements for ourselves, of the greatest utility.

When we came to read Juvenal, our declamations began, which we wrote and delivered by memory:—And after logic our syllogistic disputations.

I cannot stay to speak of his obtaining the widow's fund, his writings and improvements on agriculture for the good of farmers, whom he called the best members of society; and every scheme of greatest public utility, which were his daily employ.

From this too short and defective character, it is plain, Dr. Alison was the principal father of learning and learned men, and like Prometheus, Cadmus, or even Apollo of old, deserves perpetual remembrance, as one of the greatest benefactors, on whose urn every grateful son of science will drop a tear.

SOURCE: *Pennsylvania Journal and Weekly Advertiser,* Wednesday, April 19, 1780.

A General Account of
the Rise and State of
The College of New Jersey

GILBERT TENNENT AND SAMUEL DAVIES

On a mission that would test their persuasive powers in a new way, the two evangelists, Samuel Davies and Gilbert Tennent, sailed to Britain in 1753 to raise money for the fledgling College of New Jersey. To prepare the British for their arrival Davies and Tennent wrote and sent ahead of them the pamphlet published below. To be sure, it is a money-raising pamphlet with money-raising rhetoric. Still, it is a fairly reliable account of the college and of the efforts being made by the college leaders to keep abreast of the latest in modern teaching methods, equipment, and curriculum. The pamphlet also states the three-fold ideal of the college as one of promoting religion, science, and public service. Tennent and Davies were warmly welcomed in Great Britain, particularly in

Scotland, and they returned home with a sum estimated at over £3,200.

Nothing has a more direct tendency to advance the happiness and glory of a community, than the founding of public schools and seminaries of learning, for the education of youth, and adorning their minds with useful knowledge and virtue. Hereby the rude and ignorant are civilized and rendered humane; persons, who would otherwise be useless members of society, are qualified to sustain, with honour, the offices they may be invested with, for the public service; reverence of the Deity, filial piety, and obedience to the laws, are inculcated and promoted.

The sciences have no where flourished with more success, than in our mother-country. The universities and seminaries of learning, in England and Scotland, are annually sending abroad into the kingdom, proficients in all kinds of literature; men of refined sentiments, solid judgments, and noble principles; who spread (if the expression may be allowed) a kind of literary glory over the British nation.

AMERICA remained, during a long period, in the thickest darkness of ignorance and barbarism, till Christianity, at the introduction of the Europeans, enlightened her hemisphere with the salutary beams of life and immortality. Science, her constant attendant, soon raised her depressed head, and the arts began to flourish. New-England first felt her benign influences, whose sons she inspired with a generous emulation of erecting schools and colleges, for the instruction of their youth, and instilling into their tender mind the principles of piety and learning. The southwestward colonies, except Virginia, continued a considerable number of years without any public institutions for the cultivation of the sciences. At length, several gentlemen residing in and near the province of New-Jersey, who were well-wishers to the felicity of their country, and real friends of religion and learning, having observed the vast increase of those colonies, with the rudeness and ignorance of their inhabitants, for want of the necessary means of improvement, first projected the scheme of a collegiate education in that province.

The immediate motives to this generous design, were —the great number of Christian societies then lately formed in various parts of the country, where many thousands of inhabitants, in a tract of land much larger than all Great-Britain and Ireland, ardently desirous of the administration of religious ordinances, were entirely destitute of the necessary means of instruction, and incapable of being relieved;—the urgent applications that were annually made by those vacant congregations to the clergy in their collective bodies; complaining, in the most moving manner, of their unhappy circumstances, in being deprived of the ordinary means of salvation, and left to grope after happiness almost in the obscurity of Paganism, though the light of revelation shone on their surrounding neighbours; and the great scarcity of candidates for the ministerial function, to comply with these pious and Christian demands; the colleges of New-England educating hardly a competent number for the service of its own churches. These considerations were the most urgent arguments for the immediate prosecution of the above-mentioned scheme of education.

Accordingly, in the year 1747, a petition was presented to his excellency JONATHAN BELSCHER, Esq; governor of that province (a gentleman who has long signalized himself as a patron of religion and learning) praying his MAJESTY's grant of a charter for the establishment of a public seminary of literature in New-Jersey. His excellency, with the approbation of the council and attorney-general of the said province, was pleased to comply with their request, and ordered a charter to pass the seals; incorporating sundry gentlemen, to the number of twenty-three, by the name of THE TRUSTEES OF THE COLLEGE OF NEW-JERSEY; and appointing the governor of New-Jersey for the time being, who is his MAJESTY's representative, to act as their president, when convened. This charter places the society upon the most catholic foundation: all protestants, of every denomination, who are loyal subjects to our MOST GRACIOUS SOVEREIGN (the happy effects of whose mild and equal administration the remotest colonies of the British empire sensibly experience, and gratefully acknowledge) are admitted to the enjoyment of all its privileges, and allowed the unlimited exercise of their religion.

The Trustees, thus authorized with ample powers for the execution of this laudable design, in conformity to the plan of their charter, applied themselves, with the utmost deliberation, to form and enact such rules and orders for the regulation of the methods of instruction, and conduct of the students, as might tend to prevent the entrance of vice into the society, and the introduction of idleness, vanity, and extravagant expenses amongst its members. It would be repugnant to the design of a general narrative, as well as impertinent to the reader, to enter into a minute detail of these several private regulations. It will suffice to say, that the two principle objects the trustees had in view, were SCIENCE and RELIGION. Their first concern was, to cultivate the minds of the pupils in all those branches of erudition which are generally taught in the universities abroad; and, to perfect their design, their next care was to rectify the heart, by inculcating the great precepts of Christianity, in order to make them good.

Upon these views this society was founded. Providence so far smiled upon the undertaking, in the first instance, as to point out a gentleman, possessed of every requisite endowment, to be placed at the head of such an academy. The Reverend Mr. AARON BURR has been long known in these parts of America, for his piety, affability, universal acquaintance with the arts and sciences, and his easy, familiar methods of instruction. Under his immediate tuition and government, this society has flourished far beyond the most raised and sanguine expectations. The number of students has increased, in the short space of five years, from eight or ten, to about sixty; besides near forty in the grammar-school.

As no human institutions, in a world of imperfection and error, are so completely modelled, as to exclude the possibility of farther emendation; it may be said without any intention of disparagement to other learned seminaries, that the governors of this college have endeavoured to improve upon the commonly received plans of education. They proceed not so much in the method of a dogmatic institution, by prolix discourses on the different branches of the sciences, by burdening the memory, and imposing heavy and disagreeable talks; as in the Socratic way of free dialogue, between teacher and pupil, or between the students themselves, under the inspection of their tutors. In this manner, the attention is engaged, the mind entertained, and the scholar animated in the pursuit of knowledge. In fine, the arts and sciences are conveyed into the minds of youth, in a method the most easy, natural and familiar. But as religion ought to be the end of all instruction, and gives it the last degree of perfection; as one of the primary views of this foundation was to educate young gentlemen for the sacred office of the ministry, and fit them for the discharge of so noble an employment; divinity, the mistress of the sciences, engages the peculiar attention of the governors of this society. Stated times are set apart for the study of the holy scriptures in the original languages, and stated hours daily consecrated to the service of religion. The utmost care is taken to discountenance vice, and to encourage the practice of virtue; and a manly, rational and Christian behaviour in the students. Enthusiasm on the one hand, and prophaneness on the other, are equally guarded against, and meet with the severest checks.

Under such management, this seminary, from the smallest beginnings, quickly drew the public attention, enlarged the number of her pupils, raised her reputation; and now, though in her infancy, almost rivals her ancient sisters upon the continent.

Daily observation evinces, that in proportion as learning makes its progress in a country, it softens the natural roughness, eradicates the prejudices, and transforms the genius and disposition of its inhabitants. New-Jersey, and the adjacent provinces, already feel the happy effects of this useful institution. A general desire of knowledge seems to be spreading among the people: parents are inspired with an emulation of cultivating the minds of their offspring: public stations are honourably filled by gentlemen, who have received their education: and from hence many Christian assemblies are furnished with men of distinguished talents, for the discharge of the pastoral office.

The Trustees acknowledge, with the utmost gratitude,

the several benefactions that have been made to this infant society, by the lovers of piety and learning. But notwithstanding the assistances obtained; considering the constant annual maintenance of the president and tutors;—the expense that must unavoidably attend the erection of an edifice, with a requisite number of apartments;—the building an house for the residence of the president;—furnishing the library, which is at present very small;—and procuring a proper apparatus for philosophical experiments;—the state of their treasury is altogether inadequate to those chargeable demands.†

These things, so absolutely necessary to the well-being of the society, must remain uneffected, until Providence is pleased to excite the beneficence of those who wish the prosperity of religion and literature in the uncultivated parts of the world. The members of the college, who are annually growing more numerous, for want of

---

† The Trustees have received about £1200 Sterling in America, the yearly interest of which they have voted to be applied to the support of the president and tutors; but it is hardly sufficient for that purpose; much less for the increase of their number, which is necessary even at present. The inhabitants of Prince-Town, where the college is to be erected, have also given in land for ever to the value of £400 Sterling, for the seat of the college, and to supply it with fire-wood.

The number of scholars, including those in the grammar-school, is already near an hundred; and there is no small prospect of their annual increase. They cannot therefore be accommodated in a building of less than forty rooms, with a large hall for public exercises, a library-room, a dwelling-house for the president, and other convenient buildings; the expence of which, it is thought, will amount to above £2000 Sterling. And at least the sum of £2000 more will be necessary—for enlarging the library,—furnishing a philosophical apparatus, increasing the salaries and number of the instructors;—and forming a sufficient fund for the support of youth of piety and genius, who are unable to defray the expences of a collegiate education; without which, the numerous growing churches there cannot be well supplied.

a public building for their reception, must struggle under the greatest difficulties in procuring accommodations in private families; and that too in a dispersed village, where their daily attendance on the collegiate exercises is subject to numberless inconveniencies.

From the above representation of the ends for which this corporation was founded; the happy effects of its institution; and its present necessitous circumstances; it is hoped, that the pious and benevolent in Great-Britain, into whose hands these papers may fall, will extend their generous aids, in the prosecution and completion of so excellent and useful a design. A design! upon the success of which, the happiness of multitudes in sundry colonies, and their numerous posterity, in the present and future ages far distant, in a great measure depends. A design! which not only tends to promote the weal of the British inhabitants, but also of the German emigrants; and to spread the gospel of salvation among the benighted Indian tribes, and attach them to his MAJESTY's government. A design! which is not calculated to promote the low purposes of a party,* but in its views

* The trustees of the said college have not made such regulations as may burden the consciences of any, or confine the advantages of the institution to a party; nor did they desire such a power; as is evident from the following words of the charter—"The said petitioners have also expressed their earnest desire, 'that those of every religious denomination may have free and equal liberty and advantages of education in the said college; any different sentiments in religion notwithstanding.'—Nor can the trustees exercise such power, in time coming, without counteracting, and of consequence forfeiting their charter; the words of which are these— 'The trustees of the said college are hereby empowered to make such ordinances and laws, as may tend to the good government of the said college, not repugnant to the laws and statutes of our realm of Great-Britain, or of this our province of New-Jersey; and not excluding any person of any religious denomination whatsoever from free and equal liberty and advantage of education, or

and consequences affects the Protestant interest in general, and Great-Britain in particular, both in religious and civil respects; since by this, the filial duty of her descendents will be inculcated, their manners reformed, and her trade increased; which is the basis of her empire, glory and felicity.

The inhabitants of the infant colonies, dependent upon this seminary, unable to relieve themselves, are constrained to solicit and implore the assistance of others. And to whom shall they look, but to their tender and powerful parent, the venerable church of Scotland, whose standard of faith, worship and discipline they have adopted? To move her compassion, they plead their relation as children, as fellow-subjects, as Christian and Protestant brethren with her sons that still enjoy the advantages of residing in their native country. They plead the deplorable circumstances of the church, and the exigences of the state, for want of such an institution brought to maturity. And they beg leave modestly to intimate their importance to their mother-country, as they enlarge the British dominions upon a vast continent, whither the industrious poor may transplant themselves, and find a comfortable subsistence; as they are a check upon the growth of the French power in America; engage the Indian natives to the British interest; furnish various assistances in time of war against the common enemy; and carry on sundry branches of trade, advantageous to Great-Britain; which will undoubtedly flourish more, in proportion to their improvements in the liberal arts and sciences; for history and observation as-

---

from any of the liberties, privileges or immunities of the said college, on account of his or their being of a religious profession different from the said trustees of the said college.' "—

sure us, that learning and trade mutually promote each other.

Next to the advancement of the divine honour, the noblest pursuit of man, surely nothing can afford the human mind a more pleasing reflection, than the being instrumental in promoting the general felicity of mankind. These important ends can by no means be so effectually served, as by forming the rising generation to be useful members of the community; and by diffusing the light of Christianity among the ignorant and uncivilized nations of the earth.

SOURCE: Gilbert Tennent and Samuel Davies, *General Account of the Rise and State of the College, Lately Established in the Province of New-Jersey, In America; And of the End and Design of Its Institution* (Princeton: 1742; reprinted Edinburgh, 1754).

Religion and Public Spirit

SAMUEL DAVIES

Samuel Davies was regarded as one of the most powerful orators of his time. He not only employed his rhetorical skills from the pulpit to convert sinners, he used them with great effect during the French and Indian War to raise troops to defend the frontier. His evangelistic and patriotic fervors went hand in hand. Davies became the fourth president of the College of New Jersey in 1759, where he served for about a year and a half until his untimely death in 1761. Davies delivered the sermon, excerpted below, to the graduating class of 1760.

Unmistakably a commencement address, the sermon does exemplify the inseparable connection Davies made between revival religion, higher education, and a commitment to public service.

ACTS 13:36. DAVID, *after he had served his own generation, by the will of* GOD, [or, *having in his own age served the will of* GOD] *fell on sleep, and was laid to his fathers, and saw corruption.*

Great and good characters are often formed by *imitation:* And if we would shine in any sphere, we must propose to ourselves some illustrious examples. Great generals have acquired their martial skill, by pursuing the memoirs of the *Alexanders* and *Caesars* of former ages, And *Longinus* advises us, if we would rise to the sublime in writing, always to keep in view, a Homer, a Plato, a Demosthenes or a Cicero. And how shall the more amiable, though less glaring and renowned character of the *good,* and *useful,* and *public-spirited* man, be formed? Nothing surely can contribute more towards it, than the imitation of some bright *example.* And among all the kings, patriots and prophets, whose names are immortalized in sacred history, no *example* shines with a brighter lustre, than that of *David,* who *served his own generation according to the will of God,* and then, as a weary laborer, gently *fell on sleep,* and sweetly rested from his generous and pious toils. . . .

The excellency of the example now before you, consists in two things, PUBLIC SPIRIT and RELIGION. Public Spirit, *in serving his generation,* and Religion, in doing this *according to the will of God,* or, (as it might be translated) serving *the will of God,* in his own generation. The union of these two qualities ever com-

poses the truly good and useful man; a proper member
of human society; and even of the grand community of
angels and saints. The one includes a temper and conduct agreeable to our *social* connections; and the other a
temper and conduct agreeable to our obligations to the
author of our nature. And so inseparably are these
united, that the one cannot exist, in the entire absence
of the other. Public spirit and benevolence without religion, is but a warm affection for the subjects, to the
neglect of their sovereign; or a partiality for the children, in contempt of their father, who is infinitely more
worthy of love. And religion without public spirit and
benevolence, is but a sullen, selfish, sour and malignant
humour for devotion, unworthy of that sacred name.
. . . To excite and cherish such a spirit, I can at present only illustrate this comprehensive epitome of the
history of *David.*

"He *served* his generation." To be the *servant* of the
public, was his ambition; and to perform *labors of love*
to church and state, was the favorite employment of his
life. His public spirit pushed him on to engage in the
most fatiguing, self-denying and dangerous services; he
thought nothing too hard, nothing beneath his dignity,
that was conducive to the public good. . . . In short, all
his talents, natural and supernatural, were sacred to the
church, to his country and mankind; thus becoming
universal and distinguished blessings.

THIS, my dear pupils, this is the spirit, with which
I would inspire you. A public spirit always appeared to
me of the utmost importance, this you are sensible is
not the first occasion on which I have endeavored to
fire your breasts with the generous flame. Devoid of this,
though stationed in the most public offices, your lives
will be of little use to community; and all the valuable

ends of a liberal education, will be lost upon you. But if you feel the generous impulses of a public spirit, you can never be altogether insignificant, you will never be mere cyphers in the world, even in the obscurest and most sequestered vale of life. Even in the lowest station, you will be of some use to mankind, a sufficient recompence this for the severe conflict of sixty or seventy years. It is unknown to me, and perhaps to yourselves, in what employments you will spend your future lives. But whatever it be, whether you appear in the sacred desk, as the *ministers of God,* and devote yourselves to that office, in which you can have no bright prospects of secular advantages, but only the benevolent and God-like pleasure of endeavoring to make men wise, good and happy; or whether you appear at the bar, as advocates for justice, and the patrons of the opprest; or whether you practice the *healing art* in the chambers of affliction, to alleviate the pains and sicknesses of your fellow creatures, to restore the sweets of health, and prolong the dubious duration of life; or whether you choose the serene and quiet pleasures of retirement, and glide through the world in a private station; whatever, I say, be your place, permit me, my dear youth, to inculcate upon you this important instruction, IMBIBE AND CHERISH A PUBLIC SPIRIT. Serve your generation. Live not for yourselves, but the public. Be the servants of the church; the servants of your country; the servants of all. Extend the arms of your benevolence to embrace your friends, your neighbors, your country, your nation, the whole race of mankind, even your enemies. Let it be the vigorous unremitted effort of your whole life, to leave the world wiser and better, than you found it at your entrance. Esteem yourselves by so much the more happy, honorable and important, by how much the more useful you are. Let your own ease, your own pleasure, your own private interests, yield to the common good. For this, spare no pains; avoid no labor; dread no sufferings. For this, *do* every thing; *suffer* every thing. For this, live and die. From this, let no selfish passion mislead you; no ungrateful returns, the usual returns of active benevolence, discourage you; let no opposition deter you; no private interest bribe you. To this, be your bodies, your souls, your estates, your life, your all sacred. Bravely live and die, serving your *generation,* your *own* generation. This *David* did.

"He served *his own generation."* Every man's sphere of usefulness, is limited; the beneficence of one man, can extend to but a small part of mankind: Even *David* could but serve *his own* generation. For other generations, God raised up other servants, accomplished according to the work he had to do in them: And thus, the great scheme of his providence is carried on, through the fleeting succession of human nature, and never fails of execution, for want of instruments. . . . All hands must be busy, in every period, to accomplish the designs of heaven; and no part of the destined work, shall remain undone, for want of proper agents. . . .

The other part of *David's* character, which I would propose to your imitation, is his RELIGION. He served his generation *by,* or *according to,* THE WILL OF GOD. *The will of God* was the rule of his beneficence to men; and he served his generation, because in so doing he served his God. Whatever he did, he did heartily, as unto the *Lord,* and not unto *men.* 'Tis this regard to the will of God, in acts of humanity and public spirit, that sanctifies them, and renders them true virtue and religion. Without such a regard to the divine will, they form but a monstrous, atheistical patriotism, and an un-creature-like, irreligious benevolence. Without this, all our good offices to men, as they are not intended, so neither will they be accepted, as acts of obedience to God. Certainly, it must be the height of impiety, to be capable of doing even what God commands, not *because* he commands it, but for some other sordid, selfish reason. The greatest stress is laid upon this, in the refined morality of the Gospel. To receive a righteous man, as a righteous man; to receive a prophet *in the name* of a prophet; to give so much as a cup of cold water, to the least of Christ's disciples, *because he belongs to Christ;* this is at once an act of charity and piety. But without such a regard to God, it is but a poor, grovelling, selfish humanity; and has no more real goodness in it, than the instinctive fondness of a brute for its young.

Therefore, my young friends, let religion be the source of your benevolence and public spirit; and have a regard to the will of God, in all your offices of men. Let it not be your principal end, to gratify a natural benevolence of temper; to procure honor to yourselves, or to accomplish some interested design; but to PLEASE GOD. Let this be the center, in which all the actions of your life shall terminate, and the scope to which they tend. Then you may claim a character more noble than even that of a patriot, I mean a CHRISTIAN. . . .

I MUST add farther, that great change of temper, that extirpation of the corrupt principles of nature, and that implantation of holy and supernatural principles of action, which the Scriptures express by such strong and significant metaphors as *regeneration,* a *resurrection,* a *new creation,* and the like; I say, that divine change of the principles of action, is the great foundation of true religion and social virtue; without which, you can never arrive at the finished character of good and great men. Though you should make a shining figure in life, and dazzle the world with the lustre of your name; your true character in the sight of God, will be nothing higher, than that of a worthless, odious and contemptible sinner, fit for no place but hell, for no society, but that of infernal spirits. If my temper were agreeable to my subject, and the views I have of it, I should here assume an air of peculiar solemnity; and by the manner of my address, convince you how much I am in earnest, when I inculcate upon you the vast importance and absolute necessity of entering upon public life with A NEW HEART AND A NEW SPIRIT. So deep and universal is the present innate depravity of human nature, that the sacred structure of a truly great and good man, can never be built upon that foundation. It may admit of the external decorations of a whited wall; but it is incapable of any true substantial goodness, till there be "a new creation; till old things pass away, and all things be made new." You must be "created in Christ Jesus to do good works," before you can "walk in them." "A new heart must be given you, and a new spirit put within you," before you can "walk in God's statutes, and keep his judgments, and do them." Therefore let this saying sink deep into your hearts, THE NEW BIRTH IS THE BEGINNING OF ALL GENUINE RELIGION AND VIRTUE; it is your first entrance into a new world of usefulness; and an incorporation with the society of saints and angels, and all the beneficent beings in the universe. May your minds, my dear pupils, always retain a full conviction of this great truth, in this age, when it has lost its popularity even among nominal Christians; and so, many will *marvel* and stare, with *Nicodemus,* when they hear, "a man *must* be born again."

Thus have we traced the example of *David* in Life, let us now follow him to his end. "Having served his generation by the will of God, *he fell on sleep, and was laid to his fathers, and saw corruption. . . .*"

Thus, my dear youth, though now in the prime of life, and the vigor of your strength, thus must you fall asleep in death, and see corruption. This is the end of all flesh; and the highest endowments, natural, acquired or supernatural, which even *David* was adorned with, can be no security against it. Those eyes, that have pored with so much pleasure upon the pages of knowledge, must be closed in death; and those ears, that have listened with so much eagerness to instruction, must be stopped in the dust. Stupor and insensibility must seize your limbs; and a dead sleep arrest all your active powers. Therefore enter the world with a deep sense of your mortality; and that after a few turns upon the stage, you must retire into the chambers of death. Let your prospects and expectations be confined within narrow limits; and indulge no high hopes, form no everlasting schemes, on this side death. . . .

Let me also renew my exhortation to you, to exert all your powers in doing good, before they are seized with the eternal torpor of the sleep of death; for then, all your capacities and opportunities of being serviceable to your fellow mortals, will be irreparably lost forever. Make it the great business of life, to prepare for death; and for that end, learn to familiarize the prospect. Look forward to approaching death; look downward into the gaping grave, even in the gay and giddy hours of health and youth. And oh! above all, take frequent surveys of the eternal world, that lies beyond death and the grave. There you must ere long be, ye young immortals! ye candidates for eternity! ye heirs of heaven or hell! Unless you secure a happy immortality, in the few uncertain years of life, your existence, your reason, your liberal education, your religious advantages, your all, will be your everlasting curse: And it would be better for you, to be Hottentots, or even the most abject and miserable creatures among the meanest and most noxious of the brutal tribes, than to be the Sons of NASSAU-HALL. Therefore "strive to enter in at the strait gate" and do not disappoint my eager hopes of seeing you at the right hand of the supreme judge. We are soon to part, and be dispersed through the world. But oh! let us fix upon *that,* as the sure place of interview, and the commencement of an union never to be dissolved.

Let me now take leave of you with a few particular *advices* and *warnings;* though the hurry of the present hour, will but admit of some concise hints, for your own thoughts to improve.

Do not imagine, you may now put an end to your studies, as having arrived to the utmost limits of useful knowledge. A college education does only lay the foundation; on which to build, must be the business of your future life. If you neglect this, even the foundation however skillfully laid, will gradually molder away. You will live your age *backwards;* and be less wise at sixty, than at twenty. Therefore, as you can redeem leisure from the business of your future station, diligently prosecute your studies; especially in those branches of knowledge, which are most practical, and subservient to your particular profession.

Let me also advise you, in the choice of your stations for life, to follow nature, and consult the public good; and fix upon that which is most agreeable to your natural turn, which in some measure is equal to your abilities, and may be most conducive to the service of your generation. If you mistake in your choice upon your first setting out, you will make an awkward appearance during life, and be of very little use in the world.

Allow me also to solicit the continuance of that friendship to this institution, to which you are obliged for your education, and the prospect of your future importance; and to hope that your inclinations will at least equal your opportunities to promote the interest of your ALMA MATER. Be not however prompted by the jealous and malignant spirit of rivalship, in opposition to other literary institutions; but show yourselves catholic disinterested friends of learning in general.

Finally, I advise you to enter into the wide world, which is now before you, forewarned of the dangers and temptations, in which you will soon be involved. You are about to enter into a state of dubious conflict, where all your virtue will be put to the proof; and where strength more than human, strength from God, is absolutely necessary to render you victorious. . . .

And now, my ever-dear pupils, I must dismiss you from my care, into the wide world, to shift for yourselves. You enter into it with the great advantage of a fair character; for I must do you the justice to declare, that you have always been dutiful teachable pupils to me; and this whole house can attest the regularity of your general conduct, since you have been members of it. Go on in this path; and may it shine more and more till the perfect day! . . .

SOURCE: Samuel Davies, *Religion and Public Spirit. A Valedictory Address to the Senior Class, Delivered in Nassau Hall,* September 21, 1760 . . . (Princeton: James Parker and Company, 1761), pp. 3, 4–5, 6–8, 10–11, 12–13, 15–17, 18.

The Popular Spirit

Samuel Davies wrote that in spite of "the great difference in the capacities, improvements, characters, and
stations of men, yet considered as men, they share in
the same common nature, and are so far equal."* This
egalitarian spirit surfaced in force in the Awakening
first in a new sense of religious priorities which set the
conversion experience above all else. Once aroused,
however, the popular impulse led in many directions:
toward political activism; toward a demand for religious
and civil liberties; toward a more compassionate awareness of classes of men excluded from society—Indians,
Blacks, and poor whites; and toward a widespread desire for knowledge and the skills of literacy. With the
same impulse there also appeared all the problems which
some persons, both at the time of the Awakening and
in the present, would identify as endemic to popular
culture: an impatience with intellectual complexities,
a distrust of refinement and distinctions in taste and
style, and a readiness to be swayed by emotions rather
than ideas. The documents in the following section
look at some of the positive and the negative dimensions
of the Awakening's popular impact.

* Samuel Davies, "The Rule of Equity," *Sermons on Important
Subjects* (New York: 1862), II, 65.

The Discipleship of Study

JONATHAN EDWARDS

The following sermon by Jonathan Edwards contains several points of educational interest. It is a brief and succinct statement of Edwards' theological principles, it explains his distinction between speculative and experimental, or practical, knowledge, and it spells out the connection Edwards saw between theology and other subjects of study. Of special interest, however, is the charge delivered by an intellectual aristocrat par excellence *to each member of his congregation of townspeople, business folk, and farmers to consider themselves as "scholars or learners." "All Christians," Edwards says, "are put into the school of Christ, where their business is to learn" . . . "not only ministers and men of learning," but "men of all sorts, learned and unlearned, men, women, and children." Edwards himself was certainly no democrat, but nothing seems better suited to describe the implications of his conviction, that ministers and laymen alike had a mutual responsibility to learn and to share their knowledge, than the word, democratic.*

HEBREWS 5:12. *For when, for the time, ye ought to be teachers, ye have need that one teach you again which be the first principles of the oracles of God; and are become such as have need of milk, and not of strong meat.*

DOCTRINE

Every Christian should make a business of endeavoring to grow in knowledge in divinity.

This is indeed esteemed the business of divines and ministers: it is commonly thought to be their work, by the study of the Scriptures, and other instructive books, to gain knowledge; and most seem to think that it may be left to them, as what belongeth not to others. But if the apostle had entertained this notion, he would never have blamed the Christian Hebrews for not having acquired knowledge enough to be teachers; or if he had thought, that this concerned Christians in general only as a thing by the by, and that their time should not, in a considerable measure, be taken up with this business; he never would have so much blamed them, that their proficiency in knowledge had not been answerable to the time which they had had to learn.

In handling this subject, I shall show,

1. What divinity is.
2. What kind of knowledge in divinity is intended in the doctrine.
3. Why knowledge in divinity is necessary.
4. Why all Christians should make a business of endeavoring to grow in this knowledge.

First, I shall very briefly show what divinity is.

Various definitions have been given of it by those who have treated on the subject. I shall not now stand to inquire which, according to the rules of art, is the most accurate definition; but shall so define or describe it, as I think has the greatest tendency to convey a notion of it to this auditory.

By divinity is meant that science or doctrine which

comprehends all those truths and rules which concern the great business of religion. There are various kinds of arts and sciences taught and learned in the schools, which are conversant about various objects; about the works of nature in general, as philosophy; or the visible heavens, as astronomy; or the sea, as navigation; or the earth, as geography; or the body of man, as physic and anatomy; or the soul of man, with regard to its natural powers and qualities, as logic and pneumatology; or about human government, as politics and jurisprudence. But there is one science, or one certain kind of knowledge and doctrine, which is above all the rest, as it is concerning God and the great business of religion: *this is divinity;* which is not learned, as other sciences, merely by the improvement of man's natural reason, but is taught by God himself in a certain book that he hath given for that end, full of instruction. This is the rule which God hath given to the world to be their guide in searching after this kind of knowledge, and is a summary of all things of this nature needful for us to know. Upon this account divinity is rather called a doctrine, than an art or science.

Indeed there is what is called *natural religion* or *divinity.* There are many truths concerning God, and our duty to him, which are evident by the light of nature. But Christian divinity, properly so called, is not evident by the light of nature; it depends on revelation. Such are our circumstances now in our fallen state, that nothing which it is needful for us to know concerning God, is manifest by the light of nature in the manner in which it is necessary for us to know it. For the knowledge of no truth in divinity is of any significance to us, any otherwise than, as it some way or other belongs to the gospel scheme, or as it relates to a Mediator. But the light of nature teaches us no truth of divinity in this matter. Therefore it cannot be said, that we come to the knowledge of any part of Christian divinity by the light of nature. The light of nature teaches no truth as it is in Jesus. It is only the word of God, contained in the Old and New Testament, which teaches us Christian divinity. . . .

Second thing proposed, viz., To show what kind of knowledge in divinity is intended in the doctrine.

Here I would observe:

1. That there are two kinds of knowledge of the things of divinity, viz., *speculative* and *practical,* or in other terms, *natural* and *spiritual.* The former remains only in the head. No other faculty but the understanding is concerned in it. It consists in having a natural or rational knowledge of the things of religion, or such a knowledge as is to be obtained by the natural exercise of our own faculties, without any special illumination of the Spirit of God. The latter rests not entirely in the head, or in the speculative ideas of things; but the heart is concerned in it: it principally consists in the sense of the heart. The mere intellect, without the heart, the will or the inclination, is not the seat of it. And it may not only be called seeing, but feeling or tasting. Thus there is a difference between having a right speculative notion of the doctrines contained in the word of God, and having a due sense of them in the heart. In the former consists speculative or natural knowledge of the things of divinity; in the latter consists the spiritual or practical knowledge of them.

2. Neither of these is intended in the doctrine exclusively of the other: but it is intended that we should seek the former in order to find the latter. The latter, even

a spiritual and practical knowledge of divinity, is of the greatest importance; for a speculative knowledge of it, without a spiritual knowledge, is in vain and to no purpose, but to make our condemnation the greater. Yet a speculative knowledge is also of infinite importance in this respect, that without it we can have no spiritual or practical knowledge; as may be shown by and by. . . .

Third thing proposed, viz., To show the usefulness and necessity of knowledge in divinity.

1. There is no other way by which any means of grace whatsoever can be of any benefit, but by knowledge. All teaching is in vain, without learning. Therefore the preaching of the gospel would be wholly to no purpose, if it conveyed no knowledge to the mind. There is an order of men whom Christ has appointed on purpose to be teachers in his church. They are to teach the things of divinity. But they teach in vain, if no knowledge in these things is gained by their teaching. It is impossible that their teaching and preaching should be a means of grace, or of any good in the hearts of their hearers, any otherwise than by knowledge imparted to the understanding. Otherwise it would be of as much benefit to the auditory, if the minister should preach in some unknown tongue. All the difference is, that preaching in a known tongue conveys something to the understanding, which preaching in an unknown tongue doth not. On this account, such preaching must be unprofitable. Men in such things receive nothing, when they understand nothing; and are not at all edified, unless some knowledge be conveyed; agreeably to the apostle's arguing in 1 Cor. 14:2-6.

No speech can be any means of grace but by conveying knowledge. Otherwise the speech is as much lost as if

there had been no man there, and he that spoke, had
spoken only into the air; as it follows in the passage
just quoted, verses 6-10. He that doth not understand,
can receive no faith, nor any other grace; for God deals
with man as with a rational creature; and when faith is
in exercise, it is not about something he knows not what.
Therefore hearing is absolutely necessary to faith; because hearing is necessary to understanding: Rom. 10:
14, *How shall they believe in him of whom they have
not heard?*

So there can be no love without knowledge. It is not
according to the nature of the human soul, to love an
object which is entirely unknown. The heart cannot be
set upon an object of which there is no idea in the understanding. The reasons which induce the soul to love,
must first be understood, before they can have a reasonable influence on the heart.

God hath given us the Bible, which is a book of instructions. But this book can be of no manner of profit
to us, any otherwise than as it conveys some knowledge
to the mind: it can profit us no more than if it were
written in the Chinese or Tartarian language, of which
we know not one word.

So the sacraments of the gospel can have a proper
effect no other way, than by conveying some knowledge.
They represent certain things by visible signs. And what
is the end of signs, but to convey some knowledge of the
things signified? Such is the nature of man, that nothing
can come at the heart, but through the door of the understanding: and there can be no spiritual knowledge
of that of which there is not first a rational knowledge.
It is impossible that any one should see the truth or
excellency of any doctrine of the gospel, who knows not
what that doctrine is. A man cannot see the wonderful

excellency and love of Christ in doing such and such things for sinners, unless his understanding be first informed how those things were done. He cannot have a taste of the sweetness and divine excellency of such and such things contained in divinity, unless he first have a notion that there are such and such things.

2. Without knowledge in divinity, none would differ from the most ignorant and barbarous heathens. The heathens remain in gross heathenish darkness, because they are not instructed, and have not obtained the knowledge of the truths of divinity. So if we live under the preaching of the gospel, this will make us to differ from them, only by conveying to us more knowledge of the things of divinity.

3. If a man have no knowledge of these things, the faculty of reason in him will be wholly in vain. The faculty of reason and understanding was given for actual understanding and knowledge. If a man have no actual knowledge, the faculty or capacity of knowing is of no use to him. And if he have actual knowledge, yet if he be destitute of the knowledge of those things which are the last end of his being, and for the sake of the knowledge of which he had more understanding given him than the beasts; then still his faculty of reason is in vain; he might as well have been a beast, as a man with this knowledge. But the things of divinity are the things to know which we had the faculty of reason given us. There are the things which appertain to the end of our being, and to the great business for which we are made. Therefore a man cannot have his faculty of understanding to any purpose, any further than he hath knowledge of the things of divinity.

So that this kind of knowledge is absolutely necessary. Other kinds of knowledge may be very useful. Some other sciences, such as astronomy, and natural philosophy, and geography, may be very excellent in their kind. But the knowledge of this divine science is infinitely more useful and important than that of all other sciences whatever.

I come now to the fourth, and principal thing proposed under the doctrine, viz., To give the reasons why all Christians should make a business of endeavoring to grow in the knowledge of divinity. This implies two things.

1. That Christians ought not to content themselves with such degrees of knowledge in divinity as they have already obtained. It should not satisfy them, that they know as much as is absolutely necessary to salvation, but should seek to make progress.

2. That this endeavoring to make progress in such knowledge ought not to be attended to as a thing by the by, but all Christians should make a business of it: they should look upon it as a part of their daily business, and no small part of it neither. It should be attended to as a considerable part of the work of their high calling. The reason of both these may appear in the following things.

(1) Our business should doubtless much consist in employing those faculties, by which we are distinguished from the beasts, about those things which are the main end of those faculties. The reason why we have faculties superior to those of the brutes given us, is, that we are indeed designed for a superior employment. That which the Creator intended should be our main employment, is something above what he intended the beasts for, and therefore hath given us superior powers. Therefore, without doubt, it should be a considerable part of our business to improve those superior faculties. But the

faculty by which we are chiefly distinguished from the brutes, is the faculty of understanding. It follows then, that we should make it our chief business to improve this faculty, and should by no means prosecute it as a business by the by. For us to make the improvement of this faculty a business by the by, is in effect for us to make us to make the faculty of understanding itself a by-faculty, if I may so speak, a faculty of less importance than others; whereas indeed it is the highest faculty we have.

But we cannot make a business of the improvement of our intellectual faculty, any otherwise than by making a business of improving ourselves in actual understanding and knowledge. So that those who make not this very much their business, but, instead of improving their understanding to acquire knowledge, are chiefly devoted to their inferior powers, to provide wherewithal to please their senses, and gratify their animal appetites, and so rather make their understanding a servant to their inferior powers, than their inferior powers servants to their understanding; not only behave themselves in a manner not becoming Christians, but also act as if they had forgotten that they are men, and that God hath set them above the brutes, by giving them understanding. . . .

(2) The things of divinity are things of superlative excellency, and are worthy that all should make a business of endeavoring to grow in the knowledge of them. There are no things so worthy to be known as these things. They are as much above those things which are treated of in other sciences, as heaven is above the earth. God himself, the eternal Three in One, is the chief object of this science; in the next place, Jesus Christ, as Godman and Mediator, and the glorious work of re-

demption, the most glorious work that ever was wrought; then the great things of the heavenly world, the glorious and eternal inheritance purchased by Christ, and promised in the gospel; the work of the Holy Spirit of God on the hearts of men; our duty to God, and the way in which we ourselves may become like angels, and like God himself in our measure: all these are objects of this science. . . .

(3) The things of divinity not only concern ministers, but are of infinite importance to all Christians. It is not with the doctrines of divinity as it is with the doctrines of philosophy and other sciences. These last are generally speculative points, which are of little concern in human life; and it very little alters the case as to our temporal or spiritual interests, whether we know them or not. Philosophers differ about them, some being of one opinion, and others of another. And while they are engaged in warm disputes about them, others may well leave them to dispute among themselves, without troubling their heads much about them; it being of little concern to them, whether the one or the other be in the right.

But it is not thus in matters of divinity. The doctrines of this nearly concern every one. They are about those things which relate to every man's eternal salvation and happiness. The common people cannot say, Let us leave these matters to ministers and divines; let them dispute them out among themselves as they can; they concern not us: for they are of infinite importance to every man. Those doctrines of divinity which relate to the essence, attributes, and subsistencies of God, concern all; as it is of infinite importance to common people, as well as to ministers, to know what kind of being God is. For he is the Being who hath made us all, "in whom we live,

and move, and have our being"; who is the Lord of all;
the Being to whom we are all accountable; is the last
end of our being, and the only fountain of our happiness. . . .

(4) We may argue from the great things which God
hath done in order to give us instruction in these things.
As to other sciences, he hath left us to ourselves, to the
light of our own reason. But the things of divinity being
of infinitely greater importance to us, he hath not left
us to an uncertain guide; but hath himself given us a
revelation of the truth in these matters, and hath done
very great things to convey and confirm to us this revelation; raising up many prophets in different ages, immediately inspiring them with his Holy Spirit, and con-
firming their doctrine with innumerable miracles or
wonderful works out of the established course of nature.
Yea, he raised up a succession of prophets, which was up-
held for several ages.

It was very much for this end that God separated the
people of Israel, in so wonderful a manner, from all
other people, and kept them separate; that to them
he might commit the oracles of God, and that from them
they might be communicated to the world. He hath also
often sent angels to bring divine instructions to men;
and hath often himself appeared to men in miraculous
symbols or representations of his presence; and now in
these last days hath sent his own Son into the world, to
be his great prophet, to teach us divinity; Heb. i. at the
beginning. By means of all, God hath given a book of
divine instructions, which contains the sum of divinity.
Now, these things hath God done, not only for the instruction of ministers and men of learning; but for the
instruction of all men, of all sorts, learned and unlearned, men, women, and children. And certainly if God

doth such great things to *teach* us, we would not to do little to *learn.* . . .

The name by which Christians are commonly called in the New Testament is *disciples,* the signification of which word is scholars or learners. All Christians are put into the school of Christ, where their business is to learn, or receive knowledge from Christ, their common master and teacher, and from those inferior teachers appointed by him to instruct in his name. . . .

APPLICATION

The use that I would make of this doctrine is, to exhort all diligently to endeavor to gain this kind of knowledge.

Consider yourselves as scholars or disciples, put into the school of Christ; and therefore be diligent to make proficiency in Christian knowledge. Content not yourselves with this, that you have been taught your catechism in your childhood, and that you know as much of the principles of religion as is necessary to salvation. So you will be guilty of what the apostle warns against, viz., going no further than laying the foundation of repentance from dead works, etc.

You are all called to be Christians, and this is your profession. Endeavor, therefore, to acquire knowledge in things which pertain to your profession. Let not your teachers have cause to complain, that while they spend and are spent, to impart knowledge to you, you take little pains to learn. It is a great encouragement to an instructor, to have such to teach as make a business of learning, bending their minds to it. This makes teaching a pleasure, when otherwise it will be a very heavy and burdensome task.

You all have by you a large treasure of divine knowledge, in that you have the Bible in your hands; therefore be not contented in possessing but little of this treasure. God hath spoken much to you in the Scripture; labor to understand as much of what he saith as you can. God hath made you all reasonable creatures; therefore let not the noble faculty of reason or understanding lie neglected. Content not yourselves with having so much knowledge as is thrown in your way, and as you receive in some sense unavoidably by the frequent inculcation of divine truth in the preaching of the word, of which you are obliged to be hearers, or as you accidentally gain in conversation; but let it be very much your business to search for it, and that with the same diligence and labor with which men are wont to dig in mines of silver and gold.

Especially I would advise those that are young to employ themselves in this way. Men are never too old to learn; but the time of youth is especially the time for learning; it is especially proper for gaining and storing up knowledge. . . .

I shall now conclude my discourse with some *directions* for the acquisition of this knowledge.

1. Be assiduous in reading the holy Scriptures. This is the fountain whence all knowledge in divinity must be derived. Therefore let not this treasure lie by you neglected. Every man of common understanding who can read, may, if he please, become well acquainted with the Scriptures. And what an excellent attainment would this be!

2. Content not yourselves with only a cursory reading, without regarding the sense. This is an ill way of reading, to which, however, many accustom themselves all their days. When you read, observe what you read.

Observe how things come in. Take notice of the drift of the discourse, and compare one Scripture with another. For the Scripture, by the harmony of the different parts of it, casts great light upon itself. We are expressly directed by Christ to *search* the Scriptures, which evidently intends something more than a mere cursory reading. And use means to find out the meaning of the Scripture. When you have it explained in the preaching of the word, take notice of it; and if at any time a Scripture that you did not understand be cleared up to your satisfaction, mark it, lay it up, and if possible remember it.

3. Procure, and diligently use other books which may help you to grow in this knowledge. There are many excellent books extant, which might greatly forward you in this knowledge, and afford you a very profitable and pleasant entertainment in your leisure hours. There is doubtless a great defect in many, that through a lothness to be at a little expense, they furnish themselves with no more helps of this nature. They have a few books indeed, which now and then on Sabbath days they read; but they have had them so long, and read them so often, that they are weary of them, and it is now become a dull story, a mere task to read them.

4. Improve conversation with others to this end. How much might persons promote each other's knowledge in divine things, if they would improve conversation as they might; if men that are ignorant were not ashamed to show their ignorance, and were willing to learn of others; if those that have knowledge would communicate it, without pride and ostentation; and if all were more disposed to enter on such conversation as would be for their mutual edification and instruction.

5. Seek not to grow in knowledge chiefly for the sake of applause, and to enable you to dispute with others;

but seek it for the benefit of your souls, and in order to practice. If applause be your end, you will not be so likely to be led to the knowledge of the truth, but may justly, as often is the case of those who are proud of their knowledge, be led into error to your own perdition. This being your end, if you should obtain much rational knowledge, it would not be likely to be of any benefit to you, but would puff you up with pride: 1 Cor. 8:1, *Knowledge puffeth up.*

6. Seek to God, that he would direct you, and bless you, in this pursuit after knowledge. This is the apostle's direction, James 1:5: *If any man lack wisdom, let him ask it of God, who giveth to all liberally, and upbraideth not.* God is the fountain of all divine knowledge. Prov. 2:6, *The Lord giveth wisdom: out of his mouth cometh knowledge and understanding.* Labor to be sensible of your own blindness and ignorance, and your need of the help of God, lest you be led into error, instead of true knowledge. 1 Cor. 3:18, *If any man would be wise, let him become a fool, that he may be wise.*

7. Practice according to what knowledge you have. This will be the way to know more. The Psalmist warmly recommends this way of seeking knowledge in divinity, from his own experience: Psal. 119:100, *I understand more than the ancients, because I keep thy precepts.* Christ also recommends the same: John 7:17, *if any man will do his will, he shall know of the doctrine, whether it be of God, or whether I speak of myself.*

SOURCE: Jonathan Edwards, "The Importance and Advantage of a Thorough Knowledge of Divine Truth," in *The Works of Jonathan Edwards in Four Volumes* (New York: Leavitt, Trow and Company, 1849), III, 2–4, 4–7, 7–8, 11, 14–15.

Each Man His Own Judge

NATHAN COLE

When simple, common people took seriously the challenge to search the scriptures for themselves, and when they doggedly set themselves to follow their findings in the face of all others, the old order was shaken beyond repair. Nathan Cole, whose first repsonse to Whitefield we have already seen (pages #2), was one of many such men. Cole continued his "quarrelling with God," begun with the hearing of Whitefield, for nearly twenty years, first joining a separate New Light congregation, and then, becoming convinced that infant baptism had no biblical warrant, moving into the baptist camp. The extract that follows is from a dialogue between Cole, the baptist, and a separate minister. Composed by Cole, probably from innumerable similar debates he had actually engaged in, the dialogue offers a prime example of what could, and did, happen. To the opponents of the Awakening the Coles of America offered perfect justification for their worst fears; even Edwards cringed. When each man interpreted the scripture according to his own light—old, new, or some intensity beyond—and differed with others, who was to say what interpretation was correct? A radical individualism, fragmented churches, a disdain for conventional propriety and standards of judgment, and a society in upheaval were the inevitable results when men like Cole decided

*"to lay aside all man's inventions and traditions and con-
stitutions, and take the Bible alone." Whether desirable
or undesirable, as posterity may judge, it was a great
awakening—the sleeping giant of the populace had been
roused.*

A DIALOGUE between a Separate Minister, and some
of his People and Cole; what was said to me, and my
Answers.

.   .   .

Sep. How did you come to turn baptist in your old
age?

Cole. I will tell you I have got more light about a
gospel church, than ever I had before, how it was built
by God's order, and no human contrivance, or wisdom
mixed in with God's wisdom. Now I will tell you how
I got more light, it was by searching the bible, for when
I was young, old people and the minister advised young
people to come and join to the church of Christ, and
come to the ordinance of the Lord's supper, for that is
a converting ordinance said they, and they called it a
church of Christ, and so I and many more joined to that
church, and I was in that old church about 14 years,
and then in the year 1741, God sent that blessed man,
Mr. Whitefield, through our land, and he under God,
was the means of my conversion, hearing him preach;
and now I soon see the old standing church was not in
gospel order, and then I looked in my mind, on the baptist old church, and though they had the bible most on
their side, about baptism, but I thought they was not
strict enough in receiving members, and then I looked
on the separate church, and I thought they was as near
a gospel church as we could get one, and I joined to

that church, and have been there about 14 years at Middletown; and now our minister, and some of the brethren
have got such a party spirit against the baptist, and he
printed a pamphlet against them, and prays and preaches
against them much, I hear, and there was such a noise
and bad spirit seemed to appear against the baptist, and
all three of the churches called themselves churches of
Christ, and I concluded to go to the bible, which is our
city of refuge, to flee to for our pattern, as God says to
Moses, concerning the tabernacle and ark, for God says
to Moses, *Look,* (take care) *that thou make them in all
things according to the pattern shewed thee in the
Mount.* Take notice, God says in all things; a strict
charge! must not alter the least jot or pin; and now I
conclude to lay aside all men's inventions and traditions
and constitutions, and take the bible alone, as if there
was no other man on earth, and certainly pick out the
true gospel church, ordered by God's spirit, set up by
the apostles, and no other church to be found in the
new-testament, but a real baptist church, and so I have
got more light, and have found which of the three
churches in dispute is a real gospel church, which I suppose I should not have known, if it had not been for
that sectary and party spirit, for our minister and
church have rejected several baptist churches, and will
make us offenders if we hear them preach, and deal with
us in the church, and cast us out, etc. . . . 3 John 9:10.
*I wrote unto the church, but Diotrephes who loveth to
have the pre-eminence among them, receiveth us not;
wherefore if I come, I will remember his deeds which he
doth, prating against us with malicious words, and not
content therewith: neither doth he himself receive the
brethren, and forbiddeth them that would, and casteth
them out of the church.* The brethren were baptists; and

so our minister and church have took such a vote that if
we obey, we must give up our consciences to man to be
lorded over, and not hear them good preachers, without
leave of man; *but we must obey God rather than man,
judge ye.* . . .

Sep. You say our churches are not gospel churches, we
call them so.

Cole. How can a church be a gospel church, unless it
be built upon the gospel, taken directly out of the bible,
and there is no other church to be found in the bible
or new testament, but a real baptist church, built upon
Christ, the rock with the believer's baptism; for that is
gospel, and no other churches can be gospel churches,
but them. Read the bible, and see; and read the practices of the apostles, and see; and read the examples of
all Christians in their day, and see. We are bidden to
follow their steps, as they follow Christ, and there is no
other church in the world that is to be called a gospel
church but that that God built by his holy Spirit in the
gospel. Read the bible and search carefully and certainly
pick out that true church that God built in the apostle's
day, and when you have found it, then join to it, if you
be a true believer, and come up to gospel obedience,
and do your duty according to God's command, in Solomon's Songs 1:7, 8. *Tell me, O thou whom my soul
loveth, where thou maketh thy flock to rest at noon?*
Answer, if thou know not, go forth by the foot-steps of
the flock, and feed thy kids beside the shepherd's tents.
Now if a Christian wants to know how to find the true
gospel church, God says, go forth by the foot-steps of the
flock, viz. Read the bible or new testament, and see if
you can find any other church, but a baptist church,
built upon Christ, the rock with the believer's baptism;
we read, one Lord, one faith, one baptism, viz. Believer's

baptism, not two, but one baptism; but infant baptizers have got another baptism of unbelievers which is not to be found in the bible. They say, we will baptize them, and they may believe afterwards; whose baptism will stand, do you say, God's or your's? God says one baptism, not two, directly contrary to God; what will you say, when God shall say to you, Who hath required this at your hands? Dost you say, you had it from his word in the bible? No, surely, not for unbelievers, young or old. But God says, search the scriptures, *for in them you think you have eternal life, for they are them that testify of me*, etc. . . .

Sep. You have broken church covenant in going out from us.

Cole. I came out from your errors, to keep covenant with God, and the true gospel church, and not partake with them errors, as may be seen in what is written, etc. more separate. Acts 2:39. *For the promise is unto you, and to your children, and to all that are afar off, even as many as the Lord our God shall call.*

Now take notice, not all your children, but as many as the Lord our God shall call to a saving conversion to Jesus Christ, and none but such will be saved, or be heirs to the promise. Let you baptize or not, it doth not alter the case at all, for all things that are brought into the worship of God that he hath not required, is sinful; and infant baptism is not required, and so not pleasing to him, but contrary to him or his order.

Once more. A baptist preacher said to a separate preacher, are not the ordinances of God spiritual ordinances; he said, yes. The baptist said, why then will you apply a spiritual ordinance upon one that you know not to be spiritual, which ended the dispute.

To conclude; to the law and to the testimony, if not according to that, 'tis for want of light.

AMEN

SOURCE: Nathan Cole, *A Dialogue between a separate Minister . . . and Cole* (Hartford: 1779?), pp. 9–11, 12–14, 15.

Poetry for the Masses

SAMUEL DAVIES

Perhaps all major cultural movements rooted in a new emotional awareness have produced songs and singing— from the psalmody of the Reformation to the rock music of the mid-twentieth century "counter culture." The Great Awakening, certainly, was no exception: awakened Presbyterians, Baptists, and Methodists opened, closed, and interrupted their prayer meetings and revival services with the singing of hymns, old and new. Of all the hymn writers of the Awakening Samuel Davies may have been the most prolific. He again and again composed poems and hymns for his own pleasure and for the edification of his church people. He gladly admitted that these were not great poetry; but he felt they were tailored to the interests and education of unlettered persons, whose capacity to enjoy beauty, he was convinced, was genuine and deserving of respect. As for those of more discriminating and polished sensitivities, though he did not disparage their refined tastes, he advised them to look else-

*where for their aesthetic satisfaction. The following ex-
cerpt, taken from Davies' introduction to a collection of
his poems, expresses well his own blend of religious and
educational egalitarianism.*

There is in almost all mankind an innate love of
harmony; which gives those things that are conveyed to
their minds in a poetical vehicle a peculiar relish. This
harmonious turn of mind is the stamp of heaven, the
image of the eternal author of order; and 'tis He that
teaches us to feel the charms of poetry. . . .

And no doubt this, as well as the other powers and
natural gifts of the human mind, was given for valuable
purposes; and ought to be improved as an agreeable
avenue for the introduction of divine things.

'Tis true, it is not equally vigorous in persons of different constitutions and education. It admits of improvement, as well as the other faculties of the soul; and the
disparity will appear according to the strength of the
innate principle, and the degrees of cultivation:

> Yet if we look more closely, we shall find
> Most have the Seeds implanted in their Mind:
> Nature affords at least a glimm'ring Light;
> The Lines, tho' touch'd but faintly, are drawn right.

Persons of a refined and judicious taste are conscious
of peculiar sensations, when they meet with entertainment suitable to them. They take but little notice of
those trifling appendages of poetry, which are the most
agreeable to persons of a coarse relish; as the jingling of
syllables, the equality of numbers, the ambiguous pun,
or witty turn: But they are captivated with the lively
images of fancy, the grandeur of ideas, the flowers of
language, the pomp of style, and the proper arrange-

ment of well-disposed periods. Such readers are imaginary actors of all the scenes of the poet's imagination; and a genius that can write as well as they can read, has an entire dominion over their passions. . . .

Sublime poetry is to such a series of transports; and flat and dull, is utterly intolerable, they sicken at the sight: As nice palates have a more lively relish of an agreeable dish, and a stronger disgust to what is nauseous, than persons of a coarser taste. And as their pleasure is more refined, so it is more rare; they are offended where others are pleased, and nauseate what others relish. None but an Homer or Virgil, a Milton or Pope, can furnish them with proper entertainment. And may there always be some exalted genius to profit and please such delicate minds, and refine them for celestial pleasure, which alone can satisfy their sublime aspirations! But I am convinced by a consciousness of my incapacity, that this does not belong to my province. If any such should be so curious as to look into the following poems, and receive them with but cold approbation; I shall gratefully acknowledge it as an instance of a generous candor of taste. Or if they lay them aside, I hope they will do it with that disposition which we discover towards the over-officious attempts of impotent benevolence; or with that calmness and indifferency with which we reject things that were not intended for our entertainment or molestation, but belong wholly to others.

But there are few among us of this character; as there are but few that can write for their entertainment. And to consult the advantage of such only, is as unreasonable as if the English legislature should tolerate none but silken manufactures. The generality of mankind have neither opportunity nor perhaps capacity for these refinements; and yet are capable of a glorious immortality, and the purer joys of paradise. For the sake of such I write; and to some of them my essays will not be unacceptable. They may not accurately discern the fairest charms of poetry; yet they generally are pleased with the consonance of final syllables, proportioned numbers, etc. So that they are more ready to receive and retain those things which are conveyed into their minds in this form than in heavy and tiresome prose: For (if the modern taste will pardon a citation out of that antiquated divine wit, Herbert).

> A Verse may hit him whom a Sermon flies,
> And turn Delight into a Sacrifice.

On this account I have frequently thought the divine art of poetry might be made peculiarly subservient in the interests of religion and virtue; and lamented the common prostitution of the heavenly muse to the meanest and most wicked purposes: 'Tis certainly a sacrilege that heaven will avenge; and which lascivious wits will at last regret. Many of the conquests of vice have been owing to this abuse. This has clothed her in the most fallacious charms; and given the monster a syren's voice, to enchant the unthinking into ruin. And if we can make reprisals, and allure men to the amiable glories of holiness, by the proper use of that art, which so successfully allured them to embrace even the horrid charms of sin; it will be a glorious enterprize. And may Almighty Grace dispose those whom nature has animated with this sacred fire, to kindle it on the divine altar! There it glows with the brightest lustre; and 'tis a pity it should waste itself away in pestiferous fumes in the temple of vice and impiety.

There are thousands to attempt the reformation of mankind in other more common, and therefore less pleasing ways; while there are but few qualified to attempt it in this; and therefore those that are blest with the least spark of poetic fire ought not to suffocate it. . . .

SOURCE: Samuel Davies, *Miscellaneous Poems Chiefly on Divine Subjects; In Two Books; Published for the Religious Entertainment of Christians in General* (Williamsburg: William Hunter, 1752), pp. iv, v, vi–viii.

The Reading Revivals

SAMUEL DAVIES

Again and again during the Awakening laymen took the initiative, sometimes in the face of clerical opposition, sometimes carrying their ministers with them. The Awakening in Hanover County, Virginia, as described in this letter from Samuel Davies to friends in Britain, began wholly as a lay movement, under lay initiative and with lay leadership, since at first there were no clergy to be had. After the "reading revivals" were underway young Log College graduates began moving into the area to provide ministerial support. Even then, owing to the continuing shortage of ministers, the ability to read and the availability of reading materials remained essential "private means" of sustaining the revivals.

Hanover, Virginia
June 28, 1751

Dear Sir,

As an account of the *rise, progress* and *present situation* of religion in VIRGINIA, may not only gratify good people, but animate their prayers for us, I should charge myself with a criminal neglect by delaying or refusing to publish the marvellous works of the Almighty among us.

My design, SIR, is not to boast of proselytes, or to asperse the Church of England here established; but I hope I may observe, without the umbrage of calumny, what glares with irresistible evidence, that religion has been, and in most parts of the Colony still is, in a very low state: Various vices are triumphant, and even a form of godliness is not common. I cannot find there has been a Dissenting Minister settled in Virginia, till lately, since its first plantation; and many of the populace knew little or nothing of any denomination, but that in which they had been educated.

I have reason to hope that there are a few names in various parts of the Colony, who are sincerely seeking the Lord in the Communion of the Church of England. Some of this happy character I found in and about Hanover, before the late revival of religion. Such were awakened, as they told me, either by their own *serious reflections,* suggested and enforced by divine energy; or on *reading* some authors of the last century, such as Boston, Baxter, Flavel, Bunyan, etc. and they often wondered if there were such doctrines taught any where in the world at present, as they found in the writings of these good men. In this case about ten or twelve persons, who are now members of my congregation, continued for some time.

One Mr. Samuel Morris, a person of an active, social spirit, who had been extremely anxious about his eternal state, and unweariedly seeking relief by all the means within his reach, at length obtained a discovery of that glorious method of salvation through JESUS CHRIST, to which sinners, *from all the ends of the earth,* look and are saved; and where they universally agree to fix all their hopes. After this discovery of the Gospel, his soul was anxious for the salvation of his neighbours, and inflamed with zeal to use means to awaken them; to which end he *read* to them such authors as had been most useful to himself. By these means a few of his neighbours were made more thoughtful about religion than usual, who had lived till then in a careless ignorance of it. I have prevailed, SIR, with this my good friend, who was the principal private instrument of promoting the revival of religion, to give me a narrative of its *rise* and *progress* from this period to my settlement here, which I now present to you.

In the year 1743, a young gentleman arrived from Scotland with some manuscript sermons of the Reverend Mr. Whitefield's, preached in Glasgow, taken from his mouth in short-hand; which, after I had read with great liking and benefit, I invited my neighbours to come and hear: the plainness, popularity, and fervency of the discourses, being peculiarly fitted to affect our unimproved minds, and the good Lord rendering the word efficacious, many were convinced of their guilt and misery, and constrained to seek salvation with the greatest solicitude. A considerable number met every sabbath to hear these sermons. My dwelling-house was too small to contain the people, whereupon we determined to build a place merely for *reading*. By this very mean sundry were solemnly awakened, and their conduct ever since is a living attestation of the happy issue of their impressions. When the report of these sermons, and the effect produced by *reading* them was spread abroad, I was invited to several places to read them, at a considerable distance; and by this means the concern was propagated. Thus we continued till Providence afforded us an unexpected opportunity of hearing the Rev. Mr. Robinson, a zealous, faithful Minister of CHRIST, whose labours have been greatly blessed in Pennsylvania, Maryland, and other parts.

Having some information of him, he had an invitation sent him to come and preach to us. He continued preaching to us four days successively. It is hard for the liveliest imagination to form an idea of the condition of the assembly, on these glorious days of the Son of Man. Such of us as had been longing after a Gospel-ministry were lost in an agreeable confusion of serious passions; surprised, astonished, pleased, enraptured! so that we were hardly capable of self-government. We were overwhelmed with the unexpected goodness of GOD, in allowing us to hear the Gospel *preached* in a manner that even surpassed our former wishes, much more our hopes. Many that came through curiosity were *pricked to the heart,* and but few in the numerous assemblies on these four days appeared unaffected. Before he left us, he put us into a method of *praying* and *singing* together at our public meetings, which we had before omitted.

We were afterwards occasionally visited by the Reverend Messieurs F. Blain, John Roan, Gilbert and William Tennants, etc. whose services were greatly prospered. In the absence of whom we returned to our former way of *reading,* etc. The blessing of GOD remarkably attended these *private* means; it was really astonishing to observe the solemn impressions begun and continued in many by hearing good discourses *read.* I had repeated invitations to come to many places round, some of them thirty or forty miles distant, to *read.* Considerable numbers attended with solicitous regard; and sundry were, in a judgment of charity, truly converted unto GOD: and thereupon erected Meeting-Houses, and chose *readers* among themselves; by which the work was more extensively carried on.

Being thus destitute of a minister, we were joyfully surprised to hear that the Reverend Mr. Davies, our present pastor, was sent by the Presbytery to supply us about six weeks, in spring, Anno 1747. For which seasonable instance of the divine goodness we desire to offer up our grateful praises, etc.

Being fully convinced, SIR, that Hanover stood in greater need of a minister than any place I knew, I accepted of their call to settle there, and obtained the licensure of four meeting-houses in October 1748. In some of which you will see perhaps four or five hundred hearers, and sometimes twice that number; the church-people in general being eager to hear. This I looked upon at first as proceeding from mere curiosity; but as it continues in general without abatement, and in some places seems to increase, I cannot but look upon it as an happy presage, etc.

SOURCE: *Letters from the Rev. Samuel Davies, and Others, Shewing the State of Religion in Virginia, South Carolina, etc., particularly Among the Negroes* (London: J. and W. Oliver, 1761), pp. 3–8.

Indian Missions

ELEAZAR WHEELOCK

The Great Awakening reinvigorated missionary work among the Indians—an on and off concern of the churches since the first settling of the New World. A sizable number of New Light ministers, including Edwards himself, engaged in missionary work among the Indians, preaching and conducting schools; some of them even learning the Algonquian tongue. Eleazar Wheelock's school for Indian boys at Lebanon, Connecticut, was probably the best known and most permanent of these missionary enterprises. Samson Occum, one of Wheelock's most famous Indian students, became an ordained New Light minister, served as a missionary himself to tribes on Long Island and upper New York, and in 1765–68 journeyed to England to help raise funds for the school at Lebanon. The Lebanon school was aided by various benevolent and missionary societies in Britain. The Society in Scotland for Propagating Christian Knowledge *was especially active in supporting missionaries in New England, New Jersey, and Pennsylvania. The letter printed here, however, was probably written by Wheelock to the* Society in London for Promoting Religious Knowledge among the Poor, *thanking them for their help and pleading for more.*

Boston, N.E.
May 4, 1761

Dear SIR,

Your letter came safe to hand. The generous donation of the M— of L—n has encouraged and animated me in the Indian affairs, and I believe will encourage others for the same purpose: The hearts and minds of people are more open to the furtherance of the great design than ever they were. The work of GOD is gloriously revived in several parts of *Connecticut*. After I had appointed this journey, the spirit of conviction, which before appeared in my school, and among my people, arose to such an height as would have stopt my journey had my motives to it been only secular. The worst of my *English* scholars was surprizingly, and I trust savingly wrought upon, and the most of them humbled under a spirit of bondage; and it seemed evidently spreading and increasing among my people. A joyful omen this that GOD is making a way for his mercy to a guilty land.

I am here requested, pursuant to repeated and pressing desires of the *Indians* at *Onohoquake* river, and an hundred miles back, that I would be instrumental to procure them a minister or ministers. I doubt not but that, and several other favors I have to ask for the *Indians* will be readily granted. Mr. *Occam,* my black son, preached in my pulpit five sabbaths ago to a full assembly, and to good acceptance. A rare sight indeed! He is going on a mission to the *Oncadia Indians* as soon as he can get ready, supported by a number of gentlemen in *New-York*.

The door is wide open to send the Gospel to the most distant tribes. Nothing is wanting but missionaries, interpreters, and money: As to which, we want the help of all that love the Lord JESUS CHRIST. There is much to be done, and now if ever is the time: The *Indians* are now very tame. They fear the *English* will do by them as they are conscious they would do by us, if the tables were turned. I have enough to say to fill a volume. I wish I had a collection of *books* of the right sort for my *Indian* boys, I expect my school will soon be full of them. You have heard that dear President *Davies* is no more: That dear college—alas!—but it is enough that GOD presides! I am, in haste,

Yours, etc.

E. WHEELOCK.

SOURCE: *Letters from the Rev. Samuel Davies, and Others, Shewing the State of Religion in Virginia, South Carolina, etc., particularly Among the Negroes* (London: J. and W. Oliver, 1761), pp. 31–33.

The Black Man: A Lost Opportunity
JOHN TODD

Concern for black people was never as intense among the Awakeners as was their missionary zeal toward the Indians. After the 1750's, however, and especially as the revivals moved into southern backcountry, the attention of the Awakeners was drawn increasingly to the plight of black people, who, it was noted, responded with special eagerness and warmth to the new preaching. In fact, for a time the Awakening showed signs of possessing genuine revolutionary potential for black liberation. While some Baptist and Methodist churches in the south did continue to maintain integrated churches well into the nineteenth century, the radical anti-slavery potential of the Awakening was never realized. No consistent anti-slavery position was ever developed on a wide front, and all too often the message of the equality of all men before God was compromised in the face of social practice.

In New England the most consistent New Light opponent of slavery was Samuel Hopkins, a devoted disciple of Jonathan Edwards, but his radical position was not shared by many. In the south, Samuel Davies, who worked indefatigably to bring religion and literacy to the blacks, and the one man who might have successfully mounted a campaign for their freedom, never brought himself to do so. Davies, even on occasion, sought support for his church work by arguing that religion among the blacks would dampen any insurrectionary desires they might have.

The following letter from John Todd in Virginia was also written to the Society *in* London *for* Promoting Religious Knowledge Among the Poor *in the 1750's when the Awakeners were most active in working among neglected groups of society. It is plainly the letter of a missionary designed to move his benevolent supporters to ever more heroic feats of giving. The letter is particularly interesting, however, not only for its illustration of the popular appeal of the Awakening, but also for the direct connection the writer saw between religious interest and the development of basic literacy skills. Popular religion and popular education frequently were of a piece. John Todd was also the founder of an academy in Augusta County, Virginia, that helped lay the foundation for Hampden-Sydney College later.*

Hanover, Virginia
November 18, 1758

Dear SIR,

I BEG leave to inform you that I have with unspeakable pleasure and satisfaction distributed the greatest part of the books I had the happiness to receive from that charitable SOCIETY, which I am persuaded is approved of GOD, and is inexpressibly dear to multitudes in this guilty and distant land. The blessing of many ready to perish I doubt not will rest upon the good benefactors.

With uncommon eagerness, multitudes of *negroes* and *white* people flocked to my house to get books, upon the first notice of my having them to dispose of; they received them with the utmost thankfulness, and with serious promises religiously to improve them. The poor *slaves* are now commonly engaged in learning to read; some of them can read the Bible, others can only spell; and some are just learning their letters. But there is a general alteration among them for the better. The sacred hours of the *sabbath,* that used to be spent in frolicking, dancing, and other profane courses, are now employed in attending upon public ordinances, in learning to read at home, or in praying together, and singing the praises of GOD and the Lamb. A delightful change as to many, but especially in the pious few who give good evidence that it is in them a saving change.

What joy, what transport would it afford the truly pious among you, to see a goodly number of these poor *Africans* sit down at a sacramental table! not like frozen formalists, but like affectionate, serious Christians, unable to rise up from a table appointed to commemorate a Redeemer's love, with dry eyes!

It has given me great distress, that I have been forced to turn away *empty* several of these poor creatures, who frequently come to me for *books.* I am, with most unfeigned thanks to the SOCIETY for favors received,

Yours, etc.

JOHN TODD.

SOURCE: *Letters from the Rev. Samuel Davies, and Others, Shewing the State of Religion in Virginia, South Carolina, etc., particularly Among the Negroes* (London: J. and W. Oliver, 1761), pp. 15–16.

Popularization or Vulgarization?

CHARLES BROCKWELL

*The following letter was written by Charles Brock-
well, an Episcopal minister in Salem, Massachusetts,
working under the auspices of the* Society for the Propagation of the Gospel in Foreign Parts *(S.P.G.), the missionary arm of the Anglican Church in the colonies.
Episcopalians in America appeared as arch-villains in the
eyes of the Awakeners, who considered them major perpetrators of the Arminian heresy. Not surprisingly, most
Episcopalians were implacable foes of the Awakening,
and among its most vocal critics. In his letter to the
S.P.G. secretary in England, Brockwell makes vividly
clear why he for one was convinced that the populariza-
tion of religion could only result in the vulgarization of
religion and everything else.*

Salem, February 18, 1741/2

Reverend Sir,

It is impossible to relate the convulsions into which
the whole country is thrown by a set of enthusiasts that
stroll about haranguing the admiring vulgar in *extem-
pore* nonsense, nor is it confined to these only, for men,
women, children, servants, and negroes are now become
(as they phrase it) exhorters. Their behavior is indeed
as shocking, as uncommon, their groans, cries, screams,
and agonies must affect the spectators were they never
so obdurate and draw tears even from the most resolute,

whilst the ridiculous and frantic gestures of others cannot but excite both laughter and contempt, some leap-
ing, some laughing, some singing, some clapping one
another upon the back, etc. The tragic scene is performed by such as are entering into the pangs of the
New Birth; the comic by those who are got through and
those are so truly enthusiastic, that they tell you they
saw the Joys of Heaven, can describe its situation, inhabitants, employments, and have seen their names entered into the Book of Life and can point out the writer,
character and pen. And like the Papists support their
fraud by recommending every dream as a divine vision
and every idle untruth as a revelation to the admiring
multitude. Their works may justly be called the works
of darkness as acted in the night and often continued to
the noon of the next day and the sleep of children deprived of their natural rest is called a trance, and their
uncouth dreams (occasioned from the awfulness of the
place, the number of lights, the variety of action among
the people, some praying, some exhorting, some swooning, etc.) are deemed no less than heavenly discoveries.
In Connecticut, the next government, 'tis said many
have laid their Bibles aside; and some have burnt them,
as useless to those who are so plenteously filled with the
Spirit, as to cry out enough Lord! In short Sir, such confusion, disorder, and irregularity eye never beheld. The
illusion of the French Prophets, Anno 1707, was nothing
to this, and unless as to that, some unexpected accident
put a period to this, I know not but this year for enthusiasm may be as memorable as was 1692 for witchcraft
for the converted cry out upon the unregenerated, as
the afflicted did then upon the poor innocent wretches
that unjustly suffered. Rogers of Ipswich, one of this
pseudo apostled, displayed his talent in the town on

Sunday the 24th January and continued here so doing until the Thursday following, when he left his auditory in charge to one Elvins, a baker, who holds forth every Thursday, and though a fellow of consummate ignorance is nevertheless followed by great multitudes and much cried up. But I thank God that few of my Church went to hear either of them, and those that did wholly disliked them. I having taken true pains, both in public and private to arm them against the approaching danger which was like to beset them on either side.

Provisions of all sorts have doubled the price on account of the war, and the immemorable severity of the last winter so that it is impossible for me to subsist on my present salary especially as trading is now so decayed that my people cannot punctually comply with their contract. But of this I shall give you a further account when I have the happiness of seeing you, for which I only wait the Societie's leave. I beg you would be pleased to present my duty to the Society and my Father and believe me to be,

Reverend Sir,

Your most obliged Humble Servant,

CHA. BROCKWELL.

P.S. A noted teacher in this town is suspected of forgery, of which if he next July Court should be found guilty, I am pretty confident many of his Congregation will draw off to the Church of England and those of the better sort.

SOURCE: Charles Brockwell, "Letter to the Secretary of the Secretary of the S.P.G.," Salem, Mass., February 18, 1742, in William S. Perry, ed., *Historical Collections Relating to the American Colonial Church,* Vol. III, *Massachusetts* (Hartford, Conn.: The Church Press, 1873), pp. 453–54.

Reading and Revivalism

TIMOTHY CUTLER

In 1722, Timothy Cutler, Rector of Yale College, delivered a profound shock to New England congregationalism when he and two college tutors announced their decision to join the Church of England, and to sail for London to receive ordination as Anglican ministers. Upon his return Cutler was appointed by the S.P.G. to the new Christ Church in Boston, which under his leadership became one of the chief strongholds of Anglicanism in New England.

Cutler, like many other Anglicans, steadfastly opposed the Awakening. In the following letter extract to the Secretary of the S.P.G. in London Cutler describes the Awakening as the colonial expression of the "dissenting interest" and outlook of the non-Anglican protestants of England. Despite his initial assertion of confidence that few members of Episcopalian churches would be swayed by revivalist preachers, he, nevertheless, betrays a growing sense of alarm. Of special interest is his observation—and fear—of a spreading lay interest in the reading of religious literature, and his determination to fight fire with fire.

Boston, N.E.
December 30, 1742

Dear Sir,

The Dissenting Interest now suffers greatly from the animosity and confusion which enthusiasm has spread all over this town and country and a prevailing cry among them is for sounder doctrine and regenerate converted ministers; this multiplies separations, and many have forsaken their stated places of worship and their former teachers, and heaped up other gifted men and women whom they attend on in the Sundays in private houses; besides that several new congregations are formed by it, and it is probable that by such private meetings in this town we may have a new Anabaptist conventicle set up, if not some others.

Through the goodness of God, the quiet order and number of the people of our several churches in this town is preserved and we are rather on the gaining hand, and should itinerants from whom we have been delivered for a pretty while be again let loose upon us we are little apprehensive of any troublesome effects from them, and we would hope that the loss of any would be only an exchange to advantage, as it has been for our teachers have difficulty enough to detain many of their soberest and discreet hearers from us.

However there is reason sufficient for us all to be weary of these things; the inconveniences are general and may reach many succeeding generations: order, peace, justice, and relative duties become very low prized; religion is corrupted in theory and practice and we fear many will be tempted to lay all aside. Books of this unhappy tendency, books Calvinistic, enthusiastical, and antinomian do abound; the press here never had so full employ before, nor were people ever so busy in reading. Our antidotes to them are mostly from Dissenters, without proper guards and limitations and consequently one error is assaulted by another. I therefore humbly wish for the assistance of the honorable Society in books adapted to our present case.

Most thankful & Obedt Servt

TIMOTHY CUTLER

SOURCE: Timothy Cutler, "Letter to the Secretary of the S.P.G.," Boston. December 30, 1742, in William S. Perry, ed., *Historical Collections Relating to the American Colonial Church*, Vol. III, Massachusetts (Hartford, Conn.: The Church Press, 1873), pp. 367–368.

The Sources and the Uses of Knowledge

When Jonathan Edwards and Charles Chauncy attempted in public print to justify their religious positions intellectually, they found themselves unable to remain within the categories of discussion bequeathed them by tradition. They were also forced to bring to consciousness and to lay bare their deepest philosophical assumptions about human nature and society. In so doing they produced some of the most fascinating intellectual documents of colonial America. Although not addressed to education as such, the discussions of reason and emotion, knowledge and character, learning and social organization that infuse the religious debate of the following documents touch directly on some of the most fundamental of educational issues.

An Enlightened Mind

CHARLES CHAUNCY

The Reverend Charles Chauncy of Boston was the foremost critic of the Awakening. He corresponded with anti-revivalists throughout the colonies and in Great Britain, he collected incidents from every quarter to bolster his cause, and he published and preached repeatedly against the "enthusiastical spirit." The largest and most comprehensive attack to be leveled against the Awakening was his Seasonable Thoughts on the State of Religion in New England *(1743), from which the following selections are taken. Not content merely to rely on reports from others and on what he had witnessed in and around Boston, Chauncy prepared himself for his work by undertaking a three-hundred-mile trip through New England, visiting various towns and churches in Massachusetts and Connecticut, and amassing materials on the dangers of the awakening temper. More than a massive condemnation of the emotionalism, censoriousness, and libertinism he saw following inevitably in the wake of revivalism, his work is also a firm assertion that rationalism, discipline, and civility are the only sure foundations of true religion and the good society.*

There never was a time, in this land, wherein there was such flocking after some particular ministers, and glorying in them, as though they were GODS rather than men; never a time, wherein men's professions and affections rose higher; never a time, wherein conversions, numerous conversions were so much boasted of: Would to GOD, there was no reason to suspect the truth of any one of them! But it ought always to be remembered, there may be a very specious show, where there is not the substance of religion: Nor are persons without danger of resting in the former, to the neglect of the latter: And, it may be feared, whether this danger has not been greatly increased, while so many have been encouraged to look upon themselves as in a state of grace, without that proof of the reality of their conversion, which might reasonably be expected. There has certainly been too much haste, as well as positiveness, in declaring these and those, in this and the other place, to have passed from death to life: A judgment has been too commonly formed of men's spiritual condition, more from their affections, than the permanent temper of their minds discovered in the habitual conduct of their lives; not duly considering how precarious that religion must be which has its rise from the passions, and not any thorough change in the understanding and will.

Much, I am sensible, has been said, in these days, of a work of GOD going on in the land: And I trust, this has all along been the case with this people, from the days of our fathers: And I doubt not, 'tis so now; nay, I charitably hope, there have been more numerous instances of saving conversion, in the years past, than usual: But must it not be said, at the same time, that there have been more disorders and greater extravagances than common: And what is of still more dangerous tendency, has not the great talk of a revival of religion arisen more from the general appearance of some extraordinaries (which there may be where there is not the power

of godliness), than from such things as are sure evidences
of a real work of GOD in men's hearts? I am clearly satisfied this is the truth of the case, however unwilling
some may be to own it.

Nor have people been so plainly and faithfully taught,
as it were to be wished, what a work of GOD is, or how
to distinguish between those things which are undoubted
marks of such a work, and those which are not. They
have often been told of the glorious work of GOD; his
work, so as was never before seen in our own, or father's days. . . .

These are the reasons, why I can't entertain so high
an opinion as some others do, of the terrors appearing
in strange bodily effects, which have been so common of
late in this land.

It will possibly be said, I have, in saying these things,
reflected disgrace upon the work of conviction. If I had
had such a thought of the matter, I should have suppressed what is here offered. Those, in my opinion, do
the greatest dishonor to the blessed SPIRIT, and his
influence upon the hearts of sinners in the business
of conviction, who make no distinction between those
fears that are the effect of truth duly impressed upon the
mind, and those that arise from an affrightened imagination. And to speak freely, I am clearly in the sentiment,
that the great stress that has been laid upon such terrors,
as have evidently been produced by the mechanical influence of awful words and frightful gestures, has been a
great disservice to the interest of religion. Nay, I am not
without fear, lest the tremendous threatening of GOD
have, by some, been profanely made use of, while, under the pretence of awakening men's consciences, they
have thundered out death and damnation, in a manner
more fit for the stage than the sacred desk, and so as to

astonish the imagination rather than possess the mind of a reasonable conviction of these awful truths of GOD. I am not against the preaching of terror; but whenever this is done, it ought to be in a way that may enlighten the mind, as well as alarm the passions: And I am greatly mistaken, if this has been the practice, among some sort of preachers, so much as it ought to be. And to this it may be owing, that religion, of late, has been more a commotion in the passions, than a change in the temper of the mind. Not but that, I think, a lasting change has been wrought in a number; though I could wish I had reason to say it was so great a number as some pretend. Nay, I am not without hopes, that some even of those who have been frightened into shrieks and fits, are become new-men; but then, I have no other thought, in the general, of the surprise they were thrown into than of the surprise by a terrible clap of thunder, or the shock of an earthquake: They might hereby be awakened to consideration, and put upon waiting upon GOD in his own Way, 'till a work of grace has been effected in them. . . .

The true account to be given of the many and great mistakes of the present day, about the SPIRIT's influence, is not the newness of the thing, the not having felt it before; but a notorious error generally prevailing, as to the way and manner of judging in this matter. People, in order to know, whether the influences they are under, are from the SPIRIT, don't carefully examine them by the word of GOD, and view the change they produce in the moral state of their minds, and of their lives, but hastily conclude such and such internal motions to be divine impressions, merely from the perception they have of them. They are ready, at once, if this is unusual, or strong, to take it for some influence from above, to speak of it as such, and to act accordingly. This is the error of the present day; and 'tis indeed the *proton Pseudos,* the first and grand delusion: And where this prevails, we need not be at a loss to know the true spring of other errors. As to the multitudes who are brought into such new, and (to them) unheard of circumstances, 'tis true, they are illiterate, and young people; but this notwithstanding, if the newness of their circumstances is such as is proper to new creatures, they will, in their general behavior, discover the true spirit and genius of this sort of persons. 'Tis a great mistake to think, that the new nature, or those influences that produce it, however extraordinary, are apt to put men upon making wrong and strange judgments, either of persons or things. They have contrary tendency: and 'tis a reproach to them both, to suppose otherwise. A mere passionate religion, 'tis true, has always led to this, and always will; but not that which enlightens the understanding, renews the will, and makes the heart good and honest. How far 'tis a truth, that this people have scarce heard of such a thing as the outpouring of the SPIRIT of GOD, or had no notion of it, may admit of dispute; but that the outpouring of the SPIRIT should introduce such a state of things, as that those upon whom he has been poured out should not know how to behave, will, I think, admit of no good plea in its defence. 'Tis a plain case, one of the main ends of the outpouring of the SPIRIT is to dispose and enable people to behave as Christians, in their various stations, relations and conditions of life; and if instead of this, they are thrown into such a strange state, as that they can't behave as they ought to do, not in here and there a perplexed case, but in some of the most obvious and essential points of practice; let who will call this an outpouring of the

SPIRIT, 'tis not such an one as the Bible knows any thing of. And 'tis nothing short of a gross reflection on the blessed SPIRIT, to speak of him as wonderfully poured out upon a people, and, at the same time, to suppose such a state of things arising therefrom, as that people may run into very ill conduct, and it not be thought strange, if they do so. . . .

But the wonder is, how an extraordinary discovery of the greatness and excellency of GOD, the importance of eternal things, and the preciousness of souls, and the danger of their perishing, should make men vain and conceited, full of themselves, and apt to throw contempt on others; how it should loosen men's tongues to utter such language as would not be seemly, even in those who profess no sense of GOD, or divine things; how it should lead them into wrong sentiments in religion, blind their eyes as to some of the most plain points of doctrine; and in a word, dispose them to such things as are called in Scripture, the works of the flesh.

These don't look like the fruit of extraordinary discoveries of GOD; but they are the very things which may be expected, where men's passions are raised to an extraordinary height, without a proportionable degree of light in their understandings.

Such high affections, I know, are freely spoken of as owing to the influence of the SPIRIT of GOD; and this, when there is not given "strength of understanding in proportion"; and by means hereof, the subjects of these affections may be driven, "through error, into an irregular and sinful conduct." But it may justly be questioned, whether extraordinary warmth in the passions, when there is not answerable light in the mind, is so much owing to the SPIRIT of GOD, as some may be ready to imagine. For is it reasonable to think, that the divine SPIRIT, in dealing with men in a way of grace, and in order to make them good Christians, would give their passions the *chief* sway over them? Would not this be to invert their frame? To place the dominion in those powers, which were made to be kept in subjection? And would the all wise GOD introduce such a state of things in the human mind? Can this be the effect of the out-pouring of his SPIRIT? It ought not to be supposed. One of the most essential things necessary in the new-forming men, is the reduction of their passions to a proper regimen, i.e. the government of a sanctified un-derstanding. And 'till this is effected, they may be called New-Creatures, but they are far from deserving this character. Reasonable beings are not to be guided by passion or affection, though the object of it should be GOD, and the things of another world. They need, even in this case, to be under the government of a well in-structed judgment. Nay, when men's passions are raised to an extraordinary height, if they have not, at the same time, a due balance of light and knowledge in their minds, they are so far from being in a more desirable state on this account, that they are in circumstances of extreme hazard. There is no wildness, but they are liable to be hurried into it; there is no temptation, but they are exposed to be drawn aside by it; nor has the Devil ever greater advantage against them, to make a prey of them, and lead them captive at his will. And this has often been verified by sad experience. Who can boast of greater transports of affections, than the wildest enthu-siasts? Who have had their passions excited to a higher pitch, than those of the *Romish* communion? Who have been more artful in their addresses to the passions, than Popish priests? And who more successful, by heat-ing the affections of people, to establish error and delusion? Nay, what engine has the Devil himself ever made use of, to more fatal purposes, in all ages, than the passions of the vulgar heightened to such a degree, as to put them upon acting without thought and understanding? The plain truth is, an enlightened mind, and not raised affections, ought always to be the guide of those who call themselves men; and this, in the affairs of religion, as well as other things. And it will be so, where GOD really works on their hearts, by his SPIRIT. 'Tis true, "the end of the influence of the SPIRIT of GOD is not to increase men's natural capacities." But 'tis to fit their powers for religious exercise, and preserve them in a state of due subordination. 'Tis as much intended to open the understanding, as to warm the affections; and not only so, but to keep the passions within their proper bounds, restraining them from usurping dominion over the reasonable nature. 'Tis true likewise, "GOD has not obliged himself immediately to increase civil prudence, in proportion to the degrees of spiritual light." But if it shall please GOD to visit men with the influences of his SPIRIT, it may justly be expected, that he should increase their moral or religious prudence; that, if he should give them spiritual light, it should be for their instruction in the knowledge of what is sin, and what is duty. Nor can it be supposed, that those who are favored with extraordinary measures of light from the SPIRIT of GOD, should be in gross darkness as to the knowledge of some of the most important points of Christian practice: Which yet, may be truly said of many in these days; unless they are allowed to be under the government of a vitiated will, which is much worse. . . .

I have hitherto considered ministers as the persons, more especially obliged to discountenance the bad things, prevailing in the land; and now go on to observe.

That this is the duty of all in general. Not that I would put any upon acting out of their proper sphere. This would tend rather to confusion than reformation. Good order is the strength and beauty of the world. The prosperity both of church and state depends very much upon it. And can there be order, where men transgress the limits of their station, and intermeddle in the business of others? So far from it, that the only effectual method, under GOD, for the redress of general evils, is, for every one to be faithful, in doing what is proper for him in his own place: And even all may properly bear a part, in rectifying the disorders of this kind, at this day.

Civil rulers may do a great deal, not only by their good example, but a wise use of their authority, in their various places, for the suppression of every thing hurtful to society, and the encouragement of whatever has a tendency to make men happy in the enjoyment of their rights, whether natural or Christian. And herein chiefly lies (as I humbly conceive) the duty of rulers at this day. . . . Their duty . . . lies in keeping peace between those who unhappily differ in their thoughts about the state of our religious affairs; and their care in this matter ought to be impartial. Each party, without favor or affection, should be equally restrained from outrage and insult. Those, who may think themselves friends to a work of GOD, should be protected in the exercise of all their just rights, whether as men, or Christians; so on the other hand, those who may be enemies to error and confusion, have the same claim to be protected.

And if, on either side, they invade the rights of others, or throw out slander, at random, to the hurt of their neighbor's reputation and usefulness, and the bringing forward a state of tumult and disorder, I see not but the civil arm may justly be stretched forth for the chastisement of such persons; and this, though their abuses should be offered in the name of the LORD, or under the pretext of the most flaming zeal for the REDEEMER's honor, and serving the interest of his kingdom. For it ought always to be accounted an aggravation of the sin of slander, rather than an excuse for it, its being committed under the cloak of religion, and pretence for the glory of GOD; as it will, under these circumstances, be of more pernicious tendency. I am far from thinking, that any man ought to suffer, either for his religious principles, or conduct arising from them, while he is no disturber of the civil peace; but when men, under the notion of appearing zealous for GOD and his truths, insult their betters, vilify their neighbors, and spirit people to strife and faction, I know of no persons more suitable to be taken in hand by authority. And if they suffer, 'tis for their own follies; nor can they reasonably blame any body but themselves. Nor am I ashamed, or afraid, to profess it as my opinion, that it would probably have been of good service, if those, in these times, who have been publicly and outrageously reviled, had, by their complaints, put it properly in the magistrates power, to restrain some men's tongues with bit and bridle.

Private Christians also, of all ranks and conditions, may do something towards the suppression of these errors, by mourning before the LORD the dishonor which has hereby been reflected on the Name of CHRIST, and injury done to souls; by being much in prayer to GOD for the outpouring of his SPIRIT, in all desirable influences of light, and love, and peace; by taking good heed that they be not themselves drawn aside, avoiding to this end, the company and familiar converse of those, who, by good words and fair speeches, might be apt to deceive their hearts, but especially an attendance on religious exercises, where the churches and ministry are freely declaimed against by those who have gone out from them, under the vain pretence of being more holy than they; and in fine, by a faithful performance of those duties, which arise from the various relations they sustain towards each other. As thus, if they are children, by hearkening to the advice of their parents, and obeying and honoring them in the LORD; and if they are parents, by counseling, reproving, warning, restraining and commanding their children, as there may be occasion. If they are servants, by pleasing their masters well in all things, not defrauding them of their time or labor, but accounting them worthy of all honor, that the name of GOD be not blasphemed; and, if they are masters, not only by providing for their servants things honest and good, but by keeping them within the rules of order and decorum, not suffering them to neglect the religion of the family at home, under pretence of carrying it on elsewhere; especially, when they continue abroad 'till late in the night, and so as to unfit themselves for the services of the following day.

In these, and such like ways, all may exert themselves in making a stand against the progress of error: And all are obliged to do so; and for this reason, among others I have not room to mention, because the last days are particularly marked out in the prophecies of Scripture, as the times wherein may be expected, the rise of SEDUCERS. . . .

SOURCE: Charles Chauncy, *Seasonable Thoughts on the State of Religion in New England* (Boston: 1743), pp. 2–3, 108–109, 319–329, 366–370.

The Religious Affections

JONATHAN EDWARDS

Edwards published his Treatise Concerning Religious
Affections *in 1746. This, his final work on the nature of
revivalism, is regarded by many scholars as an American
classic in the psychological study of religious experience.
This selection from* The Religious Affections *presents
Edwards' conceptions of the self and of the conversion
experience. In opposing Chauncy's strict dichotomy between rationality and emotion, Edwards argued for the
essential unity of the feeling-knowing-acting self. This
holistic understanding of human nature also was important both in his explanation of conversion as the
acquisition of a "new spiritual sense," and in his insistence that the only true signs of genuine conversion were
to be found in changed personalities and the fruits of
action.*

DOCTRINE. *True religion, in great part, consists in holy
affections.*

We see that the apostle, in observing and remarking
the operations and exercises of religion in the Christians
he wrote to, wherein their religion appeared to be true
and of the right kind, when it had its greatest trial of
what sort it was, being tried by persecution as gold is
tried in the fire, and when their religion not only proved
true, but was most pure, and cleansed from its dross and
mixtures of that which was not true, and when religion

appeared in them most in its genuine excellency and
native beauty, and was found to praise, and honor, and
glory; he singles out the religious affections of *love* and
joy, that were then in exercise in them: these are the
exercises of religion he takes notice of, wherein their
religion did thus appear true and pure, and in its proper
glory. Here I would,

1. Show what is intended by the affections.

2. Observe some things which make it evident, that a
great part of true religion lies in the affections.

I. It may be inquired, what the affections of the mind
are?

I answer: The affections are no other than the more
vigorous and sensible exercises of the inclination and
will of the soul.

God has endowed the soul with two faculties: one is
that by which it is capable of perception and speculation,
or by which it discerns, and views, and judges of things;
which is called the understanding. The other faculty is
that by which the soul does not merely perceive and
view things, but is some way inclined with respect to the
things it views or considers; either is inclined *to* them,
or is disinclined and averse *from* them; or is the faculty
by which the soul does not behold things, as an indifferent unaffected spectator, but either as liking or disliking, pleased or displeased, approving or rejecting.
This faculty is called by various names; it is sometimes
called the *inclination:* and, as it has respect to the
actions that are determined and governed by it, is called
the *will:* and the mind, with regard to the exercises of
this faculty, is often called the *heart.*

The exercise of this faculty are two sorts; either those
by which the soul is carried out towards the things that
are in view, in approving of them, being pleased with

them, and inclined to them; or those in which the soul opposes the things that are in view, in disapproving of them, and in being displeased with them, averse from them, and rejecting them.

And as the exercises of the inclination and will of the soul are various in their kinds, so they are much more various in their degrees. There are some exercises of pleasedness or displeasedness, inclination or disinclination, wherein the soul is carried but a little beyond a state of perfect indifference. And there are other degrees above this, wherein the approbation or dislike, pleasedness or aversion, are stronger, wherein we may rise higher and higher, till the soul comes to act vigorously and sensibly, and the actings of the soul are with that strength, that (through the laws of the union which the Creator has fixed between the soul and the body) the motion of the blood and animal spirits begins to be sensibly altered; whence oftentimes arises some bodily sensation, especially about the heart and vitals, that are the fountain of the fluids of the body: from whence it comes to pass, that the mind, with regard to the exercises of this faculty, perhaps in all nations and ages, is called the *heart*. And, it is to be noted, that they are these more vigorous and sensible exercises of this faculty that are called the *affections*.

The will, and the affections of the soul, are not two faculties; the affections are not essentially distinct from the will, nor do they differ from the mere actings of the will, and inclination of the soul, but only in the liveliness and sensibleness of exercise.

It must be confessed, that language is here somewhat imperfect, and the meaning of words in a considerable measure loose and unfixed, and not precisely limited by custom, which governs the use of language. In some sense, the affection of the soul differs nothing at all from the will and inclination, and the will never is in any exercise any further than it is affected; it is not moved out of a state of perfect indifference, any otherwise than as it is affected one way or other, and acts nothing any further. But yet there are many actings of the will and inclination, that are not so commonly called *affections:* in every thing we do, wherein we act voluntarily, there is an exercise of the will and inclination; it is our inclination that governs us in our actions; but all the actings of the inclination and will, in all our common actions of life, are not ordinarily called affections. Yet, what are commonly called affections are not essentially different from them, but only in the degree and manner of exercise. In every act of the will whatsoever, the soul either likes or dislikes, is either inclined or disinclined to what is in view: these are not essentially different from those affections of love and hatred: that liking or inclination of the soul to a thing, if it be in a high degree, and be vigorous and lively, is the very same thing with the affection of love; and that disliking and disinclining, if in a greater degree, is the very same with hatred. In every act of the will for, or towards something not present, the soul is in some degree inclined to that thing; and that inclination, if in a considerable degree, is the very same with the affection of desire. And in every degree of the act of the will, wherein the soul approves of something present, there is a degree of pleasedness; and that pleasedness, if it be in a considerable degree, is the very same with the affections of joy or delight. And if the will disapproves of what is present, the soul is in some degree displeased, and if that displeasedness be great, it is the very same with the affection of grief or sorrow.

Such seems to be our nature, and such the laws of the union of soul and body, that there never is in any case whatsoever, any lively and vigorous exercise of the will or inclination of the soul, without some effect upon the body, in some alteration of the motion of its fluids, and especially of the animal spirits. And, on the other hand, from the same laws of the union of the soul and body, the constitution of the body, and the motion of its fluids, may promote the exercise of the affections. But yet it is not the body, but the mind only, that is the proper seat of the affections. The body of man is no more capable of being really the subject of love or hatred, joy or sorrow, fear or hope, than the body of a tree, or than the same body of man is capable of thinking and understanding. As it is the soul only that has ideas, so it is the soul only that loves or hates, rejoices or is grieved at what it thinks of. Nor are these motions of the animal spirits, and fluids of the body, any thing properly belonging to the nature of the affections, though they always accompany them, in the present state; but are only effects or concomitants of the affections that are entirely distinct from the affections themselves, and no way essential to them; so that an unbodied spirit may be as capable of love and hatred, joy or sorrow, hope or fear, or other affections, as one that is united to a body.

The affections and passions are frequently spoken of as the same; and yet in the more common use of speech, there is in some respect a difference; and affection is a word that in its ordinary signification, seems to be something more extensive than passion, being used for all vigorous lively actings of the will or inclination; but passion for those that are more sudden, and whose effects on the animal spirits are more violent, and the mind more overpowered, and less in its own command.

As all the exercises of the inclination and will, are either in approving and liking, or disapproving and rejecting; so the affections are of two sorts; they are those by which the soul is carried out to what is in view, cleaving to it, or seeking it; or those by which it is averse from it, and opposes it.

Of the former sort are love, desire, hope, joy, gratitude, complacence. Of the latter kind are hatred, fear, anger, grief, and such like; which it is needless now to stand particularly to define.

And there are some affections wherein there is a composition of each of the aforementioned kinds of actings of the will; as in the affection of *pity,* there is something of the former kind, towards the person suffering, and something of the latter towards what he suffers. And so in zeal, there is in it high approbation of some person or thing, together with vigorous opposition to what is conceived to be contrary to it.

There are other mixed affections that might be also mentioned, but I hasten to,

II. The second thing proposed, which was to observe some things that render it evident, that true religion, in great part consists in the affections. And here,

1. What has been said of the nature of the affections makes this evident, and may be sufficient, without adding any thing further, to put this matter out of doubt; for who will deny that true religion consists in a great measure, in vigorous and lively actings of the inclination and will of the soul, or the fervent exercises of the heart?

That religion which God requires, and will accept, does not consist in weak, dull, and lifeless wishes, raising us but a little above a state of indifference: God, in his word, greatly insists upon it, that we be good in earnest, *fervent in spirit,* and our hearts vigorously engaged in religion: Rom. 12:11, *Be ye fervent in spirit, serving the Lord.* Deut. 10:12, *And now, Israel, what doth the Lord thy God require of thee, but to fear the Lord thy God, to walk in all his ways, and to love him, and to serve the Lord thy God with all thy heart, and with all thy soul?* and chap. 6:4, 6, *Hear, O Israel, the Lord our God is one Lord: And thou shalt love the Lord thy God with all thy heart, and with all thy might.* It is such a fervent vigorous engagedness of the heart in religion, that is the fruit of a real circumcision of the heart, or true regeneration, and that has the promises of life; Deut. 30:6, *And the Lord thy God will circumcise thine heart, and the heart of thy seed, to love the Lord thy God with all thy heart, and with all thy soul, that thou mayest live.*

If we be not in good earnest in religion, and our wills and inclinations be not strongly exercised, we are nothing. The things of religion are so great, that there can be no suitableness in the exercises of our hearts, to their nature and importance, unless they be lively and powerful. In nothing is vigor in the actings of our inclinations so requisite, as in religion; and in nothing is lukewarmness so odious. True religion is evermore a powerful thing; and the power of it appears, in the first place in the inward exercises of it in the heart, where is the principal and original seat of it. Hence true religion is called the *power of godliness,* in distinction from the external appearances of it, that are the *form* of it, 2 Tim. 3:5: *Having a form of godliness, but denying the power of it.* The Spirit of God, in those that have sound and solid religion, is a spirit of powerful holy affection; and therefore, God is said *to have given the Spirit of power, and of love, and of a sound mind,* 2 Tim. 1:7. And such, when they receive the Spirit of God, in his sanctifying and saving influences, are said to be *baptized with the*

Holy Ghost, and with fire; by reason of the power and fervor of those exercises the Spirit of God excites in their hearts, whereby their hearts, when grace is in exercise, may be said to *burn within them;* as is said of the disciples, Luke 24:32.

The business of religion is from time to time compared to those exercises, wherein men are wont to have their hearts and strength greatly exercised and engaged, such as running, wrestling or agonizing for a great prize or crown, and fighting with strong enemies that seek our lives, and warring as those, that by violence take a city or kingdom. . . .

2. The Author of the human nature has not only given affections to men, but has made them very much the spring of men's actions. As the affections do not only necessarily belong to the human nature, but are a very great part of it; so (inasmuch as by regeneration persons are renewed in the whole man, and sanctified throughout) holy affections do not only necessarily belong to true religion, but are a very great part of it. And as true religion is of a practical nature, and God hath so constituted the human nature, that the affections are very much the spring of men's actions, this also shows, that true religion must consist very much in the affections.

Such is man's nature, that he is very inactive, any otherwise than he is influenced by some affection, either love or hatred, desire, hope, fear, or some other. These affections we see to be the springs that set men agoing, in all the affairs of life, and engage them in all their pursuits: these are the things that put men forward, and carry them along, in all their worldly business; and especially are men excited and animated by these, in all affairs wherein they are earnestly engaged, and which they pursue with vigor. We see the world of mankind to be exceeding busy and active; and the affections of men are the springs of the motion: take away all love and hatred, all hope and fear, all anger, zeal, and affectionate desire, and the world would be, in a great measure motionless and dead; there would be no such thing as activity amongst mankind, or any earnest pursuit whatsoever. It is affection that engages the covetous man, and him that is greedy of worldly profits, in his pursuits; and it is by the affections, that the ambitious man is put forward in his pursuit of wordly glory; and it is the affections also that actuate the voluptuous man, in his pursuit of pleasure and sensual delights: the world continues, from age to age, in a continual commotion and agitation, in a pursuit of these things; but take away all affection, and the spring of all this motion would be gone, and the motion itself would cease. And as in worldly things, worldly affections are very much the spring of men's motion and action; so in religious matters, the spring of their actions is very much religious affection: he that has doctrinal knowledge and speculation only, without affection, never is engaged in the business of religion.

3. Nothing is more manifest in fact, than that the things of religion take hold of men's souls, no further than they affect them. There are multitudes that often hear the word of God, and therein hear of those things that are infinitely great and important, and that most nearly concern them, and all that is heard seems to be wholly ineffectual upon them, and to make no alteration in their disposition or behavior; and the reason is, they are not affected with what they hear. There are many that often hear of the glorious perfections of God, his almighty power and boundless wisdom, his infinite majesty, and that holiness of God, by which he is of

purer eyes than to behold evil, and cannot look on iniquity, and the heavens are not pure in his sight, and
of God's infinite goodness and mercy, and hear of the
great works of God's wisdom, power and goodness,
wherein there appear the admirable manifestations of
these perfections; they hear particularly of the unspeakable love of God and Christ, and of the great things
that Christ has done and suffered, and of the great things
of another world, of eternal misery in bearing the fierce-
ness and wrath of Almighty God, and of endless blessed-
ness and glory in the presence of God, and the enjoyment of his dear love; they also hear the peremptory
commands of God, and his gracious counsels and warnings, and the sweet invitations of the gospel; I say, they
often hear these things and yet remain as they were before, with no sensible alteration in them, either in heart
or practice, because they are not affected with what they
hear; and ever will be so till they are affected. I am bold
to assert, that there never was any considerable change
wrought in the mind or conversation of any person, by
any thing of a religious nature, that ever he read, heard
or saw, that had not his affections moved. Never was a
natural man engaged earnestly to seek his salvation;
never were any such brought to cry after wisdom, and
lift up their voice for understanding, and to wrestle with
God in prayer for mercy; and never was one humbled,
and brought to the foot of God, from any thing that
ever he heard or imagined of his own unworthiness and
deserving of God's displeasure; nor was ever one induced
to fly for refuge unto Christ, while his heart remained
unaffected. Nor was there ever a saint awakened out of
a cold, lifeless frame, or recovered from a declining state
in religion, and brought back from a lamentable depar-
ture from God, without having his heart affected. And

in a word, there never was any thing considerable brought to pass in the heart or life of any man living, by the things of religion, that had not his heart deeply affected by those things. . . .

In those gracious exercises and affections which are wrought in the minds of the saints, through the saving influences of the Spirit of God, there is a new inward perception or sensation of their minds, entirely different in its nature and kind, from any thing that ever their minds were the subjects of before they were sanctified. For doubtless if God by his mighty power produces something that is new, not only in degree and circumstances, but in its whole nature, and that which could be produced by no exalting, varying, or compounding of what was there before, or by adding any thing of the like kind; I say, if God produces something thus new in a mind, that is a perceiving, thinking, conscious thing; then doubtless something entirely new is felt, or perceived, or thought; or, which is the same thing, there is some new sensation or perception of the mind, which is entirely of a new sort, and which could be produced by no exalting, varying, or compounding of that kind of perceptions or sensations which the mind had before; or there is what some metaphysicians call a new simple idea. If grace be, in the sense above described, an entirely new kind of principle, then the exercises of it are also entirely a new kind of exercises. And if there be in the soul a new sort of exercises which it is conscious of, which the soul knew nothing of before, and which no improvement, composition, or management of what it was before conscious or sensible of, could produce, or any thing like it; then it follows that the mind has an entirely new kind of perception or sensation; and here is, as it were, a new spiritual sense that the mind has,

or a principle of a new kind of perception or spiritual
sensation, which is in its whole nature different from
any former kinds of sensation of the mind, as tasting is
diverse from any of the other senses; and something is
perceived by a true saint, in the exercise of this new
sense of mind, in spiritual and divine things, as entirely
diverse from any thing that is perceived in them, by
natural men, as the sweet taste of honey is diverse from
the ideas men have of honey by only looking on it, and
feeling of it. So that the spiritual perceptions which a
sanctified and spiritual person has, are not only diverse
from all that natural men have after the manner that the
ideas or perceptions of the same sense may differ one
from another, but rather as the ideas and sensations of
different senses do differ. Hence the work of the Spirit of
God in regeneration is often in Scripture compared to
the giving a new sense, giving eyes to see, and ears to
hear, unstopping the ears of the deaf, and opening the
eyes of them that were born blind, and turning from
darkness unto light. And because this spiritual sense is
immensely the most noble and excellent, and that without which all other principles of perception, and all our
faculties are useless and vain; therefore the giving this
new sense, with the blessed fruits and effects of it in the
soul, is compared to a raising the dead, and to a new
creation.

This new spiritual sense, and the new dispositions that
attend it, are no new faculties, but are new principles of
nature. I use the word principles for want of a word of
a more determinate signification. By a principle of nature
in this place, I mean that foundation which is laid in
nature, either old or new, for any particular manner or
kind of exercise of the faculties of the soul; or a natural
habit or foundation for action, giving a personal ability

and disposition to exert the faculties in exercises of such a certain kind; so that to exert the faculties in that kind of exercises may be said to be his nature. So this new spiritual sense is not a new faculty of understanding, but it is a new foundation laid in the nature of the soul, for a new kind of exercises of the same faculty of understanding. So that new holy disposition of heart that attends this new sense is not a new faculty of will, but a foundation laid in the nature of the soul, for a new kind of exercises of the same faculty of will. . . .

IV. Gracious affections do arise from the mind's being enlightened, richly and spiritually to understand or apprehend divine things.

Holy affections are not heat without light; but evermore arise from the information of the understanding, some spiritual instruction that the mind receives, some light or actual knowledge. The child of God is graciously affected, because he sees and understands something more of divine things than he did before, more of God or Christ, and of the glorious things exhibited in the gospel; he has some clearer and better view than he had before, when he was not affected: either he receives some understanding of divine things that is new to him; or has his former knowledge renewed after the view was decayed. . . .

Now there are many affections which do not arise from any light in the understanding. And when it is thus, it is a sure evidence that these affections are not spiritual, let them be ever so high. Indeed they have some new apprehensions which they had not before. Such is the nature of man, that it is impossible his mind should be affected, unless it be by something that he apprehends, or that his mind conceives of. But in many persons those apprehensions or conceptions that they have, wherewith they are affected, have nothing of the nature of knowledge or instruction in them. As for instance, when a person is affected with a lively idea, suddenly excited in his mind, of some shape or very beautiful pleasant form of countenance, or some shining light, or other glorious outward appearance: here is something apprehended or conceived by the mind; but there is nothing of the nature of instruction in it; persons become never the wiser by such things, or more knowing about God, or any thing contained in any of the doctrines of the gospel. Persons by these external ideas have no further acquaintance with God, as to any of the attributes or perfections of his nature; nor have they any further understanding of his word, or any of his ways or works. Truly spiritual and gracious affections are not raised after this manner; these arise from the enlightening of the understanding to understand the things that are taught of God and Christ, in a new manner, the coming to a new understanding of the excellent nature of God, and his wonderful perfections, some new view of Christ in his spiritual excellencies and fulness, or things opened to him in a new manner, that appertain to the way of salvation by Christ, whereby he now sees how it is, and understand those divine and spiritual doctrines which once were foolishness to him. Such enlightenings of the understanding as these, are things entirely different in their nature from strong ideas of shapes and colors, and outward brightness and glory, or sounds and voices. That all gracious affections do arise from some instruction or enlightening of the understanding, is therefore a further proof, that affections which arise from such impression on the imagination, are not gracious affections, besides the things observed before, which make this evident. . . .

From what has been said, therefore, we come necessarily to this conclusion, concerning that wherein spiritual understanding consists, viz., that it consists in "a
sense of the heart, of the supreme beauty and sweetness
of the holiness or moral perfection of divine things, together with all that discerning and knowledge of things
of religion, that depends upon, and flows from such a
sense."

Spiritual understanding consists primarily in a sense
of heart of that spiritual beauty. I say, a sense of heart;
for it is not speculation merely that is concerned in this
kind of understanding; nor can there be a clear distinction made between the two faculties of understanding and will, as acting distinctly and separately, in this
matter. When the mind is sensible of the sweet beauty
and amiableness of a thing, that implies a sensibleness
of sweetness and delight in the presence of the idea of
it: and this sensibleness of the amiableness or delightful-
ness of beauty, carries in the very nature of it the sense
of the heart; or an effect and impression the soul is the
subject of, as a substance possessed of taste, inclination
and will.

There is a distinction to be made between a mere notional understanding, wherein the mind only beholds
things in the exercise of a speculative faculty; and the
sense of the heart, wherein the mind does not only spec-
ulate and behold, but relishes and feels. That sort of
knowledge, by which a man has a sensible perception of
amiableness and loathsomeness, or of sweetness and
nauseousness, is not just the same sort of knowledge with
that by which he knows what a triangle is, and what a
square is. The one is mere speculative knowledge, the
other sensible knowledge, in which more than the mere
intellect is concerned; the heart is the proper subject of

it, or the soul, as a being that not only beholds, but has inclination, and is pleased or displeased. And yet there is the nature of instruction in it; as he that has perceived the sweet taste of honey, knows much more about it, than he who has only looked upon, and felt of it. . . .

Spiritual understanding primarily consists in this sense of taste of the moral beauty of divine things; so that no knowledge can be called spiritual, any further than it arises from this, and has this in it. But secondarily it includes all that discerning and knowledge of things of religion, which depend upon and flow from such a sense. . . .

Again, the reason of this expression and effect of holy affections in the practice, appears from what has been observed of "a change of nature, accompanying such affections." Without a change of nature, men's practice will not be thoroughly changed. Until the tree be made good, the fruit will not be good. Men do not gather grapes of thorns, nor figs of thistles. The swine may be washed, and appear clean for a little while, but yet, without a change of nature he will still wallow in the mire. Nature is a more powerful principle of action, than any thing that opposes it: though it may be violently restrained for a while, it will finally overcome that which restrains it: it is like the stream of a river, it may be stopped a while with a dam, but if nothing be done to dry the fountain, it will not be stopped always; it will have a course, either in its old channel, or a new one. Nature is a thing more constant and permanent, than any of those things that are the foundation of carnal men's reformation and righteousness. When a natural man denies his lust, and lives a strict, religious life, and seems humble, painful, and earnest in religion, it is not natural; it is all a force against nature; as when a stone is violently thrown upwards; but that force will be gradually spent; yet nature will remain in its full strength, and so prevails again, and the stone returns downwards. As long as corrupt nature is not mortified, but the principle left whole in a man, it is a vain thing to expect that it should not govern. But if the old nature be indeed mortified, and a new and heavenly nature infused, then may it well be expected, that men will walk in newness of life, and continue to do so to the end of their days. . . .

And as the Scripture plainly teaches, that practice is the best evidence of the sincerity of professing Christians; so reason teaches the same thing. Reason shows, that men's deeds are better and more faithful interpreters of their minds, than their words. The common sense of all mankind, through all ages and nations, teaches them to judge of men's hearts chiefly by their practice, in other matters; as, whether a man be a loyal subject, a true lover, a dutiful child, or a faithful servant. If a man profess a great deal of love and friendship to another, reason teaches all men, that such a profession is not so great an evidence of his being a real and hearty friend, as his appearing a friend in deeds; being faithful and constant to his friend in prosperity and adversity, ready to lay out himself, and deny himself, and suffer in his personal interest, to do him a kindness. A wise man will trust to such evidences of the sincerity of friendship, further than a thousand earnest professions and solemn declarations, and most affectionate expressions of friendship in words. And there is equal reason why practice should also be looked upon as the best evidence of friendship towards Christ. Reason says the same that Christ said, in John 14:21, *He that hath my commandments, and keepeth them, he it is that loveth me.* Thus if we see a man, who in the course of his life seems to follow and imitate Christ, and greatly to exert and deny himself for the honor of Christ, and to promote his kingdom and interest in the world; reason teaches, that this is an evidence of love to Christ, more to be depended on, than if a man only says he has love to Christ, and tells of the inward experiences he has had of love to him, what strong love he felt, and how his heart was drawn out in love at such and such a time, when it may be there appears but little imitation of Christ in his behavior, and he seems backward to do any great matter for him, or to put himself out of his way for the promoting of his kingdom, but seems to be apt to excuse himself whenever he is called to deny himself for Christ. So if a man, in declaring his experiences, tells how he found his heart weaned from the world, and saw the vanity of it, so that all looked as nothing to him, at such and such times, and professes that he gives up all to God, and calls heaven and earth to witness to it; but yet in his practice is violent in pursuing the world, and what he gets he keeps close, is exceeding loath to part with much of it to charitable and pious uses, it come from him almost like his heart's blood. But there is another professing Christian, that says not a great deal, yet in his behavior appears ready at all times to forsake the world, whenever it stands in the way of his duty, and is free to part with it at any time to promote religion and the good of his fellow creatures. Reason teaches, that the latter gives far the most credible manifestation of a heart weaned from the world. And if a man appears to walk humbly before God and men, and to be of a conversation that savors of a broken heart, appearing patient and resigned to God under affliction, and meek in his behavior amongst men; this is a better evidence of humiliation, than if a person only tells how great a sense he had of his own unworthiness, how he was brought to lie in the dust, and was quite emptied of himself, and saw himself nothing and all over filthy and abominable, etc., etc., but yet acts as if he looked upon himself one of the first and best of saints, and by just right the head of all the Christians in the town, and is assuming, self-willed, and impatient of the least contradiction or opposition; we may be assured in such a case, that a man's practice comes from a lower place in his heart than his profession. So (to mention no more instances) if a professor of Christianity manifests in his behavior a pitiful tender spirit towards others in calamity, ready to bear their burdens with them, willing to spend his substance for them, and to suffer many inconveniences in his worldly interest to promote the good of others' souls and bodies; is not this a more credible manifestation of a spirit of love to men, than only a man's telling what love he felt to others at certain times, how he pitied their souls, how his soul was in travail for them, and how he felt hearty love and pity to his enemies; when in his behavior he seems to be of a very selfish spirit, close and niggardly, all for himself, and none for his neighbors, and perhaps envious and contentious? Persons in a pang of affection may think they have a willingness of heart for great things, to do much and to suffer much, and so may profess it very earnestly and confidently, when really their hearts are far from it. Thus many in their affectionate pangs, have thought themselves willing to be damned eternally for the glory of God. Passing affections easily produce words; and words are cheap; and godliness is more easily feigned in words than in actions. Christian practice is a costly, laborious thing. The self-denial that is required of Christians, and the narrowness of the way that leads to life, does not consist in words, but in practice. Hypocrites may much more easily be brought to talk like saints, than to act like saints.

SOURCE: Jonathan Edwards, *The Works of Jonathan Edwards in Four Volumes* (New York: Leavitt, Trow and Company, 1849), III, 2–7, 71–72, 108–109, 112–113, 188, 195–197.

Douglas Sloan is Associate Professor of History and Education at Teachers College, Columbia University. He received his B.A. from Southern Methodist University, his B.D. from Yale University Divinity School, and his Ph.D. from Columbia University. Mr. Sloan is also a Research Associate in the Institute of Philosophy and Politics of Education at Teachers College, Columbia University. Mr. Sloan is the author of *The Scottish Enlightenment and the American College Ideal* (1971).